Conditional Tense

THE AFRICA LIST

ANTJIE KROG

Conditional Tense

MEMORY AND VOCABULARY
AFTER THE SOUTH AFRICAN TRUTH
AND RECONCILIATION COMMISSION

LONDON NEW YORK CALCUTTA

The Africa List

SERIES EDITOR: ROSALIND C. MORRIS

Seagull Books, 2013

Images in Chapter 4 (pp. 260–84) reproduced from *Suske en Wiske: Kaapse Kaalkoppen*, No. 284, with permission from the publisher.
© Standaard Uitgeverij / WPG Uitgeverij België nv, 2012

Image on p. 276 reproduced from Scott McCloud, *Understanding Comics*: *The Invisible Art* (New York: HarperCollins, 1993) with permission from the author.

Images on p. 316–17, *The Man Who Sang and the Woman Who Kept Silent* (1998), from the collection of the Constitutional Court of South Africa, reproduced with permission from artist Judith Mason.

ISBN 978 0 8574 2 174 6

British Library Cataloguing-in-Publication Data
A catalogue record for this book is available from the British Library.

Typeset in Dante MT by Seagull Books, Calcutta, India
Printed and bound by Maple Press, York, Pennsylvania, USA

it was mostly slurry

a pit filled with dead bodies
and the living clawing away
some with plastic bags wrapped round their hands

with a hacking sound one grabs a bracelet of his mother
another pulls a skeleton towards her face
    as if kissing is what she wants to do
her father's amulet is what she recognizes
some sit staring at a shoe

*

I circle slowly
only the tips of my stretched-out wings are moving
the wind creaks in the hollows of my ears
far below drifts the landscape that makes me possible with
    the all-of-you
that it should be so, this equilibrium
the all-of-you calling the single I into existence
the I imagining itself through the all

for so long had I longed for this melting through
had I been halved without it
now my eyebrows, ears, my neck you rinse clean
I comfort all of your elbows I bandage the bleeding legs
vertebra by vertebra the deepest memory of spine is
    caressed

I take all blood, so light that it could have been dust
and it is my own

*

to become always towards and thus
beyond the brief banks of the single body
to become of the bodies, the vulnerability of them
of the hearts calibrating
of being included
with all unprotected hissing skins
fragmentary eyes

to see oneself plural
as you see an us-ed me

to begin between the fingers
rolling a silksoft thread towards a word to whole us

*

the rain picks us up
the rain has our scent
the rain holds us tightly
light filters through
it encompasses everything

Contents

ix
Acknowledgements

1
INTRODUCTION
Unlearning the Past while Trying to Live with Harmed Tongues

39
CHAPTER ONE
Ways of Knowing Mrs Konile:
TRC and the Problem of Translation

89
CHAPTER TWO
Revisiting Mrs Konile:
The Problem of Knowing

118
CHAPTER THREE
Archived Voices:
Refiguring Three Women's Testimonies Delivered to the TRC

148
CHAPTER FOUR
Shards, Memory and the Mileage of Myth

176
CHAPTER FIVE
Redefinition and the Battlefield of Guilt and Shame

193
CHAPTER SIX
'This Thing Called Reconciliation':
Forgiveness as Part of an Interconnectedness-towards-
Wholeness

218
CHAPTER SEVEN
The Letters in the Body:
Manifestations of Interconnectedness and an Indigenous
Humanism

237
CHAPTER EIGHT
A Vocabulary of Grace

260
CHAPTER NINE
Suske en Wiske:
Sequential Comic Panels and the Iconization of
Nelson Mandela

285
CHAPTER TEN
Reading with the Skin:
Liberalism, Race and Power in J. M. Coetzee's Age of Iron
and Disgrace

307
CHAPTER ELEVEN
Pieces in the Anatomy of Loss

322
Works Cited

Acknowlegements

Versions of Chapters 1 and 2 appeared in various journals until they found their final form in Antjie Krog, Nosisi Mpolweni and Kopano Ratele (eds), *There Was This Goat: Investigating the Truth Commission Testimony of Notrose Nobomvu Konile* (Scottsville: University of Kwazulu-Natal Press, 2009). Chapter 3 appeared in the journal *Tulsa Studies in Women's Literature* 28(2) (Fall 2009). Parts of Chapters 4, 5 and 8 appeared in the *Mail and Guardian*, *Cape Times* and the *Sunday Times*. Chapter 4 also appeared in Jacob Dlamini and Megan Jones (eds), *Categories of Persons: Rethinking Ourselves and Others* (Johannesburg: Picador Africa, 2013). Chapter 6 appeared in the *South African Journal of Philosophy* 27(4) (2008). Chapter 7 appeared in John W. de Gruchy (ed.), *The Humanist Imperative* (Stellenbosch: Sun Press / A STIAS, 2011). Chapter 9 appeared in Afrikaans in *Tydskrif vir Nederlands en Afrikaans* 18(1) (2011). Chapter 10 appeared in Kader Asmal, David Chidester and Wilmot Godfrey James (eds), *South Africa's Nobel Laureates: Peace, Literature and Science* (Cape Town: Jonathan Ball, 2004). A Dutch translation of Chapter 11 appeared in the journal *Nexus* 39 (2004). Some fragments about Rwanda in the opening poem are by Martien Schotsmans.

Unlearning the Past
while Trying to Live with Harmed Tongues

It was the year 1995, in Cape Town, South Africa. My country's first democratically elected parliament opened with blaring trumpets, festive crowds, jet planes of triumph—old rituals now transformed by inclusivity—and a vintage Nelson Mandela speech. I was there. I was reporting—as part of the 'new' radio team reporting our 'new' Parliament in all its languages to the nation. (Yes, we used words like 'nation' and were both thrilled and perplexed as we tasted it on our tongues for the first time.) There were eight of us in the team—keen and multilingual, we worked under editor Pippa Green and our voices, energized by the wealth of potential all around us, were regularly heard across the country.

Under the leadership of President Mandela, Parliament wasted no time. It prioritized two tasks that would influence the country for decades to come: the drafting of a new constitution to protect and guide a young democracy; and legislation that would establish a body, the Truth and Reconciliation Commission (TRC), to deal with the past by giving amnesty to perpetrators and compensating victims. The Justice Portfolio Committee became my beat.

In my memory of these times, several things stand out. First, the feeling that everything was possible—every good and wonderful thing. Mandela was putting across to the country a coherent way of being at grace with one another, creating benign spaces of togetherness instead of separateness and instilling immense hope for a profound, inclusive change. There was an upsurge of goodwill, of pride, with Mandela creating our most beautiful face, our best face, and, in the process, changing us from polecat to crown-prince country.

We were, suddenly, also a 'country-in-training'. It felt as though we had to learn a completely new vocabulary. For our reports, we regularly had to find experts to explain never-heard-of-before or never-understood-before terms in ordinary language. What actually is a 'human right' and a 'bill of rights'? Is hate speech defendable as freedom of speech? What does 'integrity of the body' mean, or 'productive rights'? If gay people have the same rights as everyone else, can they marry and have children? What are the implications when Parliament is no longer the highest authority but is instead subject to the Constitutional Court—no longer *Salus rei publica suprema lex est* (the law of the state is the highest law) but something entirely different? When is something a crime against humanity? What is the difference between interrogation and torture? What is the difference between amnesty and indemnity? What precisely is pornography?

Those of us working in our mother tongues had to find terms for these concepts new to us. I remember how, during a radio interview, the head of the South African Reserve Bank had to find Xitsonga words to explain interest rates and the Gini coefficient. He left the radio booth bathed in sweat.

One of my colleagues reported on hearings regarding the legislation about pornography. 'What is "pornography" in Xhosa?' asked Green. 'I made up a word which basically means "dirty pictures",' the journalist said. 'No, that already contains a value judgement. Let's phone somebody who works on the Xhosa dictionary.' We were learning, our languages were learning and everyone was catching up.

Another thing I remember of these times was the intensive consultation process round the TRC legislation. For months on end, different groups, individuals, societies and representatives appeared before the Justice Portfolio Committee, putting forward their requests and formulating their fears. All political parties were represented on this committee and we reported on how their often conflicting demands were accommodated in legislation that more and more resembled a patchwork quilt.

I remember how one of the civil servants who worked through the night to turn the day's discussions into draft legislation complained about the cumbersomeness of the consultation process: 'If I were allowed to draft this law, we would have been finished long ago with a short, slick piece.'

The draft bill was distributed to NGOs all over South Africa; seminars and workshops were held to help people understand the philosophy behind the TRC; the findings of these workshops and seminars were made available to the people working on the bill; thousands of booklets explaining the main ideas of the commission were distributed; and a number of programmes on the TRC were broadcast on radio and television (Boraine 2000: 50).

The slow compilation of this law was reported daily on radio and television and in all the newspapers. So why is it, I cannot help wondering after so many years, that the TRC process was eventually so astonishingly misunderstood, mishandled and mistrusted in turn by *all* political parties?

When the commission started its work, the Afrikaner-dominated National Party, the conservative Freedom Front, their newspapers, and the Zulu-dominated Inkatha Freedom Party (IFP) immediately began to brand the commission an Afrikaner/Zulu witch-hunt, with Anglican archbishop Des-mond Tutu as the instigator and former Methodist minister Alex Boraine as the typical British Afrikaner-hater/white- liberal. Tutu was cartooned in the Afrikaans newspapers as a witch with long pointed shoes, the nose he so often joked about curled, his glasses black with menace.

Why did these parties, which duly participated and were specifically accommodated in the legislation, choose not to explain to their constituencies what was about to happen, but instead decide to use the TRC as a rallying point to sidestep their responsibility to rebuild a country laid waste by themselves? If such a consultative process did not prevent dishonest opportunism, what would?

★

The idea of a truth commission for South Africa first came from the party of the country's biggest liberation movement, the African National Congress (ANC). As soon as the ban on the ANC was lifted in February 1990, accusations were levelled against the party that it had committed human rights violations in some of its training camps in Tanzania and other southern African countries. The response of the ANC was to set up its own internal investigation commissions (for example, the Stuart, the Skweyiya and the Motsuenyane Commissions). These commissions confirmed that gross human rights violations had indeed taken place in the camps during the time of exile, findings that were accepted by the party's National Executive Committee (NEC). However, in response to the Motsuenyane Commission report, the NEC called on the government to 'set up, without delay, a Commission of Inquiry or Truth Commission into all violations of human rights since 1948' (ibid.: 12).

It was Professor Kader Asmal who, at his inaugural lecture at the University of the Western Cape on 25 May 1992, gave form and content to the ANC's proposal to establish a truth commission once a political settlement had been reached. It was also in 1992 that others started to consider the idea of a truth commission for South Africa—for instance, members of the Institute for a Democratic Alternative for South Africa (IDASA) after their visit to Eastern Europe.

The notion of a truth commission was increasingly regarded as part of a process of transitional justice when a society wants to move from a past of injustice, discrimination and intolerance to a future founded on the recognition of human rights, democracy and equality (Bloomfield et al. 2005: 37). The transitional phase in

South Africa comprised the release of Mandela and other political prisoners and the unbanning of political parties—so that everyone could participate in negotiations about a new dispensation. These negotiations had to put in place an interim constitution which would regulate the country and the all-important free elections. After the elections, the new, democratically elected political leaders would then write the country's new 'real' constitution.

The elections were therefore the key to our democracy. They had to take place. But what police or defence force would protect elections which might well lead to the top brass and many ordinary Afrikaner foot soldiers being put on trial for human rights violations? There was an urgent need to signal to the army and the police that there would not be negative consequences for them in the new dispensation. The last clause added to the Interim Constitution was intended to put such fears at rest:

> The adoption of this Constitution lays the secure foundation for the people of South Africa to transcend the divisions and strife of the past, which generated gross violations of human rights, the transgression of humanitarian principles in violent conflicts and a legacy of hatred, fear, guilt and revenge.
>
> These can now be addressed on the basis that there is a need for understanding but not for vengeance, a need for reparation but not for retaliation, a need for ubuntu but not for victimization.

In order to advance such reconciliation and reconstruction, amnesty shall be granted in respect of acts, omissions and offences associated with political objectives and committed in the course of the conflicts of the past. To this end, parliament under this Constitution shall adopt a law determining a firm cut-off date [. . .] and providing for mechanisms, criteria and procedures, including tribunals, if any, through which such amnesty shall be dealt with at any time after the law has been passed (South African Government Information 1993: n.p.).

After the elections, on 27 May 1994, the newly appointed minister of justice, Dullah Omar, announced to Parliament the decision of the government to set up a truth commission and the drafting of the bill began. It took about four months (127 hours and 30 minutes) of consultation, negotiation and legislation before all the political parties reached an agreement. In November 1994, the Promotion of National Unity and Reconciliation Act (No. 34 of 1995) was published. It was signed into law in July 1995 and came into effect on 15 December 1995 (Boraine 2000: 71). This act is regarded as the most sensitive, technically complex, controversial and important legislation ever to be passed by Parliament.

The commission itself consisted of 17 members (chosen from more than 40 nominees), 350 staff members, 4 offices across the country and a budget of $18 million. The TRC dwarfed previous truth commissions elsewhere in the world in its size and reach:

- It could grant individual amnesty
- It could search premises and seize evidence
- It could subpoena witnesses
- It ran a sophisticated witness-protection programme

Its complex task was to establish a complete picture of the causes, nature and extent of the gross violations of human rights which were committed during the period from 1 March 1960 to 5 December 1993 (later extended to 10 May 1994); facilitate the granting of amnesty; establish and make known the fate or where-abouts of victims and restore their human and civil dignity by granting them an opportunity to relate their own accounts; recommend reparation measures in respect of them; and compile a report providing a com-prehensive account of the activities and findings of the commission with recommendations of measures to pre-vent the future violations of human rights.

The commission comprised three committees: the Human Rights Violations Committee, the Amnesty Com-mittee and the Reparation and Rehabilitation Committee. By the end of its life, the Human Rights Violations Com-mittee had gathered close to 22,000 statements covering 37,000 violations, which is more than any previous truth commission had achieved (Graybill 2002: 8). Two thou-sand people testified publicly. Special hearings were held focusing on a theme, institution or event: medical services; media; big business; the Soweto uprisings; the group of youth called the Mandela United Football Club, who had claimed to protect Nelson Mandela's wife Winnie while he was in jail; and so on.

The first human rights public hearing took place in East London, in the Eastern Cape, on 15 April 1996. From then on, hearings were organized all over the country in locations as diverse as local churches, town halls and schools. All in all, nearly 90 hearings took place in more than 60 places.

The Human Rights Violations Committee is one of the most impressive aspects of the TRC. Hundreds of apartheid victims were given a voice and were offered a platform to talk about their experiences of the past and many suggest that the whole TRC exercise was justified by the powerful testimonies coming from this committee alone.

The Reparation and Rehabilitation Committee had to make recommendations to the president on reparation for and rehabilitation of victims and on measures to be taken to restore their human and civil dignity. This committee was not meant to compensate the apartheid victims; it could only formulate non-committal recommendations. The final decision lay in the hands of the government. As members of the committee were often locked in infighting and individual compensations came to seem more and more controversial, the committee's attention shifted to collective or symbolic reparations, such as the building of monuments, issuing of death certificates, organizing of ceremonial reburials and the renaming of streets, schools and buildings after fallen heroes. After much fighting and a number of pending court cases, interim and long-term compensation was reluctantly paid out by the government to some victims.

In many other countries where truth commissions have been established, the amnesty procedure was often a separate legal mechanism (see Hayner 2001) or political leaders received an overall blanket amnesty. In South Africa, however, the amnesty legislation not only individualized amnesty but also made the Amnesty Committee an integral part of the TRC. Consisting of three high court judges and two TRC members, it was given the power to decide independently who was to be granted amnesty. Whereas a person on trial in court would most likely plead innocent, the TRC amnesty process was only interested in applicants who acknowledged their culpability and guilt.

Amnesty could be given when the deed was associated with a political motive and not carried out for personal gain, personal malice, ill will or hatred (ibid.: 43); brought full disclosure, including the naming of those who had ordered the offence; and was proportionally in step with the goals of the political organization. Remorse was not required to receive amnesty. The task was clearly also an effort to establish a political ethics on the basis of a recognition that even liberationist states and the victims they represent can become perpetrators.

When amnesty was granted, applicants were to be free of all civil and criminal liability. Facts disclosed and revelations made at the hearings could never be used as evidence against the accused in a court of law. If amnesty was refused, the accused ran the risk of being prosecuted in the future. The Amnesty Committee received more than 7,000 applications and granted amnesty to just over a thousand.

A five-volume final report was handed over to former president Mandela in October 1998. An interdict by apartheid president F. W. de Klerk to block out particular accusations against him was granted, but the ANC's request for postponement of the report because of their unhappiness about findings on human rights abuses by the ANC was turned down in court.

The TRC became a phenomenon that not only marked a new era in the country's history but also led to a worldwide interest in the potential of peaceful conflict resolution and restorative justice. The commission continues to be analysed and discussed, with scholars, journalists and artists trying to grasp its consequences and its effects not only on present-day South Africa but also on other countries in transition.

The effects of the TRC contributed to the worldwide tendency in the final years of the twentieth and the beginning of the twenty-first century to approach conflict resolution from a restorative rather than a retributive perspective. In the past 15 years, the International Centre for Transitional Justice (ICTJ) has worked in close to 30 countries, either to help set up truth commissions or to follow up on truth and reconciliation processes that had already taken place. The activities of the ICTJ proved that establishing reconciliation in a divided country was a burning desire in many parts of the world (Bloomfield et al. 2005: 7).

★

When it was announced that Tutu was to be the chairperson of the still-to-be-established TRC, I was sent, with my colleague, Manelisi Dubase, to interview him for radio on the estate of the Anglican church in Bishopscourt, Cape Town, where he lived at the time.

It was the first time that any of us had interviewed Tutu. We were surprised when, after we had taken our places and set up our equipment, he stopped us, bowed his head and began to pray—a short, quick, rather soft prayer praising God for his goodness and asking for his blessing. It came across as a small ritual, yet it took us some minutes afterwards to regain our professional control as political journalists.

During the interview Tutu and Dubase discussed the appropriate isiXhosa translations for 'reconciliation', 'amnesty' and 'gross human rights violations'. I had to find out the proper Afrikaans terms for 'perpetrator', 'gross violations', etc. Journalists are often at the coalface where events and word-making meet, and not always geared for this or equipped with a hotline to those better placed to handle the challenge.

I would like to think that the TRC's concern for radio stemmed from the day we interviewed Tutu and emphasized that if this interview were to be broadcast only in English, it would reach 450,000 English listeners—a larger audience than that of any South African newspaper. But if Tutu could repeat what he had said in all the other languages that he knew, he could add 6 million isiZulu speakers, 1.6 million isiXhosa speakers, 1.5 million Sesotho speakers and 700,000 Afrikaans speakers.

So right from the outset, the TRC paid special attention to radio. Its earliest business plan stipulated:

> In considering the best means of making sure
> that as many South Africans as possible are
> enabled and empowered to participate in the life
> and work of the Commission, it has judged radio
> the most effective communication medium for
> its proceedings to the widest number of people
> [. . .] In addition radio broadcasts penetrate all
> corners of the country in the home languages of
> the majority of South Africans [. . . also] for those
> who are not literate and for those in rural areas
> (TRC 1998: 1.357).

The strategy on radio was put in practice. Money for
radio coverage was raised. The South African Broadcasting Corporation (SABC) appointed a team representing
the majority languages and Pippa Green asked me to lead
it. Every hearing had a special room allocated to radio
journalists (also for private radio stations). Feeds from the
different translations on the floor were relayed to this
room so that all languages could be accessed. Special
phone lines were installed (cellphone networks were not
as efficient at the time) in order to feed radio reports
straight to news desks and current affairs shows. This
allowed radio journalists to participate in call-in and talk
shows and do Q&A sessions from anywhere in the country, delivering good-quality sound without disturbing
print or television journalists. A special sound technician
accompanied the team.

For the TRC, the strategy paid off. In an interview
with the *Sunday Times* in December 1996, Tutu said:

One of our most substantial achievements, however, has been to bring events known until now only to the immediately affected communities [. . .] into the centre of national life [. . .] Millions of South Africans have heard the truth about the apartheid years for the first time, some through daily newspapers but many more through television, and especially radio [. . .] (quoted in Boraine 2000: 89).

Boraine put it as follows:

Although it was not easy to be under constant public scrutiny, I think the Commission owes the media an enormous debt of gratitude. Through their very conscientious work they involved the whole country in the work of the TRC. Unlike many commissions, this one was centre stage, and media coverage, particularly radio, enabled the poor, the illiterate, and people living in rural areas to participate in its work so that it was truly a national experience rather than restricted to a small handful of selected commissioners (ibid.).

At least initially, journalists were not exactly falling over themselves to be assigned to reporting on the TRC. The country was writing its new progressive constitution; Mandela, the triumph of the country, was touring the world; South African sports teams were winning; the politics were new and exciting—so why would anyone want to report on people raking up the past? Sometimes I think 'underestimated' was the word I heard most often during the first year of the TRC's life. It seemed that everyone, from commissioners to staff, certainly us journalists, politicians and ordinary South Africans, completely underestimated the effects, the work, the consequences, and the breadth and depth of the challenges this commission would unearth and confront us with.

A specific strategy had to be designed for radio. We would use all the radio 'genres', but in order for TRC stories to get adequate space in the current affairs programmes, they had to be on the news bulletins. This may sound like a matter of course but there was serious doubt whether 'old stories' would be regarded as newsworthy by news desks. To be on the news was important for two reasons: first, radio stations prefer that the content of their programmes link directly to the latest news; and second, people listen to the news for a variety of reasons, such as to hear reports on the weather or the markets— even music radio stations have news bulletins—so this was the avenue to reach the widest possible audience.

During the lifetime of the TRC, it often happened that one stood in a supermarket or small shop waiting one's turn to pay for an item, in a way 'trapped' into listening to the muzak pouring from the speakers, suddenly it would be news time and one would listen to a TRC item with other customers and the staff behind the tills.

Sensing the importance of the TRC proceedings being on the news, I put in a request that an expert in news bulletin stories and quality sound, Angie Kapelianis, be seconded to the team—at least for the beginning of the process. It was her sole task to provide stories for the news bulletins. Of course, initially, the bulletins didn't want to commit (some bulletin writers were openly hostile) to using TRC stories or to giving them priority, but the excellent angles and the quality of the stories that Kapelianis sent compelled the radio stations to make the TRC the main item on every news bulletin for many weeks (Krog 1998: 31–2).

We were proud to have found ways in which to put the voices of ordinary women and men in their original languages on news bulletins, making use of the excellent translation the TRC itself provided. This radically changed the sound of the news: a housecleaner was heard on the same news bulletin as President Mandela; a Tshivenda mother-tongue speaker shared the air with Bill Clinton; and suddenly people for- merly regarded as second-class citizens, because they could not speak English, now, because of the TRC's translation, sounded as vivid, intelligent, wise, angry and heartbroken as they felt.

Within three days of the first human rights hearings, reports came in of how people in remote places had heard about the TRC and were contacting the commission staff to bring their own stories. People phoned in to say how they had heard for the first time what had happened to family members or neighbours. People wrote letters to describe how their memories were ripped open while listening to the radio by chance. There were stories about men in rural areas coming together in the mornings to sit round the radio listening to the hearings, about women taking a radio to where they would do the washing.

There was also strong reaction from members of the white community who didn't want to be confronted with these stories. Some complained that their children were in the house or car listening to these bulletins and later asking questions which parents found impossible to answer properly. Others said that they didn't want to hear about blood and torture while they were eating their Post Toasties.

After the initial stages, one constantly had to think of ways to deal with the irritation of news bulletin writers (especially those from the previous dispensation) to prevent them from ignoring our stories, shifting them to late-night slots or editing them into bland copy. An early-morning bulletin story would be sent about the TRC activities for the day as well as a late-night wrap-up of events. This compelled bulletin writers to 'follow' the TRC story during the day. For this we would provide the time and place for each case as well as 20-second sound bites from the most poignant and devastating testimonies, carefully selected and introduced in a way which made their presence on the news vital instead of sensational or overdramatic.

After news bulletins, the second important 'genre' was the 'package'. This was a longer story, between three to five minutes, broadcast on the current affairs programmes in the morning, midday and afternoon shows. Zola Ntutu (isiXhosa, isiZulu and English), Darren Taylor (Afrikaans and English), Tapelo Makushane (Sesotho, Setswana and English) and Angie Kapelianis (news in Afrikaans and English) formed the core team.

This group could access absolutely anyone and daily brought in a wide variety of viewpoints, backgrounds and information often enthusiastically discussed late at night in the makeshift newsrooms. The Pringle Award for

Excellence in Journalism that the team received later was a confirmation of its reach, both in breadth and in depth. All our texts were placed on the SABC internal web so that they could be translated into any of the other languages such as Tshivenda or Xitsonga. Radio Zulu or Sesotho would phone for a live Q&A session and it was clear how well informed their hosts were in contrast to some of the monolingual English radio hosts who had to depend on only one language as source.

Although the variety of languages and cultures was a practical arrangement, it meant that in the team there was, from early on, an awareness of the existence of many truths. Some of those truths one might not like, some might simply be lies, but even the construction of that lie articulated a particular truth. We worked in pairs or groups and the pressure, emotionally and in terms of workload, brought about a kind of reconciliation among ourselves. We worked extraordinarily long hours and assumed we could not claim overtime for most of it. We looked out for each other in terms of food or help or news. Even our fights were quickly resolved, mostly out of sheer exhaustion.

In the villages, we were joined by local reporters familiar with these neglected areas. This not only transferred skills but also helped us to do quality stories. When the TRC split its hearings into 'violations' and 'amnesty', we had to form smaller units and were then joined by Dumisane Kwamba (Tshivenda), Kenneth Makatees (Afrikaans), Dumisane Shange (isiZulu), Sophie Mokoena (Sesotho), Andries Satekghe (Setswana) and Isaac Masemola (Sepedi).

The third 'genre' used was a direct nine-to-five broadcast of the hearings. Not many people listened to this but psychologically it had a big impact. People searched for their radio stations and came across Radio 2000, stayed there or perhaps quickly moved away, but they knew: people were dealing with the past. After a year, if they came across the station again, still broadcasting the hearings, even the most sceptical person would have to acknowledge: some of it had to be true. The feeds were apparently followed by perpetrators to hear whether their names were being mentioned, so that they could quickly apply for amnesty. The demand to listen to the Winnie Mandela hearings was so high that the hours of broadcast had to be extended.

On Friday mornings, I provided a wrap-up of the week: what stood out, what patterns emerged, what was new. Once a month, I took a theme and had it analysed by experts. On Sunday evenings, we had a special slot where longer stories of between six to ten minutes provided by the team, as well as live interviews, were used.

We tried to incorporate three-phase reporting: news, longer news packages and, finally, debates and analysis. Initially this was done to satisfy our own need for understanding particular events or behaviours but it also helped listeners bombarded by terrible facts of pain and suffering to process what they were hearing. We focused on concepts such as memory loss, post-traumatic stress symptoms, anomie and so on. There was also an ever-present need to analyse legal positions and terms.

But the third phase of reporting, despite our efforts, was also our biggest failure. Most reporters were so overwhelmed by the sheer volume and intensity of the testimonies that people battled to find energy to analyse or investigate a broader context.

There also seemed to be, generally, an absence of scholarly input. Finding psychologists willing (or able?) to talk about perpetrators, memory loss or the broader effect of the death of a child on a family was not easy. I also do not remember any important analysis in the print media. Books from other countries were passed round and articles about similar processes happening elsewhere helped us at times to make sense of what the TRC was uncovering, but the intellectual input (with some important exceptions, for example, from Sheila Meintjes, Andre du Toit, Fiona Ross, Mahmood Mamdani, etc.) of South African academia mainly kicked in after the process—and then in highly critical terms.

As the process continued, the team developed an institutional memory: we could immediately pick up any shift or change, or, more importantly, identify silences—no one had yet talked about rape; men used the word 'sodomy' instead of 'rape'; no woman had yet testified about her contribution as an activist; and so on.

There was only one thing I forbade any member of the team to do: to look for or initiate and then broadcast a 'live' reconciliation story. I believed, and still do, that the mere presence of a journalist could interfere with and influence the process. One has no right to interfere in such a crucial moment in a person's life and I was, and still am, hugely suspicious of people who bring together victims and perpetrators for a story.

Having said this, the devotion that journalists report-ing on the TRC displayed showed that they felt involved in a process which was not simply a story but something that resonated with and affected their very lives. One reported because one wanted a better country, one wanted the effects of the injustice of the past to come to light so that it could stop.

To have a 'mission' as a journalist is, of course, dan-gerous. But if one wants a better society, a more caring and fair society, I believe one has to think about the way in which it is possible to bring one's work into that orbit.

I also believe it is important that a country insists to report on its own human rights violations. I once watched a BBC report on former Yugoslav president Slobodan Milošević in court in The Hague and wondered about the role of the camera in making him look monstrous. How would he have been reported on if he was on trial in his own country? It was ultimately how we as South Africans reported on apartheid's former president P. W. Botha or the ANC-member-turned-*askari* killer Joe Mamasela which empowered us to decide how much injustice and arrogance we were prepared to live with and forgive. Instead of letting overseas journalists report a country's quest for justice and fairness to its citizens, it is crucial for the local media to do it, or to learn to do it. How else would a country create and own a vocabulary with more words than just 'right' and 'wrong'; or come to under-stand the links between right and feeling right or between wrong and feeling wrong? How else could the local media be aware of the treachery of painting someone 'the Devil', the sole guilt bearer, in order to become 'the

Angel', the blameless. When global media agencies tell a country what *should* be unacceptable to them, it often has the opposite effect: if CNN says X is wrong, in South Africa it often means, for many people, X must therefore be right!

The role of the media in a country emerging from an undemocratic dispensation had been emphasized repeatedly. As the media learns to respect the freedoms of everyone and report democracy, the readers/listeners/watchers learn to read, see and hear democracy in action and, hopefully, how to safeguard it. I have often been asked by groups working towards prospective commissions about some dos and don'ts if the process of transition, as it manifests in a truth commission, is to be broadly grounded in the media.

For me, it is most important that a truth commission be convinced of the importance of mother-tongue expression and translation (simultaneous interpretation, SI). Languages could use this opportunity to strengthen their own vocabularies towards a new dispensation.

Second, a core of journalists should be party to the process so that knowledge can be developed, enabling journalists to trust their own judgement instead of being dependent on the information fed by the commission or other stakeholders.

And third, strategies should be developed to retain the integrity of the narratives. The terminology, rhythm, pace and non-verbal signs of the victims' narratives can seldom be improved upon in terms of impact and integrity.

Let me give two examples.

Once I wrote a bulletin about a mother who talked about a T-shirt that was so full of bullet holes that it looked as if it had been 'eaten by rats'. The bulletin editor changed it to 'a bullet-ridden T-shirt', because 'I cannot say eaten by rats on an official bulletin. If you want to keep the image, you have to say it yourself.' So we used sound bites when it came to strong images.

Another time I came across white people who questioned the honesty of the victims: 'They wait until the camera was on them, then they cried.' Working so closely with testimonies, I was astonished that anyone could come to this conclusion. But scrutinizing television news coverage suggested an explana-tion for their thinking. The well-known team of top journalist Max du Preez reported for their own slot—*TRC Special Report* —but television news was often done by any news reporter of the area who was not necessarily grounded in the TRC story. So the news bulletin would open with an attractive young reporter, well groomed, standing in front of the building where the TRC had its hearings and reporting, 'Today Mrs So-and-so described how her son was killed by security forces . . .' and then slap-bang the camera was focused directly on a woman incoherent with grief. It truly did not seem real. The jump from the spectacularly groomed and often unengaged reporter to the victim was too abrupt to inspire empathy.

Radio did it differently. A specific structure in which the direct words of the victim could be embedded was used. A radio story would not switch from the reporter to the victim but from the reported words of the victim to the victim herself. In other words, by the time the victim's voice entered the story, her own words already prepared the listener.

Reports on the commission were often critical. In *Commissioning the Past* (2002), an important book about the TRC, Deborah Posel and Graeme Simpson note:

> The TRC's engagement with truth was significantly shaped by its role as powerful media spectacle in South Africa's reconciliation enterprise [. . .] the TRC's direct impact on the process of national reconciliation was powerfully mediated by the mass media [. . .]. The hearings were constructed as opportunities to 'uncover' pristine, uncorrupted truths about a past previously 'hidden from history' by creating safe public spaces in which victims and survivors could tell their stories directly and openly (2002: 7).

I find this remark an oversimplification of the multiple voices reporting on the commission as well as the different contacts we had inside it. There was always someone who knew which testimonies were shaky. We could, and sometimes did, ask the commission for the initial statements on which doubtful facts were sometimes marked. Is it not an unfortunate generalization to suggest that professional journalists would think that what was being uncovered was 'pristine, uncorrupted truths'?

Madeleine Fullard and Nicky Rousseau underscore the complexity at work within the commission, but they also blame the journalists for 'shallow media interpretations' on which academics built their conclusions. They say that scholars based their conclusions almost entirely [on] media images of the TRC rather than a closer study of the texts and activities of the TRC, its practices of research and investigation, and its public and private interactions with victims and perpetrators. Much of the media coverage of the TRC, commenced with enthusiasm in 1996 but largely abandoned by the end of 1998, focused on simple images and expressions, often embodied in Archbishop Tutu, as opposed to the contradictory and at times combative impulses of the TRC (2008).

I agree with Fullard and Rousseau about the failure of academics to genuinely grapple with the complexity of the TRC process but they are guilty of a similar oversight: the complexity of radio reporting—with its different 'genres', different phases, different languages, different areas with local reporters, on-the-spot Q&As by different reporters, longer wraps and series—deserves a more careful investigation. How much research went into what exactly was on air in the variety of mother tongues in the country?

★

For months after the TRC closed most of its offices across the country, it was difficult for me to admit any kind of failure on the part of the commission. But as the government grumbled and fumbled its way round the final report, I became more and more surprised by the commissioners' lack of foresight. Why hadn't they kept the government informed and on board?

Already during the last part of the TRC's life, things had started to fall apart. Some commissioners had to leave for other engagements, others were desperately looking for new jobs equal in status. Tutu had cancer which required treatment and rest. So the TRC machine was left without the original leadership which had run such a tight ship during the first years. While the TRC's research unit was drafting the final report, commissioners were supposed to work through every draft and come back with suggestions—apparently little of this occurred on a systematic basis. What did happen, however, was that selected passages dealing with the ANC were leaked to the party and the media. Although a lot of this material was changed in the final report, the harm was done—the relationship between the TRC and the ANC deteriorated into a rancorous affair. (The bad blood between the ANC and the TRC had started earlier, when the ANC, in a swanky, grandstanding move, applied for collective amnesty. When I asked ANC member of Parliament Mathews Phosa, who accompanied the comrades carrying the big box with applications, how this amnesty would work, as the legislation did not provide for collective amnesty, he said: 'Who would know better what the law says, you or I?' Indeed, Tutu threatened to resign if the party did not withdraw these applications 'giving themselves amnesty' [Krog 1998: 116]). When the news arrived that the ANC requested an interdict against the releasing of the final report, the commissioners refused to allow the ANC special treatment.

Then I thought the commissioners were right to do so; now I have changed my mind. If indeed it rests with an ANC-led government to carry out reparations, sue perpetrators, implement prevention measures for future abuses and cultivate a human rights culture, then it is crucial to get them—and keep them—on board cultivating their understanding of what is at stake. In other words, if the government is the sole body responsible for the continuation of the spirit and recommendations of the TRC, then the TRC should have spoken to the government, not once (because it spoke to the National Party once) but a thousand times if necessary.

The TRC's failure to interact successfully with the ANC-led government has done the process more harm than all the other criticisms and mistakes put together. It blocked the growth of something important; it allowed the healthy stream of accountability that was starting to flow through the country to dry up. It curtailed compassion. It left us stunted. We were no longer a country becoming.

Reparation for the trauma of the victims had—by its own admission—been the TRC's single biggest failure. During a discussion about possible victim reparation, Minister of Finance Trevor Manuel was asked whether a plan was in place through which whites could assist in reparation. He said to some applause: 'Even if we take away everything that whites have, it will not be enough to make up for the past.' 'What are you suggesting?' was the response. 'Should whites continue living as selfishly and greedily as they want, because whatever they do will never be enough?' He sighed. 'No,' he said. 'I guess what I am saying is that there is no plan to get from whites what they owe us. To really change the lives of the poor, we need a growth rate of 6%' (Krog 1998: 286).

Looking back, it seems astonishing that no one positively mobilized round this immense, powerful dynamo the TRC released into South African society. It was a golden opportunity lost, not only to find a motor to materially change South Africa but also to mould a caring South African–ness.

Over the years, it has become common cause to be told by academics, journalists, artists and commentators that the TRC greatly failed South Africa because the condition of the victims did not improve. Rereading the TRC final report, however, one is struck by how aware the TRC was of its shortcomings and how studiously it pressed the government to redress the needs not only of those classified as victims but also of the communities in the widest possible way. In fact, the report quotes opinions and lists of legal documents to convince the government that reparation and redress were *the* axis on which the new South Africa should rest.

In Volume 5 of the final report, the commission recommended that a person should be appointed in the President's Office to coordinate a fund, made up by wealth tax and contributions by beneficiaries, to pay out the reparation fees; this person should link ministries such as health, education and legal support to the needs of victims, and should report on how this assistance was being carried out. There was supposed to be interim reparation, final reparation as well as symbolic reparation to underscore the importance of human rights through keeping the memories alive.

The reaction of the post-Mandela government was the complete opposite: it didn't want to give any reparation at all, because people 'didn't fight for liberation for money'. Remarks like these prompted a furious response from Commissioner Yasmin Sooka:

> When our country accepted that we should go the Truth Commission route, we accepted that we would pursue a model of restorative justice rather than retributive justice [. . .]. This notion of restorative justice is in trouble. It is jeopardized by our failure to make changes in the material circumstances of those who came forward to tell their stories [. . .].
>
> I fear that if we do not deal with this vision and this promise we made to our people, then we may also experience what is happening in Zimbabwe. In the twenty years that have gone by, no effort was made by that government to deal with the war veterans and now that unfinished business may destroy the present (Krog 1998: 290).

Sooka also pointed out that the Constitutional Court established that amnesty was only possible because of the commitment to reparations. The absence of reparation gave the victims the right to go to court to set aside the granting of amnesty:

> It would be a tragedy if this fragile peace we experience is placed in turmoil because the bridge that amnesty was meant to be is broken [. . .]. Media reports express the view that there is no money to go around yet money has been found for arms. What is the new democracy's priorities? (ibid.)

It was indeed a wasted moment: instead of involving the beneficiaries of apartheid in a constructive way that would not only see them giving but also bind them into a new society, they were ignored and more and more alienated through blame and, what they experienced as, accusatory application of affirmative action. A proper discussion about exactly what could and should be done by the beneficiaries never took place, nor were imaginative recommendations put forward. All we had was knee-jerk formulations of blame and refusing to take blame.

★

President Thabo Mbeki, Mandela's successor, appealed to the TRC not to leave the government with 'a lot of unfinished business' but the Amnesty Committee has done precisely that: of the 7,115 amnesty applications dealt with by the TRC, 1,146 (or just over 16 per cent) were granted amnesty and 5,504 (77.3 per cent) were refused. Who, now, should be prosecuted? The prominent white army generals and the IFP warlords who scoffed at and scorned the process? Or the ordinary perpetrators who attended weeks of public hearings but had their amnesties refused?

ANC minister Kader Asmal, for years a professor of law and dean of humanities in Dublin University and deeply involved in setting up the truth commission, warned against the over-judicialization of the TRC process: 'A further area of concern is the increasing judicialization of the Truth Commission's proceedings. In fact the Commission owes its existence in part to a rejection of the judicial option for dealing with the past [. . .]' (Krog 1998: 291).

Asmal's concern was well grounded: the amnesty hearings turned into quasi-trials and judicialized procedures, with all the expense and delay they entail. This meant, of course, that arguments in favour of judicialized outcomes were preferred to arguments favouring moral or political outcomes.

The character and legislation of the Amnesty Committee made this judicializing unavoidable. The three high court judges of the Amnesty Committee didn't form part of the commission itself and did not share the general life and times of the commissioners from the beginning. They did not attend the weeks of retreat prescribed by Tutu to focus on the goals of reconciliation and healing, nor participated in formulating an ethos of trying to move out of an amoral space into a moral humane one. By not forming part of the human rights hearings, they were often cut off from political, moral, financial and media pressures.

Slowly, painstakingly, respectful of legal procedures, they set about their task—decent, honourable legal minds. In the meantime, the clock was ticking away: the TRC closed down, offices were shut, money ran out, news hounds moved on, politics changed, victims and perpetrators died of cancer or old age, with amnesty decisions dripping few and far between—out of context and without attempts to place them within the broader TRC process. In the absence of victim voices, the granting of amnesty began to sound bizarre.

★

What has been for me the most astonishing neglect in all assessments of the TRC so far is the body's extraordinary contribution *in treating all victims the same*. In contrast to the perpetrators, who were treated as acting within a just or unjust context, no victim was regarded as someone who had no 'right' to feel pain or loss. There were no first- or second-class victims before the TRC. The mother whose child died opposing apartheid testified next to the mother whose child died defending it. White and black, coloured and Indian, literate and illiterate, rural and urban—the testimony of each was respected in the same way. To understand how radical this is, is to imagine a forum in postwar Germany with a German girl and a Jewish girl testifying about the loss of their respective fathers. This is a major break with established international thinking about victimhood and it remains the TRC achievement that has been the least acknowledged.

We have been warned by members of other truth commissions that a government, no matter how young and coming from whatever moral high ground, may quickly become a 'normal' one averse to accountability and moral pressure. Chilean philosopher and human rights activist José Zalaquett has told a South African conference that after liberation one often could no longer expect morality from politicians but one should insist accountability.

During a parliamentary debate on the TRC final report, President Mbeki rejected the TRC's findings: 'One of the central matters at issue was and remains the erroneous determination of various actions of our liberation movement as gross human rights violations, including the general implication that any and all military activity which results in the loss of civilian lives constitutes a gross violation of human rights' (Boraine 2000: 321).

This created a lot of confusion among the public. If the Geneva Convention determines that the killing of combatants is *not* a human rights violation but the killing of protected people (off-duty soldiers, spies, prisoners of war etc.) and civilians (everyone who is not a combatant) *is*, then what was Mbeki talking about? 'Who is talking about gross human rights violations in Kosovo where civilians are daily being bombed?' said one ANC member to me. 'Is anyone saying America grossly violated human rights? No, they call it collateral damage.'

ANC accusations that the TRC 'criminalized' the liberation struggle left the populace at a loss: most people did not understand the reasoning but felt adamant that to criminalize the liberation movement was unforgivable. Consequently there was no debate—not on human rights, not on accountability, not on how to prevent future abuses, not on how much of the past is already happening in the present, not on collective guilt. The ANC's refusal to acknowledge violations perpetuated a fall back on easy past stereotypes: the difference between people does not lie in their ability to exercise moral choices in difficult circumstances or to uphold human rights for all people—no, the difference between the past and the present lies in colour and colour alone.

★

In many ways the TRC, like Mandela and Tutu, will never leave us. It will stand for ever as a testament to the moral imagination of the majority of South Africans, to grace, hope and a belief, despite years of experiencing the opposite, in the goodness of mankind. This is not to suggest that the TRC was an unqualified success, as an endless stream of criticism and accusations makes clear. But it grabbed the world's imagination in the most extraordinary ways. In an era in which conflicts, wars, imperial 'peace enforcements' and revenge invasions take place as a matter of course on every continent, the peaceful South African transition, with the TRC as its figurehead, has attracted an unprecedneted, formidable and extensive political and social engagement.

My initial engagement with the process was as a radio journalist. After two years of daily reporting, I tried to capture my personal response and culpability in the book *Country of My Skull* (1998). The TRC profoundly changed me and the life I led. Functioning as an Afrikaans poet steeped in Western culture and Afrikaner tradition (with an early serious bout of Ayn Rand), I (thought I) depended on my individuality and a fierce personal ethic.

Reporting on the TRC brought me face to face with something I had never encountered and, after months of hesitation, dared to describe as *superior*—or is *transcendent* the right word? Some black people, literate and illiterate, were doing and saying things more profound than anything I had ever witnessed. I have known brave and profoundly principled Afrikaners such as clerics and anti-apartheid activists Beyers Naudé, Nico Smith and several others who gave up everything, even their lives, to side with the oppressed. But what I encountered through the TRC was something else: the magnanimity of the hurt ones; a victim not wanting revenge but wanting contact. The thousands of revenge killings in Europe after the Second World War regularly crossed my mind.

Initially I could neither name nor place this feeling that I had every time I witnessed the response of some victims to the perpetrators. It was more profound than admiration. I felt how the whole framework within which I had been raised was limping, deaf and dumb. I began to accept suggestions of being over-consumed by guilt, even of being in a way traumatized and therefore not thinking straight. It was also possible, I admitted, that I was later caught in the trap of the success of *Country of My Skull* and therefore unwilling to step out of the aura of the book. I even accepted that I was naive. But it was as if my life was divided between before and after the commission—everything I did afterwards somehow stayed connected to elements I experienced there; whatever I wrote had the TRC either as its starting or its decisive central point.

After many years, I have come to the conclusion that the commission opened up the first possibility for me of a kind of inclusivity that I had never before been aware of as a South African. In fact, previously I deliberately avoided and despised any inclusiveness—I defined it as a neediness, a pathetic dependence, a desire to be a group animal, a brick in a wall within the manipulated political construct of apartheid. During the life of the commission, I somehow found myself irresistibly drawn to, and changed by, the moments of embeddedness after repeatedly traversing borders of language, culture, colour, religion and privilege. Yet I was unable to clarify whether this feeling was simply a desire 'to belong', which was anyway the driving force so symptomatic of artists and especially Afrikaners.

But something else also stuck in my mind and forced me into an academic approach. During the lifespan of the commission I had often been interviewed by scholars and other journalists. Of these interviews, three, which took place within a period of 10 days, stayed with me.

The first interview was with a film-maker from Tel Aviv. Brimming with compliments for and questions about our TRC process, he had a throwaway line: of course it would never work in Israel. 'Why not?' I asked. 'Christians,' he muttered while changing tapes. 'Christianity is what makes forgiveness tick.' This makes sense, I thought at the time.

In the same week, one of Ireland's top radio journalists interviewed me in a specially set-up studio in the Cape Grace Hotel. He had just returned from interviewing a woman living in a squatter camp in Hout Bay. His eyes were rolling with incredulity. 'This woman talked about forgiveness. We showed her the palaces of white people within walking distance from her shack, while she, after how many years, still had nothing. And she talked about forgiveness!' After the interview I asked him about the possibilities of a similar process in his country. He immediately shook his head and said: 'It will never work in Ireland, too many Protestants, never!' This makes sense, I thought at the time. The other truth commissions that have been successful were in South American Catholic countries.

The following week, I was interviewed by an Australian woman working on her PhD. It was a laborious interview overlaid with a sense of hostility that I initially found difficult to place. As she was packing up, she asked: 'Do you want to know my personal opinion on this whole thing [the TRC]?' Before I could answer she gave it to me anyway: 'I think you whites have bulldozed black people into this whole forgiveness and reconciliation bullshit. And you know what? I find it even more atrocious and unjust than apartheid ever was. For this, you are going to pay dearly one day.'

Feeling suitably guilty, I walked back to my car with her words ringing in my ears. But then I stopped. Was this true? Or had she just insulted 40 million black people who had recently overthrown apartheid? Were people like Nelson Mandela and his first democratic cabinet, the vibrant civil society, Desmond Tutu and the church, and the youth movements all stooges or at best puppets manipulated by whites?

Something felt wrong in the assumptions underlying all three of these interviews, but I couldn't work out what. It was only when I was appointed to the University of the Western Cape (UWC) that I returned to the TRC, this time academically, to take a different kind of look at particular testimonies and literature. This book is the product of that research.

I began by taking a closer look at the testimonies of victims. With UWC colleagues Professors Kopano Ratele and Nosisi Mpolweni-Zantsi,[1] we explored original

---

1 Nosisi Mpolweni-Zantsi identifies herself as Nosisi Mpolweni in Chapter 3 of this volume.

isiXhosa testimonies to trace the phases of 'making' official testimony. The first three chapters in this book have been co-written with my colleagues, versions of which form part of a book we published, *There Was This Goat* (2009).

As the TRC dealt with memory and the effect of scars on the psyche, I found myself returning to the Anglo-Boer War and thinking about post-war scarring and how young Afrikaner men were trying to redefine themselves through searching for an honourable past. This is the focus of the next two chapters in this collection.

But it was only after nearly a year and a half's research into African philosophy that I could write the keystone piece of this book: 'This Thing Called Reconciliation'. As the TRC made me aware of something undefinable at work in the commission, the research clarified that two ontologies were at work in South Africa and that, because one of them was ignored or scoffed at, this led to profound misunderstandings and distrust—not only in everyday life but also in how the TRC is being looked at and judged from other frameworks.

As this knowledge unlocked many issues for me, subsequent chapters explore the effects of these two ontologies in pieces of literature and popular culture. These chapters reflect my becoming sensitized to how we do *not* have a vocabulary to talk about ourselves or the disgraced in terms of hope and an ethic of care, and how we keep on misunderstanding what Mandela stands for and what Tutu is saying.

In the last chapter, I return to the TRC and the unsayability of grief.

CHAPTER ONE

Ways of Knowing Mrs Konile:
TRC and the Problem of Translation

ANTJIE KROG, NOSISI MPOLWENI-ZANTSI
AND KOPANO RATELE

He laughs when he tells how he braaied my son.

> (Charity Kondile, referring to apartheid
> policeman and Vlakplaas assassination squad
> commander Dirk Coetzee)

It happened fifteen years ago, now they fucking
cry for the first time.

> (During the amnesty hearing [Port Eliza-
> beth, 1998] of those who murdered anti-
> apartheid activists, lawyer Francois van der
> Merwe whispered this to his legal team and
> amnesty applicants, but it was audible on
> radio journalist Darren Taylor's head-
> phones.)

How do we read one another? How do we 'hear' one
another in a country where the past still bleeds within and
round us? How much of what we hear translates into finding ways of living together? How do we overcome a
divided past in such a way that 'the Other' becomes 'us'?

These are the questions that confronted South Africans listening to the testimonies delivered before the TRC.

To form an idea of some of the many stumbling blocks on the path to understanding one another in a society where internal division was elevated to a logic of governmentality, we—Antjie Krog, Nosisi Mpolweni-Zantsi and Kopano Ratele—want to consider some aspects of a single testimony delivered to the TRC. In examining parts of a single testimony, one can discern the full demand and drama of translation and how it can either lead to devastating translational misunderstanding or provide opportunities for an enhanced understanding born of real interlocution—the kind of relation that requires deep and sensitive attunement to the language of others.

The testimony we look at belongs to Notrose Nobomvu Konile, a mother whose son was killed by the South African security forces in 1986. The TRC hearing revealed that during the mid-1980s, seven young men were lured by *askari*s (guerrillas who secretly changed loyalties and spied for the South African Police) to receive military training inside the country in order to become soldiers of Umkhonto we Sizwe (MK), the military wing of the ANC. As they were about to embark on their first 'mission' early in the morning of 3 March 1986, they were killed in an ambush by the security forces. In contradiction to official accounts that unsuspecting policemen were attacked by terrorists, witnesses from a nearby hostel saw how some of the seven men were shot point-blank after emerging from the bushes with their hands in the air. The witnesses also reported how Russian hand grenades and guns were planted on their bodies before the national television broadcaster was summoned to capture the 'extermination of terrorists'. Those killed in the ambush became known as the Gugulethu Seven (see TRC 1998: 2.261).

One of the seven young men was Zabonke Konile. His mother was the last person to testify, after three other Gugulethu Seven mothers: Cynthia Ngewu, Irene Mtsingwa and Mia Eunice Thembiso. The testimonies of these three mothers became widely known after the TRC hearings and assumed an emblematic status for many. Thus, for example, after Mrs Thembiso saw the dead body of her son on SABC television news, she said: 'I prayed I said oh! no Lord, I wish —I wish this news can just rewind.' This pleading for the news to 'rewind' was widely quoted and became the basis of Philip Miller's composition entitled 'Rewind: A Cantata for Voice, Tape and Testimony', which was performed in St George's Cathedral on Reconciliation Day, 16 December 2006. Mrs Ngewu's words on reconciliation have become equally famous and are the focus of Chapter 6 of this volume:

> What we are hoping for when we embrace the notion of reconciliation is that we restore the humanity to those who were perpetrators. We do not want to return evil by another evil. We simply want to ensure that the perpetrators are returned to humanity [. . .].
>
> We do not want to see people suffer in the same way that we did suffer, and we did not want our families to have suffered. We do not want to return the suffering that was imposed upon us. So, I do not agree with that view at all.

> We would like to see peace in this country. [. . .]
> I think that all South Africans should be commit-
> ted to the idea of re-accepting these people back
> into the community. We do not want to return
> the evil that perpetrators committed to the
> nation. We want to demonstrate humaneness
> towards them, so that they in turn may restore
> their own humanity (TRC 1998: 5.366).

The testimony of the fourth mother, Mrs Konile,
seemed impenetrable. In *There Was This Goat*, a book
about this testimony that we co-authored, we noted that
during the two years of weekly hearings that followed Mrs
Konile's presentation to the TRC, her narrative stayed
with Krog as one of the most incoherent she had to
report on as a journalist (Krog et al. 2009: 39). She felt that
everything in it was confusing and seemed to pander to
the racist stereotype of black women that the TRC testimonies were trying to undermine. At the same time, she
suspected that Mrs Konile's testimony was important precisely because it was different from the others and that
perhaps one needed other tools to make sense of it.

During a period of three years at the University of
the Western Cape (UWC), the three of us—Mpolweni-
Zantsi from the isiXhosa Department, Ratele from the
Psychology Department and Women and Gender Studies
Department, and Krog from the Faculty of Arts—tried
to make sense of the testimony.

Coming as we do from a past divided by colonialism
and apartheid, our efforts to come to an understanding
of only parts of a single testimony reveal the extent of
the labour one has to undertake in order to arrive at some

comprehension of one another. No doubt every country where colonialism has wreaked its divisive violence is afflicted by this problem of mutual intelligibility but South Africa's organization of separateness intensified this problem to an almost unique degree. For us, the necessity of accessing indigenous languages and knowledge systems to achieve greater understanding of and respect for one another became crucial. Without recognition of the possibility of misunderstanding despite translation, we would have been doomed to continue hearing echoes of ourselves.

In addition, we had to bear in mind the fact that some testimonies do not fit the general narrative frameworks as they emerged or were anticipated in the TRC. Yet, it is precisely these 'ill-fitting' testimonies, the ones that appear strange or foreign, that can be reread in particular ways and with respect for their singularity, which can enable a fuller knowledge of who we are as we begin to say: we recognize one another.

THE TESTIMONY

The date is 23 April 1996. Notrose Nobomvu Konile testifies about the death of her son, Zabonke. Large parts of her testimony seem incoherent. Later, on the TRC website, there will be no trace of her name in the index. Under the heading of the Gugulethu Seven incident, her surname will be given incorrectly as 'Khonele'. Of all the Gugulethu Seven mothers, she alone appears without a first name. Even in her official identity document, her second name is given incorrectly as 'Nobovu'. Here is the testimony as it appeared in the official transcription on the TRC website:

> I am Ms Khonele from [*indistinct*] I have three children the fourth one who was shot, they are all daughters, they are all married. The one I was living with was my son, because I didn't have a husband, he was the one who left us, he passed away quite early. I was living with my son, just the two of us.
>
> When he came to Cape Town we were going to be given sites here in Cape Town, but he decided no we must come to Cape Town. Now—or he wanted to come here because he wanted to join his brother-in-law. We were told to go and register—to go and register all our sons, because as woman we were not allowed to have sites on our own. So he said to me I am going to work here in Cape Town, because he knew that we are going through a miserable life, he thought okay the best thing is to go to my brother-in-law in Cape Town.
>
> Indeed he went, I heard this from his brother- in-law that yes he is working, he use to usually give me a little of what he was working for. And yes I got myself a site. People's names were being called, but mine was not one of those during that process. During that process Pheza arrived, we were on our way to get pensions, if I am not mistaken it was on a Thursday, I was on my way out. Pheza said to me no here he is, quickly I was scarred.

But I never thought that because Pheza was usually coming to Cape Town I am not—I don't even know Cape Town and now we went on to the pensions. We went and came back from getting our pensions. I said oh! I had a very—a very scary period, there was this—this was this goat looking up, this one next to me said oh! having a dream like that with a goat looking up is a very bad dream.

When we saw on TV—I am sorry Pheza came in, I was very scared when I saw Pheza and I said Pheza what is it that you have to tell me. Say to me now—say it—say it now, Pheza said he asked me where is Zabonke, I said he is in Cape Town. Then he said I am here I am sent by the comrade in Cape Town the ANC.

So I asked where is that, he said among—among the shacks. I asked what happened, he told me that my son has been shot. He said let's go now, I am here to fetch you. Your son before he left, he said your name. He said because he has this shack which is his place now, he said that seeing that he left his own mother without any place, his mother must be brought into shack.

This place—this new place that he got because he is a comrade. So I asked to Pheza, I asked to Pheza—Pheza what is a comrade. I said do you know this place that you taking me to, he said yes I know this place I am taking it—I am taking you to it. These —these are the houses belonging to the comrades, Pheza didn't tell me that he is taking me to a mortuary. He just said to me—told me that he is taking me to places of the comrades.

When we left, I didn't even know what Cape Town was and I didn't even know what a town looked like. He took me to Cape Town. When he would hold my hand, I would just shiver, my whole body would just shiver. He took me to the hospital he spoke English for a long time, and I was taken, I was getting tablets and I was getting an injection. He was told that to leave me alone for a while, well I stayed there just for while.

Then I started to sweat, well I was starting now to be conscious, I wasn't sure whether I lost consciousness, I don't know when I lost consciousness. I wasn't alone we were, I was with other woman. We [*indistinct*] Cape Town I wasn't even shown what was going on. When I got there, there were lots of comrades all—it was woman and men. And young men and boys, Pheza—okay Pheza had dropped me at this place.

Then I was told that your son Zabonke has been killed, there were seven. I was told that they were in a certain forest, him and somebody else. Him and someone else were asking for forgiveness, they held their hands up asking for forgiveness. I asked them where is he now, where is this new home that he has. So they took me to his place, that is now where—where I saw the mattress.

When I saw him, I had this vision—after I was told and I regained my consciousness, I remember people were praying there. A Kombi arrived, people asked if I had arrived already and they were told yes I have. We were four mothers, then we were told to go to the mortuary. We all left for the mortuary and now my—my grandson was at work. I was asked who will accompany to the mortuary.

Now these men, these men in the mortuary says he will—one of them will accompany me. When we got there—when they opened the door I felt this cold breeze that's when I lost my consciousness. Then they took me to some place that I don't know, they took me some pills and they asked me do you still want to back there. I said yes I do, so I went and I saw him.

When I looked at him, his body, I couldn't see his body. I didn't want to look at his body. One of his eyes was out, there was just blood all over. He was swollen, his whole head was swollen. I could only identify his legs, because they were just thrown all over the place, one of his eyes was out. His whole head was swollen.

What I can only remember now are his feet, I could only identify his feet, that's how I could see my son. They asked if I am satisfied, I said yes I am. And in the morning, in the morning we were told that these children should be buried now because after all—after all these dogs have been dead for a long time.

So this—the comrades went I don't know where they went, they came back they said you don't have to bury him whenever—when somebody else says you must bury him, bury him when you want. So we decided we will bury him on Saturday. We went to fetch him at the mortuary. Zabonke was the first one, they were arranged according to the—to their lengths.

Zabonke was the first one because he was the tallest. He stood out of everyone else. Now I—what I don't know was he was already working or he had stopped working by the time he died. Okay we chose the boxes of our children, we could see the *boers* had—somewhere at the back there, on the gravel road.

The youth—the youth just was scattered all over the—all over. The youth now was throwing stones to the police, we were left on the gravesides with the priests and the youth were throwing stones to the police. After that now we went back—the funeral was a big-big occasion.

I wanted to go back with my son—the *boers* told me that you can never go back [*indistinct*] these *boers* have already communicated with the other *boers* at [*indistinct*]. They said that my son has a bomb, they said he will never—that's how I gave up. So now this comrade said okay he will be buried where he was shot, that is what I know about my son. I don't know all the other details that's all I know.

After that I was so miserable. I had no where to go, I wanted that house, that shack, it was very difficult. Something told me to go and pick up coals, it was on a Thursday. I was knocked down by a rock, and this big rock hit me on my waist. I tried to move so that I can get some air, it was at eleven at that time, but they could only get me out of that rock around 5pm.

When I woke up, I felt like I was just getting out of bed. And there was a continuous cry that I could hear. It felt like I was going down—down—down. When I looked, I was wet—wet—wet—I was wet all over the place. I asked for water, they said no we don't have water. I said—I was talking to one of the women who was with me. I said please—please urinate on a plate so that I can drink, she did and I—then regained consciousness, I woke up.

When I was awake they put me into a van and I was taken to hospital. The doctors said to me I must just go away, I must go back under those rocks where I was before, I am no-one—I am nothing, what is ANC, what is ANC.

He said this woman's son is the one who was—who appeared on TV. You must be aware that I didn't even see my son on TV, I don't even have a TV, I still—I didn't have it then. Somebody pleaded with the doctor and then they admitted me. On Christmas I spent my Christmas in the hospital, I even spent New Year in the hospital, two months there. My children were trying to fend for themselves while I was—while I was in hospital.

It's very difficult in the township if you have no-one to take you. And now I haven't left out anything, I have said anything—everything right now (TRC 1996a).

BACKGROUND

To begin our work, we decided to focus on the place where the testimony lost us for the first time: the paragraph about the goat. What we subsequently discovered was that although we were all perplexed by the goat episode, we each responded to its enigma in different ways.

It was immediately clear that the nature of our responses reflected the different disciplinary, cultural and intellectual traditions in which each of us was formed. So, before proceeding to an account of those distinct reading practices, we have to specify a few markers.

Whenever one speaks of the effects of colonialism, it is inevitable that the representation of the colonizing and the colonized intellectual traditions will tend to be oversimplifications. The 'Western' philosophical tradition underlying the forms of capitalism which came to dominate Africa is vast and complex, containing within itself many counter-traditions, not least of all the many forms of thought and practice which have tried to encompass a perceived continental homogeneity called 'Africa'.

One also has to acknowledge the continuous influence, for over two millenia, of Greek philosophical practice, Roman jurisprudence and Judaeo-Christian monotheism. Perhaps the most powerful and destructive element of that complex tradition was its privileging of acquisitive individualism, based on a modular conception of the autonomous subject—in all domains, from law to religion, from economics to politics (Degenaar 1995). The colonial legacy in South Africa bears the marks of this privileging, as the philosophy borne by the architects of colonialism and apartheid was radically different from the philosophies that informed life for indigenous peoples.

In large parts of the continent, it was not the individual but the principle of a collective protective layer that dominated thought. In the many rich traditions of orature and performance and visual 'art', and in the plurality of religions and languages, there is a repeated emphasis on the value of communality and a view of the human being which presupposes interpersonal relationships as the basis of existence. The principle is sometimes expressed in the following Zulu idiom: 'umuntu ngumuntu ngabantu', which means 'a person is a person through other persons' (Degenaar 1995; see also Gyekye 1987 and Hountondji 1983).

African indigenous traditions are, of course, constantly changing and are also influenced by dominating European traditions. Nonetheless, everyday life, while it was radically transformed, has maintained a grip on the ethical and philosophical commitments to communality which today often go under the name of 'ubuntu'. This happened despite the systematic efforts at transforming Africans into the kinds of economic subjects that capitalism would benefit from. Indeed, in many ways the whole notion of separateness, apartness and, finally, apartheid is the absolute antithesis of what communalism or interconnectedness was all about.

Moreover, an argument can be made that apartness was used to change the concepts of labour and exchange in order to make subjects available for capitalist exploitation. These efforts were resisted by giving value to all kinds of cultural deviations in order for rural lives to be maintained in the absence of men. Ironically, that enabled tradition, or brutalized or truncated forms of it, to survive—so also the idea of communality.

Though systematic discrimination and racial exploitation had existed since the first Westerners set foot in southern Africa, the National Party that came to power in 1948 transformed it into a total legal system in which every aspect of political, economic, cultural, sports and social life was segregated. The legal bedrock of the apartheid state—the Population Registration Act of 1950 —provided for the classification of every South African into one of four racial categories: black, coloured, Indian and white. Apartheid brought about a

> social engineering project of awesome dimensions through which the inherited rural and urban social fabric of South Africa was torn asunder and recreated in the image of a series of racist utopias. In the process millions of black people and a handful of poor whites were shunted around like pawns on a chessboard. Forced to relocate to places that often existed only on the drawing boards of the architects of apartheid

entire communities were simply wiped out. These included urban suburbs and rural villages, traditional communities and homelands, schools, churches and, above all, people. Sometimes the demolition was total. These deeds may not have been 'gross', as defined by the TRC Act, but they were, nonetheless, an assault on the rights and dignities of millions of South Africans [. . .] amongst apartheid's many crimes, perhaps its greatest was the power to humiliate, to denigrate and to remove the self-confidence, self-esteem and dignity of its millions of victims (TRC 1998: 1.30–4).

The first set of hearings on human rights violations was held in April 1996 in the Eastern Cape, where much of the harshest human rights abuse took place over the years. The second set of hearings took place in Cape Town and it was there that Mrs Konile testified in front of the Human Rights Violations Committee.

STARTING TO WORK

We obtained the tape with the original isiXhosa version of Mrs Konile's testimony from the South African National Archives[1] and used our different disciplines, backgrounds, cultures and languages to gradually devise a way to 'hear' her speak. We met weekly to share and discuss the results of our individual analyses, and we believe that

1 The sound recording of this testimony is on Tape 08 of the TRC cassette tapes. The video recording is on Tape 6B, Cape Town Day 2, of the TRC videotapes.

our method of working was as important as what we found. We first discussed the official version of Mrs Konile's testimony on the TRC website, and all three of us found it largely incoherent and incomprehensible. Among the possible explanations were faulty translation or an unintelligible witness, which in turn opened up another set of questions. Was Mrs Konile unintelligible because she was traumatized or because she simply did not understand what had happened and what was happening round her?

Mpolweni-Zantsi then transcribed Mrs Konile's original isiXhosa testimony, joining a group of students under Zannie Bock at UWC who were the first to transcribe isiXhosa testimonies in full. Then Mpolweni-Zantsi and Ratele retranslated Mrs Konile's testimony into English. It soon became evident that incomprehension had been created at different stages of the process towards an official version. There were common ordinary mistakes in interpretation and transcription as well as a third category that we called 'cultural untransferables'—in other words, cultural codes and references that did not survive the interpretation process.

The process we engaged in was rather like an archaeological excavation—every weekly session unearthed a new reality that seemed to us closer and closer to a multifaceted and complex original. We were guided in our efforts by Vivien Burr's warning that an individual's understanding of the world is temporally and spatially contextualized and not a static entity with a stable core (cited in Ratazzi 2005: 23). We therefore tried to avoid the temptation to find in one or another utterance a key to the entire system in which Mrs Konile's voice would make sense. More importantly, we tried not to make her the explanation of her own enigma. We were searching for relationships between her speech and the language of others, between her language and the world where it resonated.

Even so, Mrs Konile's testimony was so ill fitting, so strange and incoherent, that we were initially tempted to assume that the testimony was more of an intuitive and spontaneous expression of her inner self than a deliberate and conscious construction of a narrative identity addressed to others from within an agreed-upon framework for such narration. This was the temptation against which we would continually struggle.

Deeper analysis showed that Mrs Konile was not only narrating coherently within particular frameworks but she was, perhaps without being aware of it, also resisting some of the frameworks being imposed on her by the TRC process itself.

But this deepening understanding was only achieved when we consulted the original recording of Mrs Konile's testimony. Listening and re-listening to its often difficult discourse strengthened our sense that the meta-codes which might have transmitted her shared reality with many other South Africans had been greatly hampered by language and, equally important, by an absence of cultural and psychological context. In other words, we could only begin to work out how to listen to Mrs Konile when we recognized the extreme partiality of the translation with which we had begun our inquiry.

In this chapter, we undertake three distinct readings. Our purpose is to stage the kinds of understanding that can be produced or that are likely to be produced given different assumptions and methods. In the first section of this chapter, Krog performs what we have come to term, with the caveats mentioned above, a 'Western' reading of the testimony. Her analysis, which follows the traditions established for reading trauma testimony in the West more generally, emphasizes fragmentation and partiality and remains with the surface of the translation to show readers how the failure to account for cultural context distorts the analysis of what Mrs Konile was trying to say.

The second reading is offered by Mpolweni-Zantsi, who explores in considerable detail the original isiXhosa narration, focusing on translational errors and locally specific idioms in order to retrieve from Mrs Konile a more coherent and, in our estimation, revelatory testimony.

Finally, Ratele offers us an alternative conception of psychic life and attempts to reclaim Mrs Konile's integrity from the tendency to psychopathologize, which is so common to Western readings of testimony. In this way, we move towards a collective understanding of Mrs Konile's predicament and suffering, one that makes of her enigmatic story an object lesson in the task of translation and in the challenge of understanding others.

READING THE GOAT INCIDENT:

THE ENIGMA OF REFERENCE

ANTJIE KROG

> [B]earing witness is . . . not just a linguistic but
> an existential stance (Des Pres 1977: 32).

With her appearance before the TRC, Mrs Konile bore witness to her son's death. Fiona Ross suggests that the TRC testimonies were at best co-creations in which commissioners, audience and the TRC framework of truth and reconciliation all played a role (2004: 62). In other words, as Mrs Konile was testifying, those round her bore witness to how she was busy constituting an identity for herself at that moment within that particular context.

But this co-creation was not the only process taking place. Everyone listening to Mrs Konile was interpreting her narrative: relatively literally by an interpreter and relatively figuratively by an audience. The interpreter was labouring to find precise lexical matches for her utterances; the audience was trying to calibrate her tale with those which they had already heard or anticipated hearing. Listeners could reformulate their own identities in response to the testimonies because the stories they were listening to, related to them in first-person mode, could become their own private story.

A story made and told by someone else can become deeply one's own. Moreover, one can locate oneself within other larger public narratives, whether those narratives concern suffering under apartheid or a more personal form of suffering brought about by familial rupture or parental loss. Mrs Konile's story, however, placed barriers in the way of empathetic interpretation of most sorts. The footage of the testimony reveals how restless and uncomfortable the other mothers became when she testified. It was as if they themselves were experiencing problems in listening to her with empathy.

The goat incident in Mrs Konile's narrative was identified by all three of us as the place where we felt that confusion was setting in. In the preceding paragraph she says: 'During that process Pheza arrived, we were on our way to get pensions, if I am not mistaken it was on a Thursday, I was on my way out. Pheza said to me no here he is, quickly I was scarred [*sic*].'

Without any introduction, Pheza enters Mrs Konile's narrative. From the testimony of one of the other mothers, we had already learnt that Pheza was an ANC activist on the Cape Flats. He says to Mrs Konile: 'Here he is'. Who is this 'he'? Why was she 'scarred'? By whom, how?

> But I never thought that because Pheza was usually coming to Cape Town I am not—I don't even know Cape Town and now we went on to the pensions. We went and came back from getting our pensions. I said oh! I had a very—a very scary period, there was this—this was this goat looking up, this one next to me said oh! having a dream like that with a goat looking up is a very bad dream.

For the first time in the testimony, Mrs Konile locates herself: she is in Cape Town. But she says she doesn't know Cape Town. People living on the Cape Flats (the sprawling townships round Cape Town) often feel cut off from Cape Town proper and generally only refer to the name of the township in which they live. Mrs Konile, by contrast, keeps mentioning Cape Town. Pheza is coming 'to Cape Town'. She doesn't 'even know Cape Town'. In the next paragraph, she suggests that the ANC is living in Cape Town ('sent by the comrade in Cape Town the ANC').

Mrs Konile's inability to pinpoint herself in a township on the Cape Flats as part of a city stretching out round her seems to suggest problems with spatial perception, or at least a sense of dislocatedness.

When one reads the word 'scary', one wonders whether the word 'scarred' in the previous paragraph should not have been spelt 'scared'? In other words, one wants to ask whether this is a transcription mistake rather than an incoherent remark. The video of the hearing confirmed that we were indeed dealing with a transcription mistake. This made us aware of another factor: mistakes not only happened in interpretation or translation but also in transcription—with potentially enormous consequences for any understanding of what a testifier was attempting to say.

Who went with Mrs Konile to get her pension? Pheza? A friend? Could we assume that she was addressing Pheza when she described a goat looking up at her? Who or what was this goat? Was it a real goat she saw that day, which she simply made part of her TRC narrative? Was she using it (or being used by it) as a psychic device, a condensational image with which the unconscious might appear to the conscious? Was she living in a world where goats and people alternate or metamorphose into each other? Why would 'this one' suggest it was a dream? Was Mrs Konile known for daydreaming or 'seeing things'? Was 'superstition' a word to be used in this context? Did Mrs Konile see a goat and was she now retrospectively seeking signs indicating an event which, had it been known in advance, might have been avoided?

Those who advocate the reading of such signs according to a universal code, or within the particular but universally aspiring iconologies of Christianity, would perhaps see in the goat a sign of evil or disaster. The goat as displaced image of the devil might be inferred here. Other traditions would read it as a symbol of energy and creative vitality, but in either case they offer their readings on the basis of a code which has no intrinsic relationship to the history and living traditions of the symbolic and metaphoric practice in which Mrs Konile's goat had to signify.

She mentioned that the goat was 'looking up'— where? At her? At the sky? Why was 'looking up' bad? Was the goat pointing towards Pheza as the harbinger of death?

> When we saw on TV—I am sorry Pheza came in,
> I was very scared when I saw Pheza and I said
> Pheza what is it that you have to tell me. Say to
> me now—say it— say it now, Pheza said he asked
> me where is Zabonke, I said he is in Cape Town.
> Then he said I am here I am sent by the comrade
> in Cape Town the ANC.

This paragraph suggests a deepening confusion in Mrs Konile's conception of Cape Town: she is in Cape Town, Zabonke is in Cape Town and Pheza is in Cape

Town, Pheza having been sent by the 'ANC' in Cape
Town. The sense of spatial incoherence is augmented
by a political confusion when Mrs Konile said 'the comrade in Cape Town the ANC'. To Mrs Konile, the ANC
appears to have been a single comrade living in Cape
Town. Is it possible that one could have lived in one of
the most highly politicized areas of the Cape Flats during
the mid-1980s, with one's child recruited for military
action for the ANC's military wing, while at the same
time not having a clue what the ANC was? Later in her
testimony Mrs Konile seemed to confirm this by asking
'what is ANC? what is ANC?' The depth of Mrs Konile's
ignorance appeared tragic if not a matter of mental
deficiency.

Her testimony also posed problems for a possible
counter-narrative reading. For the testimonies being
solicited by and heard before the TRC were partly
intended to put forth a counter-narrative to the dominant
racist narrative of the apartheid government and its culture, a narrative that attributed to black women ignorance, lack of real maternal devotion, a failure to value
life 'properly' (and hence an incapacity to grieve fully at
the death of a child) and an over-abiding interest in monetary reward. The three other mothers testifying with
Mrs Konile provided exemplary instances of the counter-
narrative. They presented acute, albeit harrowing, detail
of their last interactions with their sons on the mornings
of their deaths. All three articulated the unforgettable
moment in which they saw on television how the police
pulled their sons' bodies with ropes into the open so that
they lay face up, exposed for the television camera. All

three could formulate precisely how they regarded these gross violations and what they wanted from the TRC. All three had a very clear perception of the moral questions at stake and of the costs of apartheid for its victims.

In contrast, Mrs Konile's testimony seemed to drift from one surrealist scenario to the next; most of her testimony seemed to have nothing to do with her son but described her own personal suffering in a disjointed and confusing way—leaving the impression that her son's primary value for her had been monetary and that she was in any case not really aware of what was happening round her. She also seemed to have no idea what to ask of the perpetrators or the commission.

If she was presenting a counter-narrative, what was its structure and what did it mean? How did it signify? Was it possible that she was exposing the TRC's counter-narrative as a new master narrative? But if so, what exactly does she propose? In the end, however, one could not dismiss the possibility that her testimony was merely an exception—a chance narrative that did not conform to expectations for a variety of reasons.

Testimony as First-Hand Knowledge

In their work on testimony in the context of post-Holocaust Europe, Shoshana Felman and Dori Laub remark that the task of testimony is to impart knowledge: a firsthand, carnal knowledge of victimization, of what it means to be 'from here', testimony is 'a firsthand knowledge of a historical passage through death and the way in which life will for ever be inhabited by that passage and by that death; knowledge of the way in which "history concerns us all"' (1992: 111).

Mrs Konile's testimony was clearly the expression of first-hand knowledge of something, but was it first-hand knowledge of the death of a son or was it perhaps more a kind of first-hand knowledge of her own life? And if the latter is true, what was it saying about her life? Little of what she said seemed to deal directly with poverty or with the death of her son, as was the case with the other three mothers. On the other hand, do listeners have an ear to 'pick up' non-straightforward references to poverty? What are the hidden ways in which poverty manifests in rural narratives?

In comparison with those of the other mothers, who formed a close-knit and articulate unit, Mrs Konile's testimony made little reference to and seemed not to resonate with the value of communality. Clearly she was urgently trying to tell the audience something, but there appeared to be little sense that what she was telling emerged from a community. Her story did not carry any mark of shared experiences. The other mothers mentioned children, neighbours, bosses, but Mrs Konile simply said 'I'. She in fact said, 'I didn't even see my son on TV,' as if she felt deprived of even the horror of a collective seeing of her dead child on television. She became the bearer of testimony describing a solitary figure thrown round in an incoherent and cruel landscape.

To use the formulation of Felman and Laub, Mrs Konile's testimony did not seem to carry the historical weight, the self-evident significance of a group experience, but rather 'embodied the insignificance of a missed encounter with reality' (ibid.: 171).

Pained Language and the Transcription of Silence

But is it not possible to understand the incoherence of Mrs Konile's testimony as evidence that her grief and pain rendered her language distorted and nonsensical? In her seminal work on the effects on language of pain through torture, Elaine Scarry claims that '[p]hysical pain . . . is language destroying' (1985: 19). One can describe many things but the moment one describes pain, language begins to falter. It is always difficult to listen to a narrative of pain, for the narrative is almost always unconvincing—as though the very capacity to speak about it is evidence of its insignificance.

Possibly, Mrs Konile's inability to contain and exteriorize her pain so that the TRC could hear it originated in the fact that pain had actually destroyed her language. Scarry observes that before destroying language, pain usually monopolizes language and eventually deepens it so much that coherence is displaced by the mere sounds of language (ibid.: 54). It becomes guttural, or onomatopoeic. Pain first takes control of the language, then renders it incoherent (because the pain suffuses everything) and then transforms language from mere incoherence into nonverbal sounds—moans, sighs, shouts, groans. According to Scarry, pain initially resists expression and then destroys the capacity for speech. It 'annihilates not only the objects of complex thought and emotion but also the objects of the most elemental acts of perception' (ibid.).

An analysis informed by Scarry's insight is foreclosed by the TRC transcripts, however. There is no indication of any nonverbal sounds in the official transcript. Only by *listening* to the original testimony or by watching the video were we able to confirm how much pain was present in Mrs Konile's testimony and these unremarked tokens of her agony revealed the degree to which it became subsequently easy to assume that she had lost her capacity to comprehend the complex events and horrors surrounding her son's death. This was an important lesson for all readers of TRC documents: the absence of any system for notating nonverbal sounds in the transcribed version of the testimony is a profound obstacle to any adequate interpreting of TRC texts.

Pain and Memory

Many theorists of trauma, particularly those engaged in memory studies, claim that the silence and stammering which afflicts language is not simply a failure to express, but actually betokens the disorientation of memory which happens in moments of extreme suffering, pain or shock.

Nanette C. Auerhahn and Dori Laub identify nine different forms of remembering trauma (1998: 23). Of these, that which they term 'fragmentation' seems most relevant for my purpose. Fragmentation occurs when memory retains parts of a lived experience in such a way that they are decontextualized and no longer meaningful.

Put differently: if all memory is somewhat selective, non-traumatic memory should permit the distillation of images and the insertion of those images into narrative form. But the fragmentation of trauma prohibits that kind of integration. The individual has an image, sensation or isolated thought but does not know to what it is connected, what it means or what to do with it. The observer sees not the memory but a derivative, a symptom that infuses the individual's life. The individual may know that the symptom is irrational, yet be unable to discount it. Although these intrusive incoherent fragments may allow a person to continue day-to-day living, they limit a person's response to immediate survival needs and inhibit their other social and long-term conceptual activities (ibid.: 29).

Is it possible that Mrs Konile's life had become, for her, an assemblage of fragments which nonetheless permitted her to survive? If this is the case, the fact that her narrative was incoherent to an outsider is perhaps of less importance than the possibility that it was precisely the decontextualized and isolated fragmentation that made it possible for her to endure the death of her son. Perhaps she mentioned the goat because she could live with the memory of the goat 'looking up'. But perhaps between the goat and the news that her son had been killed lies the unbearable tragedy of her life, the real suffering that she could not articulate, because, quite simply, living with it was not possible.

That day in April 1996, Mrs Konile had an opportunity before the TRC to have her story and her son acknowledged and her self to a certain extent restored. Yet she did not use it to glorify her son or to lay claim to the right to be compensated. Whether she did not wish to or could not do so is impossible to know. In the end, she simply put the fragments of her life on the table, and in the brokenness of it one could sense the chaos and pain. I confess that I remained unable to 'hear' her suffering. It remained opaque, obstructed by the enigma of a goat.

REREADING THE ISIXHOSA TEXT
NOSISI MPOLWENI-ZANTSI

After I had read the official English translation of Mrs Konile's testimony and listened to the cassette of her original isiXhosa testimony, I realized that there were some gaps. Some of the reasons for the gaps could be attributed to the difficulty or challenges of simultaneous interpreting but others seemed to be more problematic. One understands the daunting task of the interpreter. He/she has to listen to the speaker and internalize what the speaker says. Only then is he/she able to give an interpretation. The complexity of the work of an interpreter should not be underestimated because he/she has to restructure what the speaker says in a way that carries meaning to the audience.

Claudia V. Angelelli writes: 'The concept of visible interpreters goes beyond the fact that they are active participants in the linguistic interaction. It takes into consideration the power that interpreters possess' (2004: 9). Since it is never possible to recall everything that the speaker has said, loss of information during interpreting is always inevitable. Such losses might have occurred during Mrs Konile's testimony. The interpreters were working under great pressure, trying to keep up with the relentless pace of the TRC hearings. It is possible that a further loss of information occurred during the transcription and translation of the testimonies.

According to T. Du Plessis and Chriss Wiegand, the nature of the testimonies put an additional demand on interpreters, because 'they were heavily laden emotionally' (1998: 26). One understands that, as human beings, the interpreter and translator were sometimes unconsciously affected or had difficulty maintaining a professional detachment. Another obstacle to a good interpretation could be the fact that the techniques applied by the witnesses in presenting their narratives differed from one witness to another—for example, some witnesses provided too much detail, while others were not very coherent and still others included explicit references to taboo or crude language (ibid.: 26–7).

The challenges mentioned above must have put an additional burden on the interpreter who, despite all the problems raised above, has to generate a product that is communicable and meaningful to the listener while reflecting a picture that is as close as possible to the aspirations of the witnesses (Hatim 2001: 1).

If her testimony functioned within the terms of the TRC's implicit aims, Mrs Konile was to contribute part of what Geoffrey Bennington calls the 'narration at the centre of the nation: stories of national origins, myths of founding fathers, genealogies of heroes' (1990: 121), all those things providing a country with a history, a boundary and a name. We thought that Mrs Konile was not very successful in steering her story in terms of this 'narrating the nation' context. She tried to tell a personal story but it seemed to get lost among nightmares, seeing goats, being pinned down by a rock and collapsing.

The question that I would like to address is: If Mrs Konile's narrative sounded incoherent, as indicated earlier, could this be the result of some information that had been lost in the process of translation; or was it because the context in which she delivered her narrative did not fit in with or was outside the framework of the other mothers who testified?

What I would like to establish is how the lost information influenced intercultural communication between Mrs Konile and the TRC officials on the one hand, and the audience and other possible readers on the other. Second, I want to determine whether knowledge of another context could lead to a fuller interpretation, one that would perhaps do more justice to the person who testified.

The Surprise

The official English version of Mrs Konile's testimony on the TRC website begins as follows: 'I am Ms Khonele from [*indistinct*] I have three children . . .' What word was indicated by '[*indistinct*]'? The TRC hearing was held in Cape Town, the Gugulethu Seven incident happened in Cape Town and all the other mothers who testified lived in Cape Town. Mrs Konile herself mentioned Cape Town repeatedly in her testimony, so we all assumed that she was also from Cape Town. We assumed that the '[*indistinct*]' word(s) was 'Cape Town'.

But the rock incident that we have identified as being as inaccessible as that of the goat (it is discussed in Chapter 2) was incomprehensible within a Cape Town context. There was no coal-digging activity in and round the city. Was she referring to picking up coal in a coal yard? But where would a rock come from to pin her down for five hours?

When I listened to the original isiXhosa testimony on the cassette, I picked up that Mrs Konile was using *moshani* for 'mortuary' and *khombresi* for 'comrade'—these usages are peculiar to rural Eastern Cape. I went back to the beginning of the tape and, after listening to it several times, heard her say: 'NdinguMrs Konile, eNdwe' (I am Mrs Konile from Indwe). Indwe is a village situated near Queenstown in the Eastern Cape and is known for its coal-digging activities.

From the videotape on which both the English translation and the isiXhosa original were audible, I could hear that Mrs Konile's words were correctly interpreted. So it must have been that the TRC transcriber, perhaps unfamiliar with this small hamlet near Queenstown, could not distinguish the word and therefore used '[*indistinct*]' in the official website version.

The discovery of the word 'Indwe' was a revelation! It swung the whole testimony from the realm of the incomprehensible to the comprehensible and was the single biggest contributor to the possibility of making the testimony more coherent. It also provided an example of how a transcription mistake in the English version could be detected through language peculiarities in the original sound recording. By listening to the isiXhosa, I was actually able to grasp a silence and an error in the English. Without it, the English would have appeared to be a perfect conserver of meaning, and thus evidence of Mrs Konile's incapacity to make meaning.

The revelation of a rural Eastern Cape context radically changed the whole manner in which we listened to and approached our analysis of the testimony. As a person living in the rural areas, Mrs Konile would most probably not have been as politically conscious as her fellow testifiers from Gugulethu and was almost certainly more closely connected to traditional rural life instead. This was evident throughout her original testimony, not only in particular pronunciations and expressions but also in symbols, references and gestures.

The Goat Incident

Clarity round the goat incident became possible after I discovered another omission, one that constituted a very serious error of interpretation. The isiXhosa word 'dream' was not interpreted but the original isiXhosa made it clear that it was not an *incident* with a goat but a *dream* about a goat that Mrs Konile was talking about.

The other three mothers described how they learnt of their sons' deaths through comrades and the television; Mrs Konile, however, started her testimony with a dream. A careful reading reveals that this dream is also an account of how she learnt of her son's death: 'Heyi! Yhaz' umbilini wam, undiphethe kakubi. Phezolo ndiphuphe kakubi.' (Heyi! You know what, my heart is palpitating with a strange feeling, and it persists.) She constantly interrupts her testimony by talking to herself in the way rural story-tellers often do. Although these references to a bad dream may seem irrelevant, they are the markers predicting pain, desperation, loss and distress.

Official Version

We went and came back from getting our pensions. I said oh! I had a very—a very scary period, there was this—this was this goat looking up, this one next to me said oh! having a dream like that with a goat looking up is a very bad dream.

isiXhosa Version

Sihambe sibuy' epeyini. Ndithi kulo ndihamba naye, ndithi, 'Heyi! Yhaz' umbilini wam, undiphethe kakubi. Phezolo ndiphuphe kakubi. Ndiphuphe apha ngasemnyango, kukho ibhokhwe emileyo, eyenjenje, ehh—emileyo ethe', ahleke athi lo, athi 'Eyi! Uphuphe kakubi nyhani'. Ngasemthini!

The retranslation is as follows (the direct words of Mrs Konile and those of her friend are indicated by quotation marks):

We [*Mrs Konile and her friend accompanying her*] went and came back from the grants office. I said to her, the one I was going with, I said, 'Heyi! You know what, my heart is palpitating with a strange feeling, and it persists. Last night I had a terrible dream. I dreamt that here at my door there was a goat that was standing, like this, ehh—standing like this' [*gesturing with her hands*], and my friend laughed and said, 'Eyi! You really had a bad dream.' Next to the tree!

Slippages in Translation

In the official version, the word 'dream' was missing. Only the words 'a very scary period' appeared and the transcript then continued: 'there was this—this was this goat looking up'. There seemed to be no clear connection between the scary period and the goat. The remark of Mrs Konile's friend—'having a dream like that [. . .] is a very bad dream'—confused things further: Was it a scary period or a bad dream, or was the scary period like a bad dream?

Bringing in the lost information via the original text allowed for a more conclusive reading. First Mrs Konile dreamt about the goat. Then she went with a friend to get a grant. There she saw Pheza, who would tell her in the following few hours about her son's death. The dream of the goat led her to regard Pheza's presence as ominous. As the story unfolded, her foreboding plus the dream seemed to take on greater significance in terms of cultural tradition.

Mrs Konile made use of exclamations to express her feelings about the terrible dream, such as, 'Heyi! Yhaz' umbilini wam, undiphethe kakubi. Phezolo ndiphuphe kakubi'. As she related her story, she seemed to have a vivid picture of the events, and she even demonstrated how the goat was standing. For example, she said, '. . . emileyo, eyenjenje, ehh—emileyo ethe . . .' [. . . that was standing, like this, ehh—standing like this . . .]. The way in which the goat was standing seemed to be very strange to her. On the videotape, we watched Mrs Konile demonstrate with her hands to show that the goat was standing on its hind legs. In other words, the goat was not looking up, but was standing up. She used repetition in the form of three consecutive synonyms to emphasize the strangeness in the way it was standing, namely: *emileyo, eyenjenje, ethe*. Her friend further highlighted the strangeness of the appearance of this goat when she said, 'Eyi! Uphuphe kakubi nyhani' (Eyi! You really had a bad dream).

The word *umbilini* in the original isiXhosa testimony meant 'a very strange feeling' and could be read as a kind of foreboding—implying that the goat dream was being attributed crucial cultural implications. By omitting these cultural allusions, the interpreter effaced important information. Indeed, this information could be seen from Mrs Konile's perspective as pointing to the tragic death of her son, Zabonke. She was not only talking about her personal forebodings but was trying to express her pain.

Christina Schaffner and Helen Kelly-Holmes warn that 'translators [and interpreters] have to be aware of the fact that cultures not only express ideas differently, but they also *shape concepts and text differently*' (1995: 6; emphasis added). In terms of Mrs Konile's testimony, an interpreter who is familiar with her culture would have understood that the sighs, repetitions and exclamations in her speech conveyed important information about her emotional state. But how were these indicators to be transferred into spoken English and afterwards into written text?

Mrs Konile connected the goat with Pheza, who frequently travelled between Cape Town and Indwe. Her own son was at that stage in Cape Town. She associated the strange feeling with the appearance of Pheza and it seemed to haunt her as she remarked, 'Xa ndizawuphuma, ndibon' ukuthi, ath' uPheza, "Hayi nguye lo". Ndi—kuthi dwe ngumbilini.' (Just when I was on my way out, I saw Pheza and he looked at us and said, 'No, it's this one'. I—my heart just throbbed.)

On their way back from the grants office, they met Pheza for the second time and the strange foreboding persisted. She became increasingly impatient about this: 'Xa sithi thu, Tyhini! Nank' uPheza kwakhona. Hee! Yhaz' uba yintoni na lent' izawuthethwa nguPhe za kum.' (Just when we were approaching the houses, would you believe it! here was Pheza again. Hee! I wonder what is it that Pheza wants to say to me?) In the end, she anxiously burst out, 'Yintoni lent' uzayithetha kum? Yithethe, yithethe ngoku!' (What is it that you are going to say to me? Say it, say it now!) Immediately after her remarks, Pheza related the news about the death of her son.

The sequence of forebodings every time Mrs Konile saw Pheza, coupled with the story of the goat dream, indicated that culturally these incidents were connected for her. Mrs Konile was communicating a message to the TRC audience that effectively said, 'Long before I heard of my child's death, I was already in pain through the premonitions and the bad dream.' But the interpreter seemed to have either missed the cultural codes or was unable to find a way to transfer them effectively into English.

In normal circumstances, a goat in rural Xhosa culture is associated with ancestral rituals. These rituals are a way of maintaining a bond between people and their ancestors. Some families slaughter a goat when a child is introduced to the ancestors; other families might kill a sheep. The persistent strange feeling and the strange stance of the goat might be understood as techniques of the ancestors to prepare Mrs Konile emotionally to receive the bad news about her son. Similarly, her concern about the strange feeling would also prepare other Xhosa listeners at the TRC hearings: the goat was foreshadowing her son's death.

Conclusion

At first glance it appears a simple matter: the recovery of two words, 'Indwe' and 'dream'. And yet, through them a radical rereading of Mrs Konile's entire testimony became possible. These two words opened a cultural universe, made an apparently incoherent testimony sensible and revealed not only a profound depth of grief about the loss of a son but also the painful predicament of a woman whose child has entered a social and political universe very far from her own.

The above discussion makes clear that the processes of interpreting, translating and transcribing are freighted with cultural assumptions and should also be seen as acts of cross-cultural communication. Because of the slippages in the interpretation of Mrs Konile's testimony, the valuable information and deep significance of her feelings and aspirations could not reach many of the TRC officials and the audiences assembled at the hearings. They are even more inaccessible to the readers of the TRC reports. Apparently innocuous slippages in translation can lead to enormous misinterpretations and misrepresentations of a testifier, and while there can be no guarantee of a complete or perfect transmission of intention in any translation, intimate cultural knowledge can—it should now be clear—lead to a fuller and more just interpretation of a mother-tongue testimony. This justice in translation is also, we believe, justice for the testifier, whose dignity is partially restored in the moment that her world and her experience of it can at least be recognized through the gesture of culturally informed translation.

AN AFRICAN PSYCHOLOGICAL READING

KOPANO RATELE

A Forewarning

On the eve of the day the news of Zabonke Konile's death was brought to her, Mrs Konile had a dream. In the dream she saw a goat. The animal was in a strange pose and stood under a tree next to her door. A goat in a strange pose next to a door was construable as an unto-ward sign. In her testimony, Mrs Konile said that on the day after the night of the dream, she felt out of sorts, and it was the dream with which she associated her funny feeling.

At the level of deep affect or unconscious, it was not strange when Mrs Konile said an animal was the sign of what she would learn about the next day. But the dream also functioned at a much simpler level. As we have seen, the word 'dream' was the vital missing link, whose presence could have made Mrs Konile more intelligible. A single line missing from the official English text (seven English words: 'Last night I had a terrible dream') brought Mrs Konile back from the psychopathological wilderness into which a reader of the English text might have put her—a cultural embeddedness. Even if the sentence failed to make her wholly imaginable as an adult psychological subject, these words rendered her into someone whose story was 'followable'. She had a dream, a bad, or strange, dream. It portended bad things.

In identifying and calling the mothers and other family members of the Gugulethu Seven to give testimony, the TRC was looking for a certain kind of story: that of a brutal regime, stoic struggle, resilient mothers and families, and an eventual triumph over evil. To a large extent, the commission had already acquired parts of this grand narrative from the other women. But it did not get this from Mrs Konile.

Mrs Konile began her testimony by sighing heavily six times within five rather short sentences, as if she was saying, 'I am so tired—I'm tired even before this process, of which I already despair, begins.' While the TRC hearings were meant to deal precisely with 'telling', its cathartic effect, and thus forgiveness, the commissioners appeared unprepared for and uneasy about Mrs Konile— they hardly interrupted her testimony and addressed very few questions to her. On the video footage, the discomfort of the other mothers with her testimony is also clearly visible. It was as if her story was resisting the imposed framework of the hearings, as if her mind resisted easy readings. She seemed to say, 'Mine is not part of what you want to hear. I will tell you of my dreams, my miserable life. I want to do my own kind of accounting.'

In the Realm of Dreams
Many African people use dreams to help interpret their waking lives. Dreams are part of the existential methods many use to make sense of their existence. It was therefore a perfectly ordinary thing for Mrs Konile to come to the hearings and speak of a dream. It made so much sense, yet it would be easy for some readers to miss this

part of her psychological make-up: how things were causally related to one another in her world.

When we recognized the dream of the goat and its place in the story, much of Mrs Konile's testimony became clear. The dream was a central part of the story, it was also a central part of Mrs Konile's psyche and her world—and both these were connected to language. In accessing Mrs Konile's testimony in the language in which she told her story, it became clear that underestimating this fact (of the centrality of the dream) is likely to contribute to a misunderstanding of her and her world. We need to understand what the dream meant for Mrs Konile and her mainly African audience. Mrs Konile's culture and world view originated, accommodated and carried the dream of the goat.

The dream was the connection to the ancestral world. The goat and the dream were messengers from the other world. Dreaming of a goat, Mrs Konile was suggesting, was like receiving a letter from the ancestors informing her that something was amiss. The dream of the goat also meant that the ancestors were not too far away—they were not far from her mind, nor from her lived reality. Any contact with the ancestors was not only psychological but also cultural, spiritual and, given the history of South Africa, political. The dream of the goat connected Mrs Konile to herself, her culture, her gods. Culturally and spiritually, that is, the dream meant that her ancestors were communicating to her that they were still around, irrespective of the nature of the news they were about to bring to her door. What was much more important was that she was reminded that she was connected and interrelated to a wider world of her people and to still other worlds.

But, politically speaking, the dream also connected her to what was happening elsewhere in the world. That is to say, the dream brought politics into her life, since her son was murdered in the struggle to liberate his country.

The dream of the goat was a guide and a warning, yet it led her at once to her people, her son and those in the other world. The dream was also part of a psychological world, a culture, of unspoken politics. The dream developed out of its very specific cultural symbology into a psychological meaningfulness and from the culturally decontextulized meaninglessness of the translated version into the psychic coherence of the original text, where it made perfect sense that the dream was there and told in that way.

From a discursive psychological perspective, Mrs Konile was also in the middle of (re)constituting her self and her world as an individual person of African heritage.

An Individual within Africa: A Psychology of Relations

There was no way of understanding Mrs Konile without understanding how the dominating modes of knowing brought by colonialism and institutionalized under apartheid could rupture indigenous modes of knowing— in this case, how capitalist Western psychology violently interrupted African indigenous psyches.

A simple and dominant definition of what psychologists do is to say they study individual behaviour. A vital point grows out of this definition—namely, that the discipline of psychology, formed in the particular context of the European and American university, presumes a lot of things about what an individual is, what the individual can do and what his or her relation to the world is.

Let me present an example. Most African students from rural areas or townships who come into contact with the discipline of psychology at South African universities (which is not very different from that taught at other English-speaking European and especially North American universities), or for that matter most social sciences and the humanities (which are also largely the same as they are in universities in Western societies), at first appear terribly confused.

What confuses them? Well, we teach students to get rid of everything they have been taught about the nature of social relations, about themselves and about other persons. If the students do not quickly shed their notions about what a person is and how people relate to one another, they are bound to struggle and, in fact, drop out. Recent studies show that 50 per cent of students who enter universities never finish their undergraduate degrees, and I suspect that, beyond money problems, cultural alienation contributes to this high drop-out rate. What students from rural areas or townships have to learn in the very first week of their studies to stand a chance of mastering their new world is that they cannot regard their teachers as their 'fathers' or 'mothers', 'ooms' or 'tannies'. That is, they have to get rid of one of the central lessons they have been taught from their earliest moments in most of their families: that any older person was your *mme* or *nkgono* (mother or grandmother), *ntate* or *ntatemoholo* (father or grandfather), *abuti* or *ausi* (brother or sister); they have to turn away from the lesson they received at home that any person of similar age to you was your sibling (*ngwaneso* or *kgaitsedi*). This has far-reaching implications in terms of how one learns and, in turn, whether one passes or fails.

Students have to learn not only to treat their teachers as unrelated to them, not deserving respect for living to a certain age, but also to be critical about what their teachers tell them and 'critique' in a way defined by white Western thought. If they do not get all of this into their African heads, they will fail their assignments; their teachers, who are not interested in being called fathers, mothers, uncles, aunts, sisters or brothers, and in fact are likely to find it strange and offensive to be regarded as 'familiars', will punish students for not treating them (the teachers) for all intents and purposes as strangers.

Given all of this, then, if one talks about African psychology, one always feels a bit exotic. The 'exotica' of African psychology derives from the fact that it is not treated as psychology proper. The same, naturally, applies to sociology and economics. It is as if anything other than Western/European/American psychology (or sociology or economics) is a mere analogy, something 'Other' cultures do, not the real psychology (or sociology or economics)—at best a derivative version, at worst a bad approximation.

In other words, the African psychologist and the African psychology student, like the African economist and sociologist and the African economics and sociology students, conduct their work and studies in the horn of paradox. They either have to disavow what they had been taught growing up in rural areas to stand a chance of being taken seriously by the world or they struggle to make the world understand the legitimacy of their culturally embedded world views that are always regarded as marginal to true (Western) science.

With respect to psychology, particularly ego psychology and its derivatives, its definition of its task is that of studying the individual mind—not the North American or the sub-Saharan African or the Chinese or the German individual mind. It rests on the presumptive universality of the form of subjectivity that Western society produces. Here, then, is the problem: How could one analyse Mrs Konile's so-called incoherence if one assumes that there is no difference between her and the North American psyche?

The cultural idea 'motho ke motho ka batho' (a person is made into being a person by other persons) is seldom fully appreciated—even African intellectuals (because of the paradox we have alluded to) do not fully apprehend what is borne in that concept and the values it implies. Nhlanhla Mkhize (2004a; 2004b) may be an exception in this regard, being one of the few psychologists to have tried to formulate a theory of the psyche from the perspective of this cultural life-constituting idea. Mkhize argues that if we are unable to understand the self-in-community and the unity-of-the-world, we are likely to misunderstand the individual or psyche and the world in which it gets structured and in which it functions. It is because we do not understand the self-in-community (I am because we are here) and the unity-of-the-world (we are all interconnected, even if we don't always know in what ways) that Mrs Konile sounds incoherent.

Indeed, what racism, colonialism and apartheid did and still do is to erode those specific values because, within the terms of economic rationalism and the acquisitive individualism that capitalism requires, it is often incomprehensible that one lives for others. It is very difficult within such a system to accept that others *make* one. The forms of psychologism that underlie capitalism put the individual first; from that perspective, the individual is foremost, the family being constituted by individuals and the world made up by individual minds.

But what Mrs Konile brought to our attention is this very fact that for some people this idea of 'me first' does not quite hold—does not hold them together as persons or keep their world intact. In fact, it is the other way round: if Mrs Konile, or any other person, wanted to perform a ritual in which she slaughtered a goat, she could not simply get up one morning and declare, 'I have had a dream and I am going to buy a goat and offer it as a sacrifice to my ancestors and invite you people.' No, instead she would have to tell people about her dream. They would help her to decipher it. If she wanted a ritual, they would have to agree and find a date suitable for all. One cannot simply slaughter a goat and say, 'I have a dead goat, I have my ritual, come and eat.' People would stay away, for they would ask themselves, 'Who is this person who acts alone?'

On a deeper, philosophical level, I interpret the dream as telling Mrs Konile about her interconnectedness with others being threatened, because she is not an individual, not in the way it is defined in the dominant frameworks of psychology. Rather, the dream revealed that she was still whole, in that she was part of a world where she was in contact with the living and the dead. They were assisting her in preparing her for her loss, appearing through signs that she could recognize and helping her to encode a world being violently torn asunder.

There was little existential loneliness in the moment of the dream's narration. It was only later, on learning of the death of her son, that her wholeness was ruptured, that she felt she was becoming an individual in a terrible way.

Mrs Konile's son's death introduced her to a deep loneliness. She experienced it as being cut off from the community. She was sighing because she had become an individual through the death of her son—selected, as it were, to become an individual. We can imagine her saying: 'I am suffering, because I have been forced to become an individual. All the other mothers are together there in Gugulethu, they talk and support one another, but I am outside of it all.'

I would like to suggest that the word 'I' was not actually indicating a real psychological individuality. Rather, Mrs Konile was using 'I' as a form of complaint. She was saying: 'I don't want to be "I". I want to be "us", but the killing of my son made me into an "I". This deed has removed me and I can't get back to where I belong. The last time I was whole was when the goat spoke to me. Since then I have been simply removed, cut off.'

Thus, to understand Mrs Konile—however partially we can understand her on the basis of one testimony in relation to one event—to accord her a psychological comprehensibility, our approach needs to be founded on her reality, her notion of her position in a universe of people, animals and things, and her thoughts and feeling of how she relates to others and the environment. In other words, meaning systems undergird the possibility of being understood by others.

CONCLUSION

ANTJIE KROG, NOSISI MPOLWENI-ZANTSI
AND KOPANO RATELE

One of the specific tasks of the South African TRC was to begin restoring the personal dignity of victims. A first step towards restoration and reconstitution was to allow people to testify in their mother tongues, thereby drawing on and accessing the dignity and wisdom of themselves and their cultures. The testimonies were simultaneously interpreted, which meant that people's mother tongues were no longer treated as cul-de-sacs, but were specifically used to open up hitherto unknown and silent spaces. Restoration could only begin when the testimonies were 'heard' and 'understood', including—perhaps especially—those that fell outside the norm.

In 'restoring' the official English translation and doing critical qualitative research into Mrs Konile's ontological framework(s), we have come to radically new conclusions and have left behind the kind of easy assumption that silence is equal to trauma or that incoherence in a testimony is the transparent sign of incomprehension on the part of a testifier. The consequences of this recognition are, we believe, profound for any treatment of the TRC archive and must give pause to those who would too quickly import the analytic assumptions of Western trauma theory.

By analysing Mrs Konile's testimony through reference to an African conception of individuality as that which is constituted in and through community, we have taken a radical step. We are saying: within a postcolonial context, a woman might appear either incoherent because of severe suffering or unintelligible because of oppression—while in fact she is neither. From within her own conceptual and affective framework, her testimony is logical and resilient in her knowledge of her loss and its devastating consequences in her life. She was not too devastated to make narrative sense. On the contrary, she was devastated because she intimately understood the tragedy that had befallen her. However, the forum she found herself in and the way official versions of narratives are being arrived at made it very difficult for her to bring the depth of this devastation to her listeners.

In this context, we want to re-emphasize the importance of our working method, because we think it has crucial implications for the study of truth commission testimonies in general. In a country emerging from a divisive past, some narratives, such as that of Mrs Konile, are likely to reproduce old cultural, racial and geographical divisions. To overcome that, as well as the inevitable interpretation and transcription mistakes, we suggest that there is almost no other way to proceed than by collaboratively working within a communally orientated human-centred methodology. Our method was, in this sense, coextensive with the ethical principles of the universe we were trying to access, in order that Mrs Konile appears to us in all her dignity. This method does not guarantee a perfect translation or even the full presence of Mrs Konile to our knowledge. But it does promise to overcome the overt violence of reading what does not conform to the dominant narrative as mere incoherence.

CHAPTER TWO

Revisiting Mrs Konile: The Problem of Knowing

ANTJIE KROG, NOSISI MPOLWENI-ZANTSI
AND KOPANO RATELE

We are still ignorant of what Mrs Konile has to tell us and what we have to learn in order to hear her.

We have seen how one can move, through a culturally inflected translation, towards some understanding of this unmentioned, incorrectly identified, misspelt and incoherently translated woman. We want to pursue the question further, taking up once again a moment of apparent meaninglessness in her testimony in order to test our method and to challenge our assumptions. Through this process, we hope to give her testimony the significance with which she tried so valiantly to infuse it.

Mrs Konile was the last of the four mothers to testify about the deaths of their sons before the TRC in Cape Town. Here we look at the most puzzling paragraphs in her translated testimony, taken from the official transcript on the TRC website:

> After that I was so miserable. I had no where to go, I wanted that house, that shack, it was very difficult. Something told me to go and pick up coals, it was on a Thursday. I was knocked down

by a rock, and this big rock hit me on my waist. I tried to move so that I can get some air, it was at eleven at that time, but they could only get me out of that rock around 5pm.

When I woke up, I felt like I was just getting out of bed. And there was a continuous cry that I could hear. It felt like I was going down—down—down. When I looked, I was wet—wet—wet—I was wet all over the place. I asked for water, they said no we don't have water. I said—I was talking to one of the women who was with me. I said please—please urinate on a plate so that I can drink, she did and I—then regained consciousness, I woke up.

When I was awake they put me into a van and I was taken to hospital. The doctors said to me I must just go away, I must go back under those rocks where I was before, I am no-one—I am nothing, what is ANC, what is ANC (TRC 1996a).

As with the goat incident, our confrontation with Mrs Konile's narrative of the rock left us perplexed. As we did before, we followed the method that began with re-examining Mrs Konile's original isiXhosa testimony, undertaking a retranslation and then pursuing our own respective analyses, before returning to share our conclusions and to forge a new, collective understanding of what we had learnt.

REREADING MRS KONILE: TRANSGRESSIONS OF THE
TRANSCRIPT

ANTJIE KROG

Following our initial work on the goat incident, I now
knew that much of what had previously seemed incoherent in Mrs Konile's testimony could be explained through
reference to the material fact that she lived in Indwe and
the corollary fact that her life experience was that of a
rural woman living in desperate poverty, relatively ignorant of the political struggles convulsing the nation. This
allowed me to explore her testimony beyond merely
focusing on what I perceived to be inconsistencies and
incoherencies in her speech. My 'new' knowledge led me
to a much freer exploration of the text, which was now
demanding its own forms of being comprehended. I also
felt for the first time that I could go back to the official
transcript (instead of our own new transcript), which I
liked despite its errors. From the very beginning, I felt
myself drawn to the rhythm of the translation based on
the primary testimony and wanted to explore what a bet-
ter-informed 'ear' would be able to hear.

Narrative Structure: Forms of Expectation

The task of the TRC's Human Rights Violations Committee dictated the form of victim narratives. The beginning
of a testimony usually consisted of some biographical
detail, leading to the middle part about the circumstances
and content of the violation. After clarifications, the
desires and/or needs of the victim would be established,
upon which the commissioner chairing that specific
evidence would conclude the interaction.

Testifying last, Mrs Konile found herself in a complex narrative situation. She had to tell her own story within the framework of four broader narratives: personal, communal, regional and national.

First, her testimony had to give voice to her personal experience out there in Indwe as well as her deepest pain. One can assume that she had certain personal expectations of what and how she would present. Second, her testimony formed part of those of the mothers of the Gugulethu Seven. One can assume that the other mothers expected from her that her testimony should fit in with, verify, affirm and broaden theirs. Third, her narrative formed part of the Western Cape hearings on human rights violations. The Gugulethu Seven incident was selected by the Western Cape TRC office to form part of its very first hearings as emblematic of what happened in the region. As the first round of human rights hearings was to receive heavy media attention, every region selected cases which displayed the variety of abuses as well as the variety of communities involved in gross human rights violations. Fourth, her narrative formed part of the bigger narrative 'gathered' by the TRC in order to arrive at a national picture that was 'as comprehensive as possible' of the wrongs of the past.

The Gugulethu Seven incident formed an integral part of the national liberation struggle. The death of these seven young men was announced on apartheid's national television as a 'breakthrough against terrorists' and footage was shown of how weapons of Russian origin were found when ropes pulled the corpses round from a safe distance in case a grenade exploded. This footage was shown on the seven o'clock news of the day and, as we shall see, played a substantial role in the testimony of the majority of Gugulethu mothers.

Add to this the fact that the two white journalists who exposed the lies of the apartheid police by publishing an eyewitness account of the incident were themselves going to testify before the TRC. In the years subsequent to the incident, both of them had become quite senior and much-respected journalists, which brought extra media attention to the hearings. Thus, in the glare of the media, Mrs Konile had to steer her testimony through the four-tiered structure of personal, communal, regional and national narratives.

Initially, I thought that she could not manage that at all. She tried to tell a personal story but its thread seemed to get lost amid nightmares, the apparitions of goats, her entrapment by a rock and her collapse. In contrast to the other mothers, she produced no meta-narrative formulation of any meaningful relationship with her son. Nor did she project a sense of herself as the general innocent victim confronting a brutal state. She also tried to link herself to the other three mothers ('We were four mothers, then we were told to go to the mortuary'), but coming from Indwe, she obviously found it difficult to produce a story fulfilling regional Western Cape and national expectations. Not once did she acknowledge the purpose of the TRC or mention the political significance of her son's death.

Our investigation into the dream sequence brought much clarity, but the incident of the rock felt out of place and impenetrable. I decided that in order to grasp the logic of what she was saying, I needed to consider her testimony in terms of the oral traditions whence it came and where its repetitions and forms of self-marking were part of relatively familiar genre conventions. Being a rural woman, Mrs Konile was unaccustomed to the forms of representation more typical and dominant in the urban world of Cape Town, where the other mothers of the Gugulethu Seven lived.

'Oral narrative,' says Isabel Hofmeyr, 'is largely shaped by the prerogatives of oral memory and its need to create mnemonic systems' as core images to enable the narrator to fulfil his or her task. The mnemonic systems may include 'a plot that is more episodic than climactic [. . .] and the use of formulaic images through which story segments can easily be retrieved' (1993: 106, 109). In the Gugulethu Seven narratives presented to the TRC, there were obvious mnemonic or core moments that were narrated by more than one mother:

- last contact between son and mother (Ngewu and Miya; not Konile)
- hearing of the news of the death (all four talked about it)
- seeing the body of the son on television (Ngewu, Miya and Mtsingwa; not Konile)
- identifying the body in the mortuary (Ngewu, Miya and Konile)
- funeral (all four talked about it)
- harassment and inquest (Ngewu, Miya and Mtsingwa; not Konile)

Interestingly, Mrs Konile apppeared to lack three of the most important core narrative elements: last contact between mother and son, seeing the incident on television and the inquest and further harassment by police. Not having had access to three of the most core elements must have influenced Mrs Konile's testimony in significant ways.

It is important to recognize here that the absence of these elements in Mrs Konile's testimony is not simply a function of her narrative; it reflects the very distinct experience that she had of the mediated public sphere and, consequently, her blocked access to communication— both interpersonal (with her son and other relations, including her ancestors, as well as with the harassing police) and mass-mediated (via television).

With her rural background, she must have been acutely aware that her own narration was in danger of not doing justice to her own and her community's experience. I want to argue that the rock incident functioned in her narrative to affirm the other mothers' stories while simultaneously testifying to the severity of her suffering.

Richard A. Wilson (2001: 50–1) reminds us that seemingly irrelevant details can often be enormously significant, even constituting key events upon which whole segments of narrative hang: 'Sometimes they can seem quite bizarre and expressive of states of extreme psychological dissonance. They are the personalized symbols upon which the structure of the narrative hinges and emotional associations tend to pivot.'

Mrs Konile's narrative ran parallel to Mrs Miya's (and the other women's) in many ways but, at certain moments,

Mrs Konile substituted the events of Mrs Miya's story with seemingly arcane or unreal elements whose relationship to the overall meaning of the narrative was oblique at best and nonsensical or irrelevant at worst. The list below identifies the points of contact and departure, in order that we can begin to address the possible reasons for and meaning of the differences that Mrs Konile's story might make and signify:

Mrs Miya	*Mrs Konile*
saw son live	saw son dead
at station	at mortuary
his clothes	bleeding body
last words of son to her	last words of son to policeman
TV	rock
harassment	urine

Between a Rock and a Hard Place

The television news broadcast of the killing of these seven young men provided the pivotal element of the Gugulethu Seven incident. In fact, the SABC's news footage became something like a signature or 'brand' for the Gugulethu Seven hearings and was featured prominently later in two documentaries about the Gugulethu Seven: *Long Night's Journey into Day* (2000) by Frances Reid and *The Guguletu Seven* (1999) by Lindy Wilson.

The broadcast itself must have confronted Mrs Miya, Mrs Ngewu and Mrs Mtsingwa with a bizarre mix of gothic horror and postmodern media elements: sitting in front of a television, seeing one's dead child being used as a prop in a killing that was staged as terrorist action, complete with planted Russian weapons, and then presented as 'The News' on television. Many clues might have warned a media-savvy viewer that the whole incident had been staged, except that the young men, these women's sons, although used as props in a make-believe event, were truly dead. Mrs Konile did not see the news broadcast because she did not own a television set; her poverty and isolation rendered her doubly deprived.

How could she effectively bring her suffering in rural isolation across to this TRC audience? How could she explain her marginal, television-less life in isolated Indwe? How could she convey that her life had become part of the margin itself? Hofmeyr suggests that the fantastic resides at the centre of oral memory (1993: 35). I want to suggest that within the small space left to her by the other three testimonies, Mrs Konile had no choice but to resort to a technique of the fantastic in order to do justice to her part in this group testimony. She created her own core image. She used the rock of metaphor and fantasy to do justice to her very different experience while at the same time affirming the central narrative of the mothers.

While the other mothers could move round looking for their sons, she was pinned down by a rock, she said. While they were catching trains according to modernity's precise scheduling of the working day (leaving at specific times, such as 4.20 a.m.), she was pinned down by a rock. She spoke of her endurance of this captivity, from eleven o'clock until four (translated by the interpreter as five), in terms that appeared precise but could only approximate the rigours of the clock that the train obeys. While the other mothers were attending an inquest where Afrikaans was a noise in their ears, she was lying under the rock, hearing a continuous cry. While they were safe and sound in their houses, she found herself drenched and so thirsty that she had to beg for urine to stay alive. While they were involved in commemorating their sons as political heroes, a doctor was taunting her: 'What is ANC? What is ANC?'

Identifying the rock as a core image opened up the metaphoric quality of this scene. The poetic rhythm and repeating words expressed her despair and loneliness like few sequences in the broader Gugulethu narrative:

> And there was a continuous cry that I could hear.
>
> It felt like I was going down—down—down.
>
> When I looked, I was wet—wet—wet—
>
> I was wet all over the place.
>
> I asked for water, they said no we don't have water.
>
> I said—[. . .] I said please—please urinate on a plate so that I can drink [. . .]
>
> I am no-one—I am nothing, what is ANC, what is ANC.

I am not suggesting that Mrs Konile was imagining these things or that she was making them up in a competitive spirit so that her listeners could 'travel [her] imaginative and emotional landscape' (Coplan 1994: 205) but, rather, that she was clustering particular incidents in order to form her own core moment in her own narrative of desperate isolation and poverty. Instead of the TV moment, Mrs Konile put forward her life immobilized by a rock.

Mrs Konile's excessive focus on the rock expressed her state of 'extreme psychological dissonance' (Wilson 2001: 50–1). (Or so I initially thought until my colleague's cultural analysis). One way to read this compulsive repetition of the rock and its association with urine is to read the urine also as a symptom of distress. Urine can be accorded polluting qualities by virtue of its association with bodily orifices, or what Mary Douglas refers to as liminal areas, and waste processes. According to Douglas' analysis, anything oozing from these liminal areas where interiority and exteriority meet—blood, milk, urine, faeces—is polluting (2002: 149). In several human rights violations hearings, victims testified how warders and police often urinated or shat on detainees in order to humiliate and torture them. So, at least for the perpetrators, the association of human waste with pollution was strong.

Begging to receive the rejected fluid of another body, Mrs Konile might also have been saying: 'I'm so marginal, so rejected, devastated, give me urine to drink, let me make humiliation, devastation and torture part of myself. Let me internalize my completely degenerated life.'

But one could also focus less on the fact that urine was requested and more on the thirst that was expressed. According to John L. Comaroff and Jean Comaroff, thirst is sometimes a key signifier of affliction in black religious communities: it 'connotes dissipation by means of very general images of physical depletion, images that imply an imbalance in relations between person and context'. To be thirsty means to be 'desiccated by the disruption of the regular, fluid interchange between one's being and the world' (1992: 82). Mrs Konile seems to have desperately wanted the connection between her and her world to resume its previous flow. Her testimony suggests that she felt depleted and desiccated after her son's death. The use of the word 'wet' six times in the original isiXhosa transcript, followed by 'I asked for water [. . .] so that I can drink,' may indicate her desperate desire to be replenished.

By creating her own core images, images that had abso-lutely nothing to do with the TRC's core image of the woman-as-mother-of-the-hero, Mrs Konile effectively undermined both the regional and the national frameworks imposed on her during the TRC hearing.

One must also consider the issue of 'awakening' in trauma studies. What does it mean 'to awaken'? asks Cathy Caruth, writing about the dream of one of Freud's patients:

> Awakening, in Lacan's reading of the dream [of Freud's patient], is itself the site of a trauma, the trauma of necessity and impossibility of responding to another's death [. . .] To awaken is thus to bear the imperative to survive: to survive no longer simply as the [mother] of a child, but as the one who must tell what it means not to see [. . .] (1995: 100–05).

Mrs Konile's constant references to becoming conscious, to waking up, to feeling like being asleep are all signs of efforts to deal with the encounter of the real, to wake up to the external world, to awaken to the death of her child. During her testimony, Mrs Konile was dealing with this imperative to survive in order to tell of her son's death.

Conclusion

I could only have come to this reading after my co-researchers found the isiXhosa testimony to be coherent and dignified and after they were able to attribute the apparent incoherence in the testimony to slippages in the simultaneous interpretation. The place name 'Indwe' greatly mitigated the spatial confusion that was implied in the English translation, recontextualizing the narrative as rural and thus linked to an oral tradition. With the barrier of incoherence out of the way, I could read the rock incident anew. And in this new context, I recognized in it such evocative and poetic beauty that my initial misgivings changed to admiration and empathy. In fact, the repetitions, the inclusion of small cameos of direct speech, the metaphors of goats and rocks pushed this narrative of the Gugulethu Seven beyond its entrapment in harsh township life and relentlessly unchangeable television footage. It concluded the group of testimonies with a deepening of content through the exceptional power of metaphor and the beauty of poetic language forged in pain.

TRANSLATIONS AND CULTURE

NOSISI MPOLWENI-ZANTSI

One cannot understand Mrs Konile's testimony without the context of her sociocultural background. Aspects that helped my 'reading' of her included Xhosa linguistic and paralinguistic information: repetition, direct speech, exclamations, crying, sighs and pauses.

Mrs Konile's Sociocultural Background

Mrs Konile is a mother from Indwe, a village near Queenstown. As a rural person, she is more closely connected to a traditional way of life, although heavily interrupted over the years by Christianity, colonialism and apartheid. This link to tradition is reflected in the testimony.

By listening to the original isiXhosa, we learnt that Mrs Konile had wanted her son to be buried at home (i.e. at Indwe) but the security police had refused that because, according to them, he 'had bombs'. They resisted her request so fiercely that her son, Zabonke, was buried with the other members of the Gugulethu Seven in Cape Town. It is important to note that after Mrs Konile had told the TRC about the police refusal of an Indwe burial, she used and emphasized the following words: 'Kwabe ke ngoku ndiyancama' (I gave up). This statement reveals that not even a hero's funeral with many comrades participating was more important to her than that he should be buried in Indwe. She arrived at the sentiment 'I gave up' not after her son's death but after she learnt about his burial place.

The desire to have her son buried at Indwe has deep cultural foundations. In traditional Xhosa culture, it is important for one to be buried near one's ancestors. This is seen as a way of safeguarding the channel of communication between the deceased and the ancestors, rooted in the belief that the deceased person will be protected by the ancestors. For Mrs Konile, this also meant that the bond between mother and child would be kept intact, because she could visit her son's grave. But more than that, her own bond with the ancestors would not be

broken. Her unsuccessful attempts must have left her
with a deep wound.

After the funeral, Mrs Konile returned to Indwe (this
was not clearly indicated in the official transcript). On her
return, she found life very difficult. The loss of her son
was compounded, first, by a disturbed relationship with
ancestors and, second, by the loss of her only financial
support; even the house that Zabonke had left her was
never given to her. According to Willy Jansen, the misfor-
tunes and complaints of women who are left behind as a
result of death, war, migration or desertion indicate at
once dislocation and poverty (1987: 4). Mrs Konile was
no exception. The death of her husband left her a
widow—but with a son. The death of her son left her destitute. The burial of her son in a faraway town left her
without any recourse. Even access to a house became
impossible. Her desperation is reflected in her halting
isiXhosa words 'a-ndi-akukho cebo, ndiyayifuna la ndlu,
ela bala. Ndadedisw' umva' (I don't—there's no plan—
and I want that house, that site. I was driven back). In
apartheid South Africa, only males were entitled to own
houses. This meant that the absence of her son had
plunged her deeper into poverty. She exclaimed: 'Eyi!
Akusenzima!' (Eyi! It was hard!).

In the official TRC transcript, this exclamation is
missing. Its omission tones down the severity of Mrs
Konile's plight and the affect of her speech. Her desperation becomes even more evident in her decision to go and
dig for coal. Yet, one could say that she resorted to digging coal in order to sustain her sense of hope. Reading
this part of Mrs Konile's testimony reminded me of a

Xhosa folk tale about an impoverished grandmother who was looking after her grandchildren, keeping them happy by telling stories while they were sitting round the fire. Since there were times when they had nothing to eat, she managed to sustain life by keeping a pot of water on the fire. The children would stay filled with hope that food was coming as they saw steam coming from the pot. Gradually the children would fall asleep.

In the case of Mrs Konile, however, her attempts to sustain a sense of hope seemed to have failed, for instead of finding warmth, she got hit by a rock and lost consciousness. At this point in her testimony, Mrs Konile started to cry but the official transcript does not reflect that she was no longer in control of her emotions. Her original isiXhosa testimony, followed by my translation, runs as follows:

> Ndabethwa loo mini, kwakungoLwesine. Ndabethwa lilitye, wabuy' umgodi. Kancinci, okokuba mawungandigqumeleli. Wahlal' es' nqeni . . . Ndabethwa ngoleveni, ndakukhut-shwa . . . ngo . . . fo. Ndathi mabandiph' amanzi, kwathw' akekhw' amanzi. Ndathi mna, 'Tsho kweny' inkosikazi endikunye nayo apha nakula madoda, a—a—' Ndathi—ndathi kwamna, ndathi, 'Chama ndisele, uchamel' epleytini le sikhupha ngay' amalahle.' Ndasela, ndaqabu—ka (*walila cwaka okwethutyana, isingqala*).

> I was hit by a rock on that day, it was a Thursday. I was hit by a rock, the rock fell on me. I was nearly buried by the rock. The rock landed on my

waist . . . I was hit at eleven and was recovered at
fo . . . ur. I asked for water, they said there's no
water. I said, 'Ask from one of the women who
are with me and from the men out there.' I said .
. . I said, I said, 'Urinate in the plate that we use to
dig coal so that I can drink.' I drank, I recovered
(*pause, crying, deep breathing*).

The rock seemed to symbolize and make visible her
sense of pain and powerlessness to the extent that in
order to crawl out of her misery, she had to drink urine
to regain consciousness. A consulted sangoma (traditional
healer) practising in Gugulethu confirmed that, in Xhosa
culture in particular, urine is associated with healing. It
holds potency and can be used to treat eye problems or
insect stings.

In the original version, Mrs Konile gradually
regained consciousness but then heard a persistent cry,
'Yho! Yho! Yho!' This cry seemed to symbolize her pleas
for help. She also mentioned that she found herself soak-
ing wet and this obviously shocked her, because she
repeats it six times: 'ndathi ndawujonga, ndajonga, ndimanzi, ndimanzi, ndimanzi, ndimanzi, ndimanzi. Ndimanzi ndonke' ('when I looked, I saw that I'm wet, I'm
wet, I'm wet, I'm wet, I'm wet. I'm wet all over'). Research
done into possible trauma among teenage Xhosa girls
found that incontinence is often an indication of post-
traumatic stress (see Booi 2004). This part could be read,
then, as a description of the manifestation of Mrs Konile's
trauma as well as her desire to be healed through the life
force of urine.

The Omission of Quotation Marks

After the incident Mrs Konile was taken to hospital. In the official translation it seemed as if Mrs Konile herself asked in despair, 'What is ANC? What is ANC?' But from the original isiXhosa tape it became clear that the doctor, who turned her away, had been told that her deceased son belonged to the ANC (perhaps in an attempt to convince him to treat her? Or, if told by the police, to not treat her?). In response, the doctor asked: 'What is ANC (anyway)?' Here is my transcription of the original isiXhosa testimony, followed by my translation:

> Xa ndifik'esibhedlele ndagxothwa ngugqirha. Wath' ugqirha mandihambe (*with emphasis*), ndiye phants'kwamatye kulaa ndawo bendikuyo. Bendingengom-nto yanto kakade, 'Yintoni iANC? Yinton' uANC?'

> When I arrived at the hospital I was chased away by the doctor. He said I should get OUT! OF! his SIGHT!, I should go back under the rocks where I was. I am nothing! 'What is ANC anyway, what is ANC?'

The official transcription omitted to indicate that Mrs Konile, in her retelling of her experience, was quoting the doctor. The lack of secondary quotation marks made one assume that Mrs Konile didn't know what the ANC was. By adding the quotation marks, the question is rendered entirely different: rather than a politically naive utterance from a distressed woman, it becomes the question of a suspicious third party—the doctor.

This is a prime example of how incomprehension was created in and through the accretion of several layers as the original testimony moved towards the official translation. Mrs Konile told the story. The interpreter translated it without indicating either by voice or any other marker that these words were spoken by the doctor. The reader of the official transcript assumed that an ANC activist had a mother who didn't know what the ANC was. In fact, Mrs Konile narrated the rejection of the doctor, his remarks about the liberation movement her son gave his life to, in an effort to tell the TRC about how terrifyingly vulnerable were the circumstances in which she had to live.

Conclusion

The coal story, the episode of the rock and the references to urine were real manifestations of Mrs Konile's trauma: her dire poverty, her sense of loss, her helplessness and the state of despair that she found herself in. Since her son was her only source of support, the depth of her personal devastation seemed to know no end. And this was the biggest obstacle the official transcript presented: it effectively effaced the extent of her poverty and her subsequent vulnerability from the narrative. In contrast to the other mothers, Mrs Konile suffered extreme circumstances of poverty and despair but this fact could only be picked up in her rural references, the points in her testimony when she cried, and in her references to the culturally specific practices associated with Xhosa life in such circumstances. Restored to a context that included these attributes, she became 'legible' as a woman suffering not only the violent loss of her son but persistent and repeated deprivation as well. None of this would have been graspable had we stayed with the English translation;

only the isiXhosa testimony retained the traces of these facts, and hence the fullness of Mrs Konile's humanity.

PSYCHOCULTURAL RUPTURINGS

KOPANO RATELE

Unable to always follow her testimony with ease, I found myself asking, why can I not readily understand Mrs Konile? This question lay at the bottom of my engagement with her isiXhosa testimony. In addition to *why*, I also asked *what* it was that I could not understand. What prevented me from readily apprehending her sense of things—her relationship with her son, the commissioners and the audience, with herself? Was it because she was psychologically disturbed? The answer to that was negative—she did not seem to suffer from any recognizable psychopathology.

My desire to effortlessly fathom Mrs Konile's testimony was countered by the terror of incomprehension regarding what the testimony suggested about a shared history of oppression, African culture and understanding itself. It is often assumed that those who share the same language and who are ostensibly from the same 'culture' and, especially, those who are subject to the same political process will be mutually intelligible, that they share a deep essence. My incomprehension of Mrs Konile challenged this easy assumption.

Provoked by this incomprehension, I came to postulate a general notion of what might be loosely called a 'psychocultural rupturing' at the heart of the TRC. This rupturing manifested itself in the tear or incommensurability between the multiple truths of Mrs Konile and the truths recorded by the TRC—indeed, between the psyche of Mrs Konile and the psyche of a body commissioned to hear her truth.

The TRC acknowledged the problem of dichotomizing truth into objective and subjective and instead opted to differentiate between four notions of truth: forensic, personal, dialogical and healing truths (TRC 1998: 1.110–14). It is interesting how Mrs Konile, deliberately or not, moved from one to the other. For example, she said, 'Ndabethwa ngoleveni, ndakukhutshwa . . . ngo . . . fo' (I was hit at eleven and was recovered at fo . . . ur). According to a forensic conception of the truth, this statement should have remained under suspicion until one knew whether any of the women round her at the time of the rock incident had a watch. When it came to the other kinds of truth, however, whether she was under the rock for about six hours was not really the point.

Entrancing Confusion

Mrs Konile made the work of her audience and subsequent readers difficult. Commissioner Boraine asked her to 'tell us where you come from, where you've been, about your family before you tell us what happened in 1986.' In the official translation she responded:

> I am Mrs Khonele [*sic*] from [*indistinct*] I have three children the fourth one who was shot, they are all daughters, they are all married. The one I was living with was my son, because I didn't have a husband, he was the one who left us, he passed away quite early. I was living with my son, just the two of us.

Mrs Konile connected her deceased spouse with her son. 'The one I was living with was my son,' she said, 'because I didn't have a husband [. . .].' She was not saying that she had children outside her marriage but that her husband died a while ago and that she was a widow. Even with this little bit of biographical information, Mrs Konile made it hard for us to follow her.

Let me insert some unease here. One of my co-researchers seemed to have no significant difficulties with 'hearing' Mrs Konile. Being a lecturer in isiXhosa as well as a Xhosa person with deep links to rural culture enabled her to access the way rural women speak. My other co-researcher, after some input from us, departed from what we could label 'a white place' and seemed also not to have further problems 'hearing' Mrs Konile. In contrast to them, I had problems. For me there was both a familiarity and a stunning strangeness to her testimony. What did she mean when she said that 'something told her to go and pick up coals'? Was that a common way of talking among rural people? Or did it indicate that within her world, Mrs Konile oriented herself 'irrationally' through signals and portents? Similar questions were provoked for me when I read that she had said, 'When I woke up [under the rock], I felt like I was just getting out of bed'. It was inexplicable to me how getting out from under a rock could be like getting out of bed. How should we explain all the 'going down', the wetness, the 'continuous cry'? To read Mrs Konile's truth literally did not deliver much.

These sentences had a dreamlike quality of magic and hallucination. Was it indeed about magic elements in real life, the fantastical used to render the everyday explicable, liveable? The rock was at once literal, metaphoric and metonymic. It referred to and stood in for the burden of a reduced life and living without a son (and husband and daughters). It did not really matter that it did not make ready and immediate sense. It was one of the truths—Mrs Konile's personal truth. She went digging for coal because she was poor, was felled and covered by one of the many boulders on the hill where the poorest inhabitants of Indwe scraped coal with tin plates from small quarries.

How should one explain with such an ordinary yet painfully material fact of loneliness, poverty and suffering? This, it might be said, was another truth, where language became too common and one needed to find other means of communicating.

Conclusion: Botho ke tiro—*Living with the Strange*

We need to find other ways to examine the truth of testimonies. What could these be? Given our history, any attempt to analyse the past or the present by anyone who values intercultural understanding must assume that a subject from another cultural group is both familiar and strange. More significantly, however, I want to argue that even subjects from one's own cultural group are both familiar and strange.

Let us then re-approach the testimony of Mrs Konile. Let us seek in her story a personhood that is as familiar as it is estranged. It is precisely in how she went about telling us of her life in her curious way that the possibility of her psycho-cultural wholeness lies. It is out of her

112 | *Conditional Tense*

strangeness and ordinariness that we are able to re-suture her self-in-culture wholeness, as well as her Xhosaness. Her narrative was composed of what must have been to her strange (indeed terrorizing) events but was conveyed in a familiar manner, and only by recognizing this could we re-suture her back into the fabric of a cultural whole, the kind of whole in which a self is also constituted through the totality of its relations with others. The form of her Xhosaness lay there.

To paraphrase what Comaroff and Comaroff have said about the Batswana, Mrs Konile's testimony revealed an aspect of *botho ke tiro*: how personhood is fabrication-in-progress (2001). The Comaroffs remind us of the process in which one makes oneself in the act of working in the world and in which working with others in the world makes oneself. This understanding of working and self-making is strange to most people who inhabit the worlds that capitalism has created. As anthropologists, the Comaroffs have offered a model for familiarizing the strange while African intellectuals such as A. C. Jordan have theorized the problem of how to relate to that which is strange.

Thus, to rephrase Jordan on ubuntu, the task of the intellectual is to be an advocate for that which is strange (discussed in Sanders 2002: 119–28). Strangeness should not be such a terrifying thing. In spite, or because, of the difficulty of following Mrs Konile, it was ultimately her elusiveness which achieved that point: that another person, regardless of her group or belonging, is always strange to some extent. Membership in a 'shared culture' does not mean total sameness and hence total mutual intelligibility. Indeed, when looking at an 'African self', an intra-African strangeness needs to be part of it. In the face of intransigent stereotypes fostering exclusivity, Africans need to re-accept that we have always been strange to one another. This should instruct us to be much more cautious about what we claim to know about one another, about what we say Africans are or are not and what African culture is or is not.

My conclusion has two phases: I had to verify whether Mrs Konile's strangeness was authentically hers or whether she was 'made strange' by the TRC's framework and/or simultaneous interpretation. Only the original isiXhosa version of the testimony could verify if Mrs Konile was embodying the idea of Martin Heidegger: 'The colonized does not exist as a self; the colonized *is*, but in the same way as a rock *is*—that is, as nothing more. And anyone who would make him/her express more finds nothing' (quoted in Mbembe 2001: 187; emphasis in the original). The original isiXhosa version established for me that, despite some slippages, her strangeness was entirely her own. Mrs Konile was coherent but strange.

The second phase was to embrace the strangeness, because the self is a work in progress. Through Mrs Konile one can learn to advocate for that which is strange. By accommodating strangeness, one contributes to the spaces first opened up by the TRC, by articulating a nuanced South African–ness that speaks of tolerance and diversity.

One of the specific tasks of the TRC was to begin restoring the personal dignity of victims—in many ways an impossible task in the light of how black people

in South Africa and Africans in general were (are) treated
and perceived before, during and after colonialism.
But at the very least, we should perhaps refrain from
'un-strange-ing' the strange and allow it to be strange—
but within its original logical and coherent context.
Accommodation of strangeness would keep the spaces
of tolerance open for many people emerging from contexts of conflict and estrangement.

CONCLUSION

NOSISI MPOLWENI-ZANTSI, KOPANO RATELE
AND ANTJIE KROG

The African, says Achille Mbembe (2001: 3), stands for 'a
headless figure threatened with madness and quite innocent of any notion of center, hierarchy, or stability', and
he/she is usually portrayed

> as a vast dark cave where every benchmark and
> distinction come together in total confusion, and
> the rifts of a tragic and unhappy human history
> stand revealed: a mixture of the half-created and
> the incomplete, strange signs, convulsive move-
> ments—in short a bottomless abyss where every-
> thing is noise, yawing gap, and primordial chaos
> (ibid.).

A small step towards reconstituting the sensibility of
Mrs Konile and restoring her dignity was to allow her to
testify in her mother tongue so that she could sound as
dignified, articulate and wise as she inherently is. A second step was to interpret her isiXhosa testimony simultaneously into English, thereby asserting that listeners,

especially the commissioners, valued the content of her contribution. But perhaps a bigger step towards restoration could only come about if the testimonies were 'heard' and fully 'understood', especially those that fell outside the norm.

Attention to an irregular or marginalized testimony is also a step towards liberating ourselves. It provides an opportunity for the ideas, techniques and issues from non-Western communities to become part of intercultural exchange and genuine scientific innovation.

In order to avoid Mbembe's accusation that recent academic output suggests that sub-Saharan Africa is wrapped in a 'cloak of impenetrability' and has become a 'black hole of reason' (ibid.: 7–8), it is important to deal with precisely those texts that seem to beg these kinds of descriptions. The roots as well as the 'ground around the roots' of TRC testimonies should be extensively dealt with before submitting them to various theories. For example, one could have regarded the question 'What is ANC? What is ANC?' as sufficient ground for a whole series of existential, alienation and/or liminality theories, while the presence of quotation marks rendered it into a sceptical and/or nasty remark.

Looking Back

Without perhaps realizing it at the time, we have strayed with our analysis of the testimony of Mrs Konile into postcolonial territory. While doing research on translation, the work of Gayatri Chakravorty Spivak (1988) suddenly became relevant to the effort we made to 'hear' Mrs Konile from Indwe.

Spivak posed the famous question: Can the subaltern speak? According to her, it is the woman who lives below the radar of news gathering, research and government, who finds herself in 'a space outside of organized labor, below the attempted reversal of capital logic. Conventionally, this space is described as the habitat of the *sub*proletariat or the *sub*altern' (1993: 78).

Mrs Konile was such a person. We came to realize that the incident of coal-gathering was told to the commission in an effort on her part to explain precisely how poor she had become after the death of her son. The coal pickers from Indwe who scrape coal with tin plates to sell for a pitiful amount to the brick makers at the edge of the township are the truly desperate and destitute ones, beyond telling or speaking, unable to move their dry lips and mouths parched and bleeding through lack of water.

As a coal picker, Mrs Konile would have stayed off the South African radar, until a truth commission was tasked to gather the narratives of those whose human rights had been violated through their political stance. Instead of focusing on the famous stories, the commission deliberately set out to travel across the country to find more marginalized narratives. Through its extensive translation set-up it became the first South African institution which provided a space for people from far-flung isolated areas to 'speak'. This made it possible for the experience of a subaltern to be picked up, translated and even broadcast nationally.

Spivak (cited in Williams and Chrisman 1993: 190) reiterated that she never asked: Can the subaltern *talk*? The subaltern is talking, she says, but we and the radar are not capable of picking it up—we don't hear / understand her spe(ak)ech. Therefore, although Mrs Konile was no longer regarded a subaltern (because she was being heard), the strangeness of her testimony kept her a subaltern, despite her being on the national radar, because she was not understood.

By deferring the drive to theoretical conclusion and attending to the material details of the transcript, and by pursuing the question of translation and seeking the referential basis for Mrs Konile's metpahors, we believe we were able to accord her speech something of the meaningfulness that she was trying to encode. We were not granting her dignity; we were trying to recognize it.

CHAPTER THREE

Archived Voices: *Refiguring Three Women's Testimonies Delivered to the TRC*

ANTJIE KROG AND NOSISI MPOLWENI

The South African TRC executed a vital process of transitional justice. The platform on which victims / survivors narrated their experiences turned the TRC into one of the most significant phenomena in South African history. After the testimonies, with simultaneous translations, were delivered in public, the TRC archived the audio, visual and transcribed versions of the testimonies as part of its mandate to gather evidence of human rights abuses during apartheid. This archival material has since been used to refigure some of the archives of South African history.

In this chapter, we want to explore the less obvious and more subtle refiguring that took place during the gathering of TRC testimonies. Using testimonies delivered by three women, we look at how refiguring happened not only through the processes of translation and transcription, or through who testifies and how, but also through narrating the event in a way that leaves the central moment unuttered.

The Notion of Archive in the South African Context

Since its publication, the book *Refiguring the Archive* (2002) has become an important benchmark in discussions about archives in South Africa. A collaborative effort by six of South Africa's foremost archivists and writers, accompanied by philosopher Jacques Derrida, the collection investigates the concept of the 'archive' within the broader South African context. One chapter, as well as part of an extensive interview with Derrida, is devoted exclusively to the TRC. To contextualize our analysis of three TRC testimonies, we want to focus on several arguments from *Refiguring the Archive*. Most centrally, we want to emphasize the importance of recognizing that, as Carolyn Hamilton, Verne Harris and Graeme Reid point out in the introduction, '[t]he archive—all archives—every archive—is figured' (2002: 7). Whether material was gathered by colonial or apartheid authorities or by the TRC, it was gathered within a particular context and with a particular purpose. Thus, *Refiguring the Archive* pleads for a refiguring within a new democratic dispensation and for recognizing and rethinking the patterns that manifest themselves visibly and invisibly in archived material. They want the archive-as-source also to be studied as archive-as-subject (Stoler 2002: 86) so that students can become aware of how archiving comes about. Where scholars previously 'mined' archives for fact, they should also focus on 'the particular processes by which [the] record was produced and subsequently shaped, both before its entry into the archive, and increasingly as part of the archival record' (Hamilton, Harris and Reid 2002: 9).

Most of the essays in *Refiguring the Archive* point to the different ways that archival material itself is directing us to how it could and should be refigured. Three essays in particular are helpful in explaining our methodology in working with the TRC testimonies.

First, Hamilton, Reid and Harris argue that attention should be paid to: (a) how the record has been altered over time; (b) the gaps, omissions and excisions from the record; and (c) why a particular choice for a particular trace was made (2002). Harris later warns, in 'The Archival Sliver: A Perspective on the Construction of Social Memory in Archives and the Transition from Apartheid to Democracy', that any archivist undertaking a refiguring should always be aware that the archive can only be a small trace of a whole: 'One should be wary of the claim that one or another corrective intervention can "fill the gaps" in an archive, so it is suggested that *the archive is a sliver instead of an incomplete whole*' (2002: 135–6; emphasis added).

Second, in 'Colonial Archives and the Arts of Governments: On the Content in the Form', Ann Laura Stoler suggests that scholars should try to understand the power relations that contextualized decisions about what and how to archive and to look for the mark of power struggles within an archive: 'Archives are crucial elements in epistemological challenge and experimentation. Archives are not simply sources, they are sites of contested knowledges' (2002: 98). Following Derrida, Stoler explores the term 'archive' by going to its etymological origins: *archivuum* is the Latin for 'residence of the magistrate' and *arkhe* is the Greek for 'to command'. She writes:

[T]he colonial archive ordered (in both the imperative and taxonomic sense) the criteria of evidence, proof, testimony, and witnessing to construct its moral narrations [. . .] It was in the factual stories that the colonial state affirmed its fictions to itself, in the moralising stories that it mapped the scope of its philanthropic missions, and in multiple and contested versions that cultural accounts were discredited or restored (ibid.: 90).

Third, Brent Harris takes the concept of 'official ordering' directly to the realm of the TRC in 'The Archive, Public History, and the Essential Truth: The TRC Reading the Past'. The commission officially determined what should be gathered as evidence as well as what of it should be archived and how. The TRC claimed to 'fix' knowledge, in the sense of both correcting misunderstandings and overcoming the instability of the meanings attached to the past. This official declaration of what is supposed to be true, and therefore worthy of archiving, represents two moments of perhaps temporarily displaced instability: (a) what should be archived is determined through negotiation and contestation, but the moment the decision is made, epistemological instability is contained; and (b) at the moment of archiving itself, the stasis and fixing of the material create a second overcoming of instability (2002: 161).

We take the request to refigure the archive seriously. In our qualitative analyses of the three testimonies, we use several of the tools outlined above. We explore how the archived record has been altered over time; we look at gaps and silences; and, finally, we try to determine the effect of these losses upon the 'archived truth' left behind by the process of the TRC. Mpolweni focuses on the archival impact of what is not said and on the different sorts of gaps and omissions, created by slippages in translation and transcription, between the live testimony and the archived version. Krog looks at the slippages in transcription between the initial translated testimony as it was recorded at the time of the TRC and the final archived version, also examining how the testifiers themselves refigured the event during the process of testifying.

THE ARCHIVED TESTIMONY ABOUT THE DEATH OF SICELO MHLAWULI

NOSISI MPOLWENI

On 27 June 1985, Fort Calata, Sparrow Mkonto, Matthew Goniwe and Sicelo Mhlawuli drove from Cradock, the small town where they lived, to Port Elizabeth to attend a briefing from the United Democratic Front (UDF), an anti-apartheid organization. They did not return home that evening and their burnt and mutilated bodies were found near Bluewater Bay outside Port Elizabeth about a week later. An inquest in 1987 into what has become known as the Cradock Four incident found only that the men had been killed by unknown persons. The inquest was reopened in 1993 and, after the disclosure of a top-secret military directive calling for the 'permanent removal from society' of Goniwe, a schoolteacher in Cradock, it was found that the apartheid security forces were responsible for their deaths.

The four widows of these men testified on the second day of the human rights violations hearings by the TRC on 16 April 1996 in East London in the Eastern Cape. This part of the chapter explores the testimony of one of them, Nombuyiselo Mhlawuli, the wife of Sicelo Mhlawuli. The latter suffered a particularly cruel death as he was stabbed several times, doused with acid and finally burnt to death in a fire after his hand had been cut off. Activists from the ANC subsequently testified to the TRC about the missing hand. Madoda Jacobs, former head boy of Lingelihle High School, told the commission that while he was in detention in Port Elizabeth in 1985, security police had shown him a hand in a bottle and told him it was Mhlawuli's. Another activist said: 'I saw the severed hand of a black activist in a bottle at a Port Elizabeth police station. The police told me it was a baboon's hand. They said to me, "Look here, this is the bottled hand of a Communist." But I know that Sicelo Mhlawuli was buried with his hand missing' (TRC 1996h).

How does Mrs Mhlawuli express her trauma at the loss of her husband and her concerns about being haunted by the 'unfinished business' of the missing hand? One must bear in mind that she appeared before the commission to testify about her husband. She was there not as a woman in her own right but as a struggle widow. Although women were active in opposing the discriminatory policies of the apartheid and, like their male counterparts, suffered gross human rights violations, they seldom gave public testimony about their own experiences during the TRC hearings. However, as Fiona Ross explains, despite the fact that women tended not to foreground their own experiences of suffering, references to their personal suffering were there, 'submerged, but structuring the form and cadence of their narratives, [as] women spoke of the effects on their own lives of the ruptured lives of others' (2003: 46).

Zannie Bock, Ngwanya Mazwi, Sifundo Metula and Nosisi Mpolweni-Zantsi describe how women who came to the TRC used the opportunity to express their suppressed feelings of pain (2006: 6). They verbalized the guilt they experienced when they were unable to protect and secure their families; they described the disruption of order and the diminished prospects that resulted from losing a husband or son who would have provided for them in their old age. In Mrs Mhlawuli's efforts to convey her suffering to the commission, we see the roles played by memory and emotional trauma. Differences between the original testimony delivered in isiXhosa and the archived version in English reveal further the limitations that arise with errors in translation and cross- cultural understanding. Here a newly translated version will permit us to examine the original testimony and compare that to the official archived version from the TRC website.

PART OF MRS MHLAWULI'S TESTIMONY

isiXhosa Transcription
(Made from a recording of the floor sound)
Yes Mr Matthew-Mr Smith / I went through — ndazifunda iidocuments eze post-mortem / apha ekuzifundeni kwam / ndakhathazeka kakhulu / ngoba kaloku yona ichaza in detail yonke into eyenzekayo / ndazifunda / ndafu-

manisa into yokuba lo mfo / wayenamanxeba
amaninzi angumangaliso emzimbeni wakhe /
kwi upper abdomen waye na about 25 wounds
/ iwounds ezazichaza into yokokuba different
sizes of weapons were used / to stab him /
okanye a group of people stabbed him / and the
kwi lower parts zakhe wayenezinye / but all
together iwounds awayenazo zaziyi 43 / and
enye into esiyiqondayo ukuba yenzeka kuye /
bamgalela i-acid emehlweni ache / bakugqiba
bamqhawula isih- lahla sakhe sasekunene / simngcwabe ngaphandle kwewrist yakhe yase right
/ right arm or whatever / hand actually / asazi
ukuba basithini isandla eso.

Official Archived Version
(A transcription of the English translation of the
isiXhosa testimony generated through simultaneous interpretation)

I read the post-mortem documents. Reading
them I was really worried, because it has to
explain in detail what happened. I read through
and came to understand that he had many
wounds, in the upper abdomen were five
wounds, these wounds indicated that different
weapons were used to stab him or a group of
people stabbed him. Now in the lower part he
also had wounds but the wounds in total were 43.
One other thing that we understood, they poured
acid on his face, after that they chopped off his
right hand, just below the wrist, I don't know
what they did with that hand (TRC 1996h).

New English Translation

(By Mpolweni from the recording of the floor sound)

Yes, Mr Matthew—Mr Smith / I went through— I got the post-mortem documents / as I was reading them / I got very hurt / because they stated everything in detail / I read them / and I found out that this man / had many unbelievable wounds in his body / he had 25 wounds in his upper abdomen / wounds which showed that different sizes of weapons were used / to stab him / or a group of people stabbed him / and then in his lower parts of the body he had others / but all together he had 43 wounds / and another thing that we think happened to him is that / they poured acid in his eyes / and then they chopped off his right hand / we buried him without his right wrist—right arm or whatever / hand actually / we don't know what they did with the hand.

In the above excerpt, Mrs Mhlawuli recounts the experience of reading a detailed post-mortem report about her husband's death. Although she did not physically experience the torture and the pain her husband went through, on the video clip it is clear from the tone and the pace at which she relates her narrative that she suffered intense emotional pain while reading the documents and suffers again, now, as she recalls them. This episode is the most difficult point in her testimony, evinced by the fact that she breaks down and cries after recounting it.

What is interesting is how sharp her memory is—enabling her to relate an episode that took place almost 10 years ago as if it had happened the day before. The precision of her details—the position of the wounds, the number of wounds—proves that the whole incident is still fresh in her mind. This confirms Pumla Gobodo-Madikizela's explanation that 'the struggle with trauma is a struggle with memory. It is common for traumatized people to be confronted with [and overwhelmed by] the painful traumatic memories long after the traumatic event occurred' (2006: 71).

However, the language of the translation and transcription reveals the power dynamics that mediate Mrs Mhlawuli's attempt to describe the intensity of her pain. She uses the expressive words 'ndakhathazeka kakhulu' (I was deeply hurt). But in the archived testimony, this phrase is omitted, affirming the suspicion that Mrs Mhlawuli is only there to talk about the death of her husband—her own pain is either not translated at all or translated in less emotional words: 'worried' instead of 'hurt'. Thus the archived version performs a kind of 'toning down'—a refiguring actually: Mrs Mhlawuli says she was 'deeply hurt': the interpreter interprets this as 'very worried'.

This dynamic continues into the next part of Mrs Mhlawuli's testimony, when she tells of her husband's wounds and of the distressing fact that his right hand was missing. Two things are of note: first, there is a transcription error (made by the person who typed out the simultaneous English translation of the testimony); second, a vital piece of information has been omitted from the official archived version. On the day of the hearing, the interpreter (translating through simultaneous interpretation the words of Mrs Mhlawuli from isiXhosa into English) correctly interpreted Mrs Mhla-wuli as saying that her husband had 25 wounds in the upper abdomen. However, the transcriber of the official version typed the word 'five', not '25', which underplays the severity of the wounds and the brutality of the event. In addition, at the end of the extract, the interpreter misses a very important detail—namely, that Sicelo Mhlawuli was buried without his right hand. In Xhosa culture, it is believed that if you bury someone without a body part, he or she will not rest in peace until the part is returned and there could be serious consequences for the homestead. So for a Xhosa person, the detail that he was buried without his right hand is serious and culturally significant.

Mrs Mhlawuli's own acts of omission and 'misnaming' also come to bear on the portion of her testimony that concerns her husband's lost hand. In the isiXhosa version, her sentence 'simngcwabe ngaphandle kwewrist yakhe yase right— right arm or whatever—hand actually' (we buried him without his right wrist—right arm or whatever—hand actually) is incoherent and illustrates how difficult it is—even impossible —for her to talk about it. All the detail is sharp until she reaches the point of the hand. This sentence also demonstrates how Mrs Mhlawuli subconsciously keeps thinking about the part(s) that is (are) *not* severed and still part of her husband's body (wrist, arm) and battles to find the correct word— 'hand'—for the part that was severed. Note also that she moves at that moment from the comfort of her mother tongue into English, as if she is not able to accommodate the deed, the hand, in her own language. The hand had not yet come to rest in her mother tongue. Once again, these indications of emotional distress are lost in the archived version. The closing note of this episode indicates that she is preoccupied with endless questions in search of the missing hand of her husband, as suggested by the phrase 'asazi ukuba basithini isandla eso' (we don't know what they did with the hand).

Apart from trying to avoid saying the word 'hand', another crucial aspect is reflected in the testimony: the notion of unfinished business. In one sense, Mr Mhlawuli has joined the ancestral family; in another sense, his life seems to be lingering with those who are still alive. For Mrs Mhlawuli, this scenario seems to be some kind of an ongoing torture and pain because her husband is dead but alive. There is a parallel at work here: Mrs Mhlawuli's memory is about the past and, at the same time, vividly trapped in the present; Mr Mhlawuli has joined the past (ancestors) and yet his missing hand traps him in the present. In contrast to this, the missing hand has no past, yet it may still be in a bottle somewhere. In other words, the process of healing is deferred. Mrs Mhlawuli cannot heal because her husband is not safely in the realm of the ancestors. One of her anxieties is the specific location of the hand: Where is it now? Where does it find itself at that moment of her testimony? Thinking about the different (humiliating) circumstances in which the hand once found itself (in a jar, in a jar on a desk, in a jar in a torture room, presented as a pickled hand, a baboon's hand, a communist's hand) disturbs her further.

The missing hand should also be read against the larger background of the crisis of missing body parts in the Eastern Cape (see Lalu 2009). During the colonial period, the head (according to his descendants) or ears and genitals (according to some written records) of the Xhosa king Hintsa (1789–1835) were lopped off by British soldiers and taken back to England. A Xhosa *sangoma* made world news in 1996 when he set off to Scotland to retrieve the skull of King Hintsa so that an era of peace could be ushered into the new South Africa. He said that the soul of Hintsa 'was blowing all over the world with no place to settle' (ibid.: 1). Thus, Mrs Mhlawuli tries to tell the commission that she is disturbed by the restlessness of her husband's incomplete buried body.

One should also not ignore the cultural perception based on the ubuntu world view that all people are interconnected: the living, the living-dead and the still-to-be-born. If Mrs Mhlawuli experiences herself through ubuntu as being interconnected with her husband as a human being as well as part of a married couple, then one could say that she experiences the severed hand as her own hand. She is also suffering the humiliation, torture and burning and the severance of the hand. Through him she is also maimed. Finding and restoring the hand to its rightful place would also be a kind of refiguring that would bring an end to the instability of both herself and her husband.

THE ARCHIVED TESTIMONY ABOUT THE DEATH OF
MRS DELATO

ANTJIE KROG

On 10 October 1985, Nombulelo Delato, an ANC activist, was burnt to death not by pro-apartheid operatives but by her ANC comrades in Colesberg, a small rural town in the semi-desert region of South Africa known as the Karoo. The incident was an example of some of the conflict within the ANC movement itself. During the TRC's second week of hearings into human rights violations, Mrs Delato's daughter, Busiswe Kewana, and Kewana's aunt, Thomzama Maliti, came to testify on 24 April 1996.

The testimonies of these two women, like all the others, are archived in English on the Internet. There is no indication on the Web as to which of these testimonies had been translated into English and which were originally delivered in English. For any close reading of these testimonies, it is crucial to know whether, when and at what stage the text had been 'interfered' with. Hamilton, Harris and Reid correctly underscore the importance of being aware of the particular processes by which the final record was produced and shaped before its entry into the archive (2002: 9). Interpretation and transcription leave their marks, as Mpolweni has shown. Ms Kewana's testimony, however, introduces yet another problem: how meaning gets lost / altered / refigured during the archival processes—the problem of what can be heard. The testimony raises this problem in the most literal sense in that it opens with questions about the working condition of the microphone to facilitate translation:

ADV[OCATE DENZIL] POTGIETER (*on behalf of the
commission*). Thank you for coming and
thank you for being patient. Your—your evidence—your evidence—can you hear me?

MS KEWANA. No.

ADV POTGIETER. Okay, can you hear me now?

MS KEWANA. No.

ADV POTGIETER. Or perhaps the translation.

MS KEWANA. Ja I hear you now (TRC 1996d).

The faulty microphone confuses the testimony
process, making participants inaudible to one another at
several points during the proceeding. But the microphone
is also emblematic of a deeper, psychological dynamic of
needing and yet not being able to hear. Ms Kewana was
not in Colesberg when her mother was burnt and therefore did not *see* her mother's death. She is living on what
she has been told. The phrase 'seeing is believing' was
changed for her into 'hearing is (should be) believing.'

In his book *Memoirs of the Blind,* Derrida writes:

One must always remember that the word, the
vocable, is heard and understood, the sonorous
phenomenon remaining invisible as such.
Taking up time rather than space in us, it is
addressed   not only from the blind to the blind,
like a code for the nonseeing, but speaks to us, in
truth, all the time of the blindness that constitutes it. Language is spoken, it speaks to itself,
which is to say, *from / of the blindness*. It always
speaks to us *from / of the blindness* that constitutes
it (1993: 4).

These words seem to me to fit what is happening with these two women sitting in front of the commission. The daughter is 'blind'; she has not seen her mother's death. The aunt is trying to tell (or draw with the fingers in the dark) what she has seen, but is, in the moment of trying to tell, as blind as the daughter who cannot see. The aunt is addressing from blindness and her testimony is of course speaking to itself of the blindness that con-stitutes it—the terrible thing that does not want to be said, cannot be said. This blindness then becomes the very condition for both of them (and us) to finally 'see' (speak/hear). Through the commission's prompting, the death could be approximated; some marks could be finally made on paper.

The aunt, Mrs Maliti, witnessed the burning 10 years before. The TRC provided an official forum from which her seeing could become audible and the audible could become archived as we built the archives of a 'new South Africa'. Ms Kewana, the daughter, makes it clear that she had already heard formulations of her mother's death but that she has problems accepting/hearing them. 'Hearing' is a leitmotif right through the two testimonies and there are moments in which the process of telling cannot begin or continue because people are not hearing one another.

> ADV POTGIETER. You—I assume you knew the deceased well.
>
> MR [*sic*] MALITI. No I can't hear well no (TRC 1996d).

A more intentional form of hearing is 'listening'. One listens because one wants to understand. Testimonies are not monologues taking place in solitude. The word 'testimony' implies a listener. A witness is always talking to someone. In other words, the victim is *silent* because there is *no one* to listen; the victim *speaks* because there is *some one* to listen.

In their work on testimony, Felman and Laub say that the task of testimony is to impart first-hand knowledge of 'a historical passage through death', so we do not listen to a victim/survivor necessarily to get factual truth but to hear a personal truth as seen through those particular eyes and told by that particular tongue. Felman and Laub emphasize, however, that there is a dialectic between what the survivor did not know and what she knows now, what she knew and what she's telling (1992: 62).

This dialectic between past and present knowledge shaped the testimony given by Ms Kewana and Mrs Maliti. Between them, the two women should have had a rich and detailed image of the events in their minds. Ms Kewana knew about the death through family members who were witnesses to the events. Both knew that the comrades who killed Mrs Delato had prevented the family from burying her in the town where she had lived and they must have been aware of a subsequent official court case in which a person had received the death sentence for the murder of Mrs Delato. But in front of the TRC, the two women chose to refigure this knowledge. Ms Kewana foregrounded the fact that she didn't see the burning and therefore had problems accepting it. Mrs Maliti foregrounded her suspicion of the reasons given by the ANC comrades for burning Mrs Delato. Both of them avoided the detail of the death itself, busying themselves with the rationale by which it was legitimated.

When Mrs Maliti finally spoke about the burning of Mrs Delato, on the basis of her own first-hand knowledge, Ms Kewana, being then both victim and listener, began to cry with shock and horror, as if she were truly 'hearing' the detail for the first time. No wonder that two journalists, John Yeld and Joseph Aranes, reported for the *Cape Argus* newspaper the next day that it was 'the first time that the daughter, Busisiwe [*sic*] Kewana, learnt the exact details of how and why her mother [. . .] had been severely burnt in the Colesberg "location"' (1996).

It is important to realize that the daughter might not be *hearing* the details for the first time but she might be *understanding* them for the first time. We might say, following Derrida, that during the hearing, she had to turn her ears inward, had to become deaf in order to really hear (analogized Derrida's concept of blindness to that of deafness).

The request to Ms Kewana to tell her side of the story provided the conditions for the most haunting characteristic of the testimony to manifest itself: trying to describe, yet refraining from describing, Mrs Delato's killing. TRC deputy chair Alex Boraine invited Ms Kewana to relate her 'story', which was, as Brent Harris noted in *Refiguring the Archive*, 'perforated with lacunae' (Hamilton et al. 2002: 161) that, despite several attempts by the TRC, Ms Kewana was unable to fill in adequately. The commissioners were aware of these gaps because she, like all the other witnesses, had submitted a narrative to the TRC's statement takers some months before the actual hearing.

Felman and Laub have found that the survivor often profoundly fears the memory of the event and shrinks away from it, preferring silence—because even when silence is defeat, it is also a sanctuary, a home (1992: 64). Many terrible deaths had been described to the TRC but the speakers were often sustained by a particular structure: this was my son, this is what he meant to me, this is how I noticed things were wrong, this is how I heard about his death, this is where I am now. Nowhere in these two testimonies did one find any structure to carry the death of Mrs Delato. In her daughter's testimony, Mrs Delato's death became a kind of landmine, something one could not and should not dare to describe. She, Ms Kewana, had already 'heard' through different channels: 'my mother was burnt while she was pregnant,' yet she was 'not satisfied [. . .] the reason why I am here, I want the Commission to help me—to help me try and find out why they killed my mother' (TRC 1996d).

The political rationale for killing someone by means of dousing the person with petrol or other chemicals and then setting the person alight had been circulating in the townships for more than a decade. (Note that the TRC makes a difference in its final report between 'necklacing' and 'death by burning': a burning becomes a necklacing when there is a burning tyre round the body of the victim.) In an interview in the ANC newsletter *Sechaba* in December 1986, Chris Hani, the commander of the ANC's military wing, had said:

> So the necklace was a weapon devised by the oppressed themselves to remove this cancer from our society, the cancer of collaboration of

the puppets. We have our own revolutionary methods of dealing with collaborators, the methods of the ANC. But I refuse to condemn our people when they mete out their own traditional forms of justice to those who collaborate (TRC 1996i).

Earlier that same year, a few months after the incident in Colesberg, Winnie Mandela had reportedly declared, '. . . with our boxes of matches and our necklaces, we shall liberate this country.'

Ms Kewana carefully structured her testimony so that it did not reveal any first-hand knowledge. It seemed as if she wanted to keep a space open in which she still could be told that her mother was alive. She did not say that her mother was dead; rather: 'My mother was burnt.' Her non-descriptive testimony moved round the edges of an unformulated, not-heard and not-understood death. At times, it felt as if her words were drifting like debris round the black hole of her mother's death, waiting for something to be put in that space, asking for the terrible death to be described and explained to her so that she could not only hear it but also accept it as knowledge. On the one hand, the hole or gap in Ms Kewana's testimony was partly caused by the kind of power relations that Stoler warns about: archives are sites of contested knowledge in which the marginalized voices are silenced (2002). Ms Kewana was clearly holding out this space, protecting its emptiness in order to prevent others (such as the comrades, the police, the courts) from excising or filling it as they had done in the past. On the other hand, it was much more than that: the daughter was on the brink of terror—if the gap was filled, her mother was dead in the cruellest way possible.

The way the TRC helped was to assist the aunt to narrate the event in order that Ms Kewana could 'hear'. But the unsayability of the black hole affected everyone involved in that moment of truth-telling. They all knew that the case before them contained graphic detail and a careful analysis revealed that every one of them, from victims to commissioners to translators to transcribers, struggled to postpone the moment of entering the vortex of that story. Initially, Advocate Potgieter desisted from requesting any further detail from the daughter. In the second testimony, he asked for details from the aunt, and the many mistakes in translating and transcribing her response stand as a gripping record of a collective struggle for meaning:

> ADV POTGIETER. Can you tell us what you saw what happened.
>
> MR [*sic*] MALITI. He was on his way to work, two young men—young men approached at him. Now they were five, when they saw him, they chased him. He went to hide in another house, and now they took him out of that house.
>
> They took him—they took his overall; and they poured him with petrol bomb. One of them held his feet and then they started igniting her—his—her feet. They were beating him up—her up.

Suddenly the transcription jumps to the interpreter sitting in the translation booth:

INTERPRETER. I am sorry I can't hear the microphone is off. They beat her up and they put
a tire on him—on her. There was nobody
who could stop this, the police were looking
for—for her but they were lost and they
couldn't find her. She tried to go to them,
when she got there, the people who tried to
hurt her and [*indistinct*] they couldn't
because she didn't have a voice, the police
took her to Bloemfontein. In Bloemfontein
she stayed for three days, she started to mention everybody who did this to her. Then
after that, she died. They didn't allow her to
be buried in Colesberg, because they said
she was an informer. After—they said if she
was buried there, they were going to burn
the church. Then she ended up being buried
in Pilonome Hospital, that's where I will
stop for a moment.

These excerpts exposed like few others the untenable
tensions and barriers to comprehension—technical, cultural and psychological—that were often present in testimonies before the TRC. But it was only by watching the
video of the testimonies that one fully grasped how the
traumatic content and emotional delivery had put everyone under unbearable strain.

It was during the part of the testimony quoted above
that the daughter, sitting next to Mrs Maliti, uttered a wail
and fell to the side into the lap of the briefer. The *Argus*
reported that Mrs Maliti's testimony was 'punctuated' by
Ms Kewana's 'grief-stricken cries' as she learnt of the

death of her mother (Yeld and Aranes 1996). And indeed, everything was rupturing: the daughter collapsed, the witness cried, the interpreter could not hear, the microphone got shifted and, many months later, the transcriber, typing the testimony from a tape, was so distracted that she could neither indicate when the personal words of the interpreter stopped and the testimony took over nor what the gender of the testifier was.

Mrs Maliti resumed speaking with the phrase 'They beat her up,' but the print transcript made it appear as if this and the subsequent text were said by the interpreter. To my knowledge, this was the only testimony in which the veil of the interpreter was pierced for so long by the transcription of his or her direct words. What is more, it became a surreal moment when the interpreter also joined the ranks of those not able to hear.

To listen to testimony is hard. People devise ways of protecting themselves and of not hearing. Obsessive search for facts or numbness is a 'normal' form of self-protection, say Felman and Laub (1992). During the testimony, Mrs Maliti herself, as well as the advocate, the daughter, the interpreter and later the transcriber displayed signs of not hearing, of growing numb to the graphic detail of Mrs Delato's death. The paragraphs suddenly swarmed with gender confusion. In addition to the transcriber turning 'Mrs Maliti' into 'Mr Maliti', the interpreter alternated between 'he' and 'she' in the translation of the actual testimony. These slippages are partly due to the fact that there is no clear distinction in isiXhosa between 'he' and 'she', the isiXhosa word for both being *u*.

So it was up to the translator to pick the right English gender for *u*. However, more was at play here. For the interpreter did not merely make the wrong choice but battled to make any choice at all, and the horror shifted its gender focus between 'her' to 'his' to 'her'. The interpreter did not experience any confusion in the rest of the testimony; from the video, I recognized the voice of the TRC's top isiXhosa interpreter—so the failure here was not due to incompetence. My suggestion is that the emotional content was such that the interpreter had to shut down some faculties in an effort at self-protection.

Stepping into the Vortex

One could be forgiven for thinking that the hardest part was over, but Mrs Maliti and Ms Kewana, along with the commission and the audience, had only just begun to approach the unsayable. Advocate Potgieter, who became increasingly numb as the testimony continued, withdrew after the setting-alight phase. In a near-obsessional search for facts, Advocate Dumisa Ntsebeza took over.

According to Felman and Laub, a victim does not simply speak; the listener has to make the right kind of move— indicate a 'password'—that sets the witnessing in motion. This password recognizes the 'black hole' of silence that 'swallowed up the past [. . .] the past before death, before destruction', and it is at 'the place of the greatest density of silence—the place of concentration where death took place' (1992: 64).

Ntsebeza gave the right password. Sentence by sentence, he went through the 'reasons' of the burning. But as it became clear that nothing ever adequately 'explained' such a killing, the witness and the listener, with immense effort and courage, mentally supporting each other, moved as close as possible to that 'past before death, before destruction' that is densest where death takes place.

What happened after Mrs Delato was set alight?

In sparse sentences, no adjectives, no adverbs, no composite sentences, a word here, a phrase there, interspersed with misunderstandings, faulty transcriptions, confusion between the voices of advocate and victim, break-ups in language and interventions, a rare and moving attempt was made to put words to the silence of that death.

> MR MALITI. The police arrived when she was burnt already.

> ADV NTSEBEZA. What do you mean now by that?

> MR MALITI. When the police came in, they could—they were trying to find out where she was, but they could hear her crying. They saw her in the Main Road, she was already alight.

> ADV NTSEBEZA. Did she run after she was burnt?

> MR MALITI. No, she couldn't run, she was just walking slowly, her clothes were burning. She went to the direction where the police were.

> ADV NTSEBEZA. Was she walking around while she was naked?

> MR MALITI. Yes.

> ADV NTSEBEZA. Were the people afraid to help her?

MR MALITI. No one was allowed by the comrades
to help her, so she went alone to the van.

For a few moments the swirling rubble of words
somehow gravitated to form substance. A glimpse is being
caught in the darkness, an image rescued of a burning,
pregnant woman, walking and crying alone along a road
in great pain, terror and abandonment, surrounded by her
stunned community and by men, those who killed her
and those who organized her killing, calmly watching her
living out the last part of her violently demolished life.

Although it was merely a mention right at the end of
the testimony, Commissioner Mary Burton received confirmation from Mrs Maliti of the family's suspicion that
the police had instigated this burning.

The devastation, however, affected not only the testifying daughter with her silent grandmother on the stage
but also the husband who couldn't save his pregnant wife.

ADV NTSEBEZA. Do you know the husband to the
deceased?

MR MALITI. Yes, I know his name is Doti. That
day—he doesn't know anything because he
ran. He ran to Crossroads, and even today
he is not well since then.

ADV NTSEBEZA. Just to clear something up, are
you trying to say he was never well again
mentally?

MR MALITI. Yes that's what I am saying.

Refiguring was happening on a variety of levels in all three of the testimonies we have explored. In each case, the nearest family members of the deceased destabilized the official versions previously established by the apartheid courts and inquests. To reinterpret Stoler: the apartheid archives ordered the criteria of evidence, proof, testimony and witnessing in the court cases. Through its 'factual' stories, the apartheid state affirmed the fictions undergirding its authority, which was now destabilized by the testimonies of these three women. They also pitched female voices and female perspectives against the dominating narratives of men, grief against the 'facts' of the inquiries, honesty against the fabrication of the powerful.

Through their testimony, the victims/survivors were also refiguring the archives of their own memories in a way that enabled their personal needs for facts or for peace and healing to be addressed by the TRC. Mrs Mhlawuli was desperately looking for what Harris calls the 'end of instability'. Not in terms of an imposition of false closure that strategically confirmed new hegemonies but a different ending of instability in which no one is silenced but personal peace is achieved through making 'whole' the body of her husband. She wanted the commission to find out *about* the hand, *find* the hand; she wanted it buried with the body. In a sense she wanted the hand archived by the commission to be made secure, so that she could know where it was, could know that her husband was at peace in his grave, so that her 'epistemological instability' could end. The moment the hand was found and buried with its crying body, it would (could) lose its 'stasis' as an unconnected hand and became stable within ordinary safety—in other words, she could perhaps begin to 'forget' the hand and start the process of healing.

The daughter and her aunt not only refigured the 'reasons' for the killing of Mrs Delato but they attempted to resurrect the dead woman in the safe and official space of the new political dispensation. Although they knew their truth was finally heard and would be archived, its rendering in many ways was nothing but a ruin, to use Derrida's term, nothing more than a prompting to recall what was never truly there, because even the TRC hearing failed to recapture a presence 'outside of the abyss' into which the killing had sunk.

And yet, by describing the last moments of Nombulelo Delato, they made her more than a mere statistic, an empty hole or simply a ruin—a sliver, a trace of a female figure pitched against the real terror of the darknesses surrounding her. The testimony about Mrs Delato became unforgettable for its searing attempt to prevent the unsayable from being said, while at the same time trying to call forth those very unsayable words to step into the silences, however mangled, that were annihilating the lives of those trying to survive that death.

In all three testimonies, we showed examples of incorrect translation and transcription. We want to suggest that this should be read as a further form of refiguring against a background of the impossibility of recapturing: sometimes the choices are conscious, sometimes they are mere mistakes, but most often, as we have pointed out, it was the result of the trauma of listening that affected both the translation and often the transcription process.

In his interview for *Refiguring the Archive*, Derrida is asked about how his idea of the 'death drive' manifests in the TRC archives. He answers:

> I think the death drive is at work at least in two ways. One is the drive to destroy the very memory, the very trace and the very testimony, of the violence, of the murder. The perpetrator tries not only to kill, but to erase the memory of the killing, that is, to do, to act in such a way that no archive is left [. . .]. Now, another part of this effect appears on the opposite side. That is, when in order to oppose the destruction, you want to keep safe, to accumulate, the archive, as such, not simply living memory—because we don't trust the living memory, you trust the archive [. . . T]here is a perverse, a perverse, desire for forgetting in the archive itself. The death drive is not simply at work in killing, in producing death, but in trying to save, in a certain way the memory [. . . producing] forgetting by remembering (quoted in Harris 2002: 66)

The traces and ruins left by these three testimonies point to the archival presences of absences. But by remembering, shaping and refiguring their memory through and with language, Mrs Mhlawuli, Busiswe Kewana and Thomzama Maliti have tried to tell/see the darknesses that continue to engulf them—their tongues/ eyes, in agony and supplication, often could not continue;

at times nothing but contours became visible. So they (we) have found that 'deep down, deep down inside', their (our) eyes are 'destined not to see but to weep' (Derrida 1993: 126–7).

CHAPTER FOUR

Shards, Memory and the Mileage of Myth

> German memory was like a big tongue which kept on touching a painful tooth.
>
> Ian Buruma

> Normal history means: a plurality of interpretations.
>
> Ian Buruma

> (Early October 1899) [. . .] An indescribably strange feeling rises in him, as if invisible powers are at work in the night; not seen by the human eye but felt. Far off, a jackal howls and even that sounds strange and mysterious. The moon stands like a sentry, pale and aloof [. . .] Then, on the hill, a man on his horse appears, suddenly, out of nowhere. Without breathing, he stares at the figure. Horse and man like one, looking out onto the moonlit plain [. . .].
>
> Mikro

It is through this vivid image in a youth novel titled *Ruiter in die Nag* (Rider in the Night)—the image of a lonely rider in vigil over the injustice that was to be done to his people—that the war entered my consciousness as a child and became part of my earliest memory as an Afrikaner. (The term Anglo-Boer War or even Boer War was never used in my family—for us it was simply the War. If she was forced to call it something, my mother would talk about the Second Liberation War.) The Anglo-Boer War destroyed about a third of the Afrikaner population, with 26,000 women and children dying in the first concentration camps of the twentieth century. The war had always been a presence in my life: as point of reference, as explanation, as continuity, as backdrop—seldom the suffering, only the statistics, often the betrayal, always the bravery and never, never stories other than those about the Afrikaner.

During my first school year, there was a boy in my class called Hennie Nagel. I remember my father telling one of my uncles: 'She's sitting next to one of the Nagels.' To which the uncle would nod knowingly: 'Head shots—all of them—they were the best marksmen . . . used them to silence the gunners.' Then my father would turn to me: 'After the Battle of Sannaspos Oom [Uncle] Chris van Niekerk specifically measured the distance—from a thousand yards with an open sight the Nagels shot every single gunner, one after the other, right between the eyes.'

At school we learnt the names of the streets of the town in which I grew up. One of them was Colonel Thring Street. Thring was an Irishman who fought on the side of the Boers. Whenever we passed this leafy street, my father would quote from Thring's diary:

After the battle a wounded British officer asked me [Thring] where the Boers were. On having them pointed out to him, he said, 'No, no, I mean the Boers.' I replied, 'Well, here they are', pointing to the same men. The officer again said, 'No, no, you don't understand me—I mean the wild savage Boers, those looking like orang-out-angs' (Serfontein 1990: 137; my translation).

Whenever we went on holiday, my father would point out the plains, hills and farms where the war played itself out: here was where the son of General Christiaan De Wet was shot. Commandant Danie Theron hid in this farm. At this railway station on Christmas Day, De Wet raided a Khaki train. He and his men had a feast on the tinned Christmas puddings, alcohol and presents destined for the British soldiers. From this farm came the woman who was the ancestor of three Boer War generals. The meteorite crater at Ventersburg was known to me as the place where General De Wet and his commando 'disappeared'. Because of a deceptive double range of mountains, he could hide there and recuperate within an atypical ecology. We did not only name the country; we also marked it by deed and blood.

On 10 October, Afrikaners would celebrate Heroes' Day. My parents would take us to the concentration camp cemetery, where the frail harmony of a girls' choir would drift across a sparse veld and thorn trees:

> Our hearts still trill with unbearable grief,
> no blade of grass has covered this holy place,
> where earth and stone cover the pale bones.
> There are calls to forget. How dare we,
> when the naked graves shout: Remember!
>   Remember!

These mornings were cut into my memory by an icy wind. It was usually too early for summer rains; so an atmosphere of dust and dread hung over the brittle ceremony. Even the stalwarts reciting fierce, bitter poems seemed eventually to falter into despair:

Give me a gun in my right hand,
and a buck that flee,
give me a horse to carry me,
Give me South Africa.

They made you in England, little soapbox,
to serve as coffins for our children in the camps.
They found corpses for you, little soapbox,
as a coffin I had seen you myself.

The small trampled thorn tree slowly healed itself,
over the wounds seeped the ointment of own glue.
The wounds healed as the years came and went,
but that scar enlarged and kept growing.

★

After some wreaths were laid, a classmate, the plump, bespectacled and pimpled Hannes Gerber, would play the last *taptoe* on his trumpet. And the fact that somewhere in the middle he always made a mess of it became just another indicator to us, this pathetic us, that in this wide, merciless landscape, no one would ever be on our side. This was affirmed when we drove home past the town and township where we could see English and black people out in their gardens and streets to enjoy a day that was for them merely a holiday.

★

Lice-infested camp. I watched a Tommy this afternoon, taking his leggings off, unwinding them like strips of bandage. Then he used broken glass to scrape the lice from his legs (Uys 2007).[1]

People die like rats. Carts come down the rows of tents. They pick up the dead. At least twelve funerals every day.

Typhus everywhere here in the tents. Heavy rains every evening and again at midnight. We try to sleep in a few inches of mud.

No candles left. All five of my children have diarrhoea. The whole night in pitch-black darkness, the sound of stomachs going and the scary wet smell of death. My littlest ones. My littlest ones. God shall I give for soap.

In the food today: maggots, weevils, crushed glass and a fish hook.

No vegetables, no fruit. Her mouth full of sores. A gaping stench until, this morning, her whole palate imploded, teeth and all. She held it in her hand like this.

On 24 October my seventeen-year-old daughter Anna died. A day later Magdalena, the wife of my brother. Then, on 30 October, one of my daughters, Rykie: eight years old—taken by the angel of death. My only grandchild died on the 20 December and on 15 January, my fifteen-year-old daughter Alettalie.

My youngest died last night. In the pitch-black dark. I could not see his little face, nor he mine.

---

1 Unless otherwise mentioned, testimonies and letters summarized in this section are sourced from Raath (1991; 1992; 1993).

I saw fourteen coffins, three per grave. On the mounds bottles were planted with the names of the dead written on paper torn from hymn books.

She cried for food yesterday. I just held her. Johanna was dead this morning. The baby still suckling.

★

In the black clothes of the mourner she rises indestructibly from the red grass. Concentration camp, says the bend in her neck. Blood for the Fatherland, says her bosom, and the destruction that men bring. She is our Ouma. And whether we dance or long-leggedly sit to watch videos, whether we are secretaries or are combing our hair lounging on ragged bedspreads, somewhere in our family albums she sits: a black, bitter root fed by humiliation and grief.

And from her came the women of Afrikaners—moments of anxiety had just flashed across their cheeks. Anxiety combined with determination. Determination combined with submissiveness. Submissiveness combined with an unshakeable belief that 'our cause is just.'

★

'I was awake, but suddenly completely awake in my bed. It was very dark but I sensed someone bending over me . . . then these cold, kind of dry hands were at my throat.' The woman talking fastens her red hair with a golden clasp. 'I started shouting, fighting and hitting while the grip tightened round my throat. Then by chance my hand touched the prickly, shorn scalp and I immediately realized it was my bloody old grandmother! But by that time everybody was storming to my room because of my yelling.'

The grandmother was an ordinary woman. Or so her family thought. The fact that she had shaved her head ever since the Anglo-Boer War and always wore a kind of skull-cap was regarded as a sign of healthy mourning. The fact that two of her baby girls—born after the war—died seemed part of her tragic life. After the attack that night on one of her grandchildren, she was sent to an institution.

Years afterwards, the family found remnants of a diary which contained the following entry: 'The storm was raging through the night. The mortuary tent blown away. This morning they lay there. Row upon row of drenched corpses. Hair wild and eyes and mouths distended under the scorching sun. Among them I saw the rusty red plait of Aletta.'

Aletta was the grandmother's firstborn. Then the family remembered that at least one of the babies who died had red hair like Aletta, red like the hair of the grandmother herself and the granddaughter that she tried to strangle one night.

Less than a century later, another voice testified. The woman talking in front of the TRC was beautiful, articulate, smart—the daughter of a famous black Pan Africanist Congress (PAC) activist.

I was a pretty little thing in a tutu—the only daughter in a well-off family. We read, we talked politics. This was destroyed when my father became a political prisoner. Our home became cold and needy. I and my mother . . . for me there was a real war against my mother. We were so clumsy with each other . . . I felt so unloved by her. I was abused by stick, by mouth, by neglect . . .

I took that with me into my own family. I bashed my son. I almost killed my son. Today he is overseas [a brilliant musician] . . . But his sister saw him go up, he was about six, trying to hang himself in a tree, because I used to bash him so much. I sent him to the shop. I spit on the floor. You must be back before the spit dries. My son would run. My boy would run . . . and then I worry. He is too short, they wouldn't see him at the counter. Maybe someone kidnaps him. Maybe he dies. And when he comes back, I take the sjambok [whip made of hide]—I would beat him, I would beat him, I would beat him—until the neighbours jump over the fence and stop me. And this son of mine, this one so close to my heart, I hear him say to his friends: 'I don't know suffering' (TRC 1997).

How does one reconstruct a society after conflict? Is it possible to rebuild a postwar society when those who should weave the social and moral fabric are themselves maimed?

What does one do with what was made by the old? How does one break out of destructive cycles to find a past tense for the word *hurt*? How does one learn to live with scars that could not become language? How does one get released into understanding the harmed-ness within those who harmed? How do the harmers make good? How close can harmed tongues lie to tenderness, the harmed cheek to forgiving?

Can this country ever cut clean?

★

Ever since I can remember, my parents collected war stories and diaries relating to the people from our province, the Orange Free State, based on which, my mother describes the beginning of the Anglo-Boer War in her novel:

> One was so bloated with fear that one could hardly breathe without farting. Six feet to my right lay a man looking like a freshly washed potato. He stacked his bullets in front of him, tested his Mauser's muzzle, took out his watch, put it next to the bullets, followed by a neatly folded handkerchief and a packet of peppermints. He took out all the small stones under his body, put his Mauser in place and started scanning the landscape with his binoculars. On my left, someone was stuffing himself with chewing tobacco as if berserk.
>
> While spewing tobacco juice, he asked me if I knew how to distinguish a cannon shooting *away* from you from one shooting *towards* you. How should I know? He knows, he was in the war of 1880. It's simple: when the noise goes zoeiing zoeiing zoeiing catchla, it is shooting away from you; if the noise goes catchla zoeiing zoeiing zoeiing, then it is shooting towards you.

I cleaned my sweaty hands on my trousers and put my Mauser bullets next to me. The first English bullets kicked up dust round us. I shot back, blindly. Then this side, then that. Before the dust could lift, I saw a rinkhals snake coming towards me—behind him short fire tongues burning after a cannon-hit in the grass. I flapped desperately with my hat in front of me until the snake swerved sharply. My ears were deaf, my hands were shaking so much I could hardly get the bullets into the magazine. I glanced quickly towards the man who knows about cannons. He was lying turned towards me. From a small hole in his head came a stream of blood. His eyes were staring past me, his mouth hanging open like a finch nest from his tobacco-stained teeth. The man on my right had disappeared, only the packet of peppermints remained.

[. . .] It has become very quiet around me. Someone touched my arm. I turned round. 'Arsehole, pretend you're dead so that I can pick you up.' I raised my arm in protest. He hissed: 'Quiet, you stupid fool, I'm here under the white flag to pick up the dead. If you're alive, you have to go that side as a prisoner of war.' I fell forward. He threw me onto a cart. I was with those who died. Body after body piled onto the cart. The stench of death, urine, sweat, blood. The wagon creaked away. I was vomiting. I recognized some of the faces squashed between bodies. I was convinced I was dead (Serfontein 1979: 39–42; my translation).

Did all of this happen to one man? Was it true? I never asked because in a sense it didn't matter—one figured that all these tales were playing themselves out repeatedly in front of a vast backdrop, never officially or comprehensively documented by both sides. My father told me that after the Anglo-Boer War, President Martinus Theunis Steyn of the Free State Republic, General Christiaan De Wet and Klasie Havenga, private secretary to General J. B. M. Hertzog, ordered the gathering of affidavits in order to take the British to court for breaking the rules of the Hague Convention of 1899. They were requested, for the sake of nation building and reconciliation between Boer and Brit, not to pursue the case and restrictions were placed on the documentation. This prevented any officially accepted version of atrocities accommodating all sides. After the war, the issues were left initially to the devices of the nationalist storytellers within the different communities.

My mother's novel about the war ends with the main female character giving birth to a baby, the product of rape by a black man, in a cave to which the family had fled after their farm was raided and burnt down by a group of black and coloured men under the command of British officers:

> I see the tiny hands making fists, the little mouth opening to reach for breath, the little feet kicking. Then, as if in a dream, I see Aunt Bet taking a folded piece of cloth. She presses it down over the little face and keeps it there. The tiny hands grab wildly, the little back making a bowlike movement, then, slowly, everything releases, the

child lies motionless. 'It was stillborn,' says Aunt Bet in a flat voice (ibid.: 172; my translation).

The raping of Boer women was never mentioned when I grew up. When I read my mother's book, I assumed it was fiction.

But in another book, *Vroueleed* (1993), compiled by A. W. G. Raath and R. M. Louw—the fourth in a series of ten written after the restrictions on these documents were lifted— I found some testimonies.

Eighty-five affidavits of the suffering of women before they were sent to the concentration camps had been taken down in the area where I grew up: Kroonstad, Lindley, Heilbron and Winburg. Nineteen of those deal with rape or sexual assault. Seven of the accused were black.

> Two black men entered and I fled. But I became worried about my sister and returned. One was lying on top of her. The other one pinned her down. Her legs were naked, she fought but seemed exhausted. Her breathing was painful. When it was all finished I saw the bruises the next day, her arms yellow-purple and deep bruises with cuts in between her legs. (Signed M. M. de Jongh from the farm Sterling, Heilbron, before Magistrate H. Potgieter.) (Raath 1993: 122; my translation).

> He was busy for half an hour with Anna Geertruida. When he was finished, she stood up. She was very weak and came to sit next to me. I gave her some water. The black man left the

house without saying anything. It was one of the bitterest moments of my life to see my daughter like this. (Signed A. G. de Jongh from the farm Sterling, Heilbron, before Magistrate A. Potgieter.) (ibid.: 120; my translation).

The black man tore the clothes from my little daughter and took her to another room. 'If she is "onbekwaam" [inept], I want you,' he said. (Signed J. C. Geldenhuys before Commandant A. Ross.) (ibid.: 110; my translation).

One of the stories recorded by A. H. M. Scholtz in his book *A Place Called Vatmaar* (2000) describes the raiding of a farm house:

Why white people have to kill one another, I could never understand,' Auntie Vuurmaak said. 'The English said that they were giving their lives for an old woman whom they called Queen, and even if they play-fight, the Boere shot down the Queen's people like game.

. . . Then this man came to hire five boys to work for Queen. He took us to an Englishman who said that he was Lance-Corporal Lewis. They would pay us a sixpence per day, a tin of bully beef and biscuits . . . In those days there was no other work, only war work . . . We soon found out what we were supposed to do . . . At the first farmhouse there was only an *ouma*, a pregnant woman and two small girls. None of them cried or begged for mercy. Then the *ouma* remembered that the Bible was still in the kitchen. She went back into the flames. She came out of the house with the Book high above her head. The young woman ran to take the Book from her. Then the *ouma* burst into one big flame, her dress burnt—her bonnet was the last thing to burn and we just looked at that old face. Not a tear came out of her eyes or a sound from her lips. Then she fell to the ground—a black bundle of burnt meat (2000: 18).

So where did all these images go?

The English, because of a less than honourable victory, had to bury theirs in official files and personal letters in England.

And this afternoon in the course of about ten miles we have burnt no fewer than six farmhouses . . . I stood till late night before the red blaze and saw the flames lick round each piece of poor furniture—the chairs, the tables, the baby's cradle, the chest of drawers containing everything they owned; and then I saw a housewife's face pressed against the window of a neighbouring house, my heart burnt with a sense of outrage (Raath 1993: xx; my translation).

In turn, the Afrikaners turned their stories into myths of exclusion: only Afrikaners suffered, all Afrikaners were brave, the only contribution of women was their suffering. In the absence of a comprehensive multi-voiced version of the war, the stories had no choice but to stutter forth orally from generation to generation: the mightiest nation in the world had turned against us—our survival, from now on and for ever, depends only on ourselves. Even if we have to make the most unjust laws, like those officializing apartheid, even if we have to become worse than our hated enemy, we have no choice, because our survival depends solely on our own strategy. Our erstwhile honourable principles of freedom and justice have been reduced to only one—survival—and the strategy to cunning and cruelty.

A humane interaction between Brit and Boer never formed part of my memory but a positive engagement between black and Boer somehow did slip in. My grandmother would tell how her mother would go down from the caves where they were hiding and how the old black man staying on the farm would sit for hours with a knife at the spruit (stream) to spear a fish for her. She would whisper to me: 'If it wasn't for him, we would all have died.'

★

Man can be assimilated by a country. There is an x and a y in the air and in the soil of a country, which slowly permeate and assimilate him to the type of aboriginal inhabitant, even to the point of slightly remodelling his physical features. The foreign country somehow gets under the skin of those born in it (Jung 1964: 510).

★

I am moved by the photographs of Afrikaners during the 1950s and 60s taken by David Goldblatt (2007), because it is us—and everything that we are—down to the lees.

We, wrought from an overwhelming landscape, embedded in stone as we are—our eyes sweeping the sky.

Three kinds of Afrikaners look out from these photographs, of which the poor Afrikaner is the most haunting. Of this group, landscape is the essence—the limbs of their children stick like tiny spokes against an infinity. A man works with his spade against a wilderness, a house surrenders to fences rusting in the snow, a woman gets water from a stream. Small joys, small acts of survival, eating bread, sweating in isolation within a merciless landscape.

And they live simply. They look out towards the camera without a suggestion of suspicion or inferiority. The elderly sit self-mockingly, the young ones hang in blissful ordinariness over the side of a cement dam.

The most surprising are the black people in these photographs. Their body language is relaxed and they look towards the camera with the same amount of curious intensity as the whites next to them. It is as if the harsh earth turned white and black for and into each other.

Look at the man on his haunches with the pipe. He has an outward bond with the landscape. He is not a personality. He will never find a proper place in the collectivity of Afrikaners on the rise but he is at peace with where and how he is and he gives to the photographer what he has.

The dark shadow in the foreground is the photographer, *you*, who are watching us, undisturbed. You watch, as you have always been watching us. Since we can remember, we feel ourselves being watched by those speaking English: sometimes with disdain or irritation, often with scorn and, at times, pity. You watching—a secure you—safe in your history, language and myth.

But here, look at the stone wall that we erected like a bulwark against the wide desolate plains. It is we who planted the windmill like a punctuation mark against the horizon. We? Yes, 'we' willed the wall; 'they' packed it stone by stone.

Who knows what other sutures and ways of living together might have developed between 'we' and 'they' if it wasn't for another, a second group of Afrikaners?

This second group suddenly bursts from the photographs in the book. In hats and good woollen jackets they stand together—inseparable. Like a bullet they come straight. Their faces are fierce. They sell and buy.

They're the middle class. They're the mounted guard. They're the revokers of laws and the rewriters of history. On national days, they sit together behind sunglasses and hats. They know what is best for 'our' people.

They're resolute. They're defensive and, at times, aggressive when they think that they hear derision. Part of them feels ennobled by the 'righteousness' of their claim to rule the land; the other part is filled with unease.

As part of the second generation of camp and war survivors, they expect the worst, which leaves them with an 'insatiable thirst for recognition' and 'a tragic lack of civic courage' (Jung 1964: 208).

They feed on legends of betrayal and stabs in the back. They publicly suppress their dark side but it flourishes in their strategic activities (ibid.: 112). They rally their own and clamp down on the Other. They legislate for what they believe is their threatened survival.

During the time these photographs were taken, they declared South Africa a republic. They made Transkei a Bantustan, black African homeland. They celebrated the arrival of the Dutch in 1652, 300 years ago, with extra police forces deployed in the peri-urban townships where black people lived—their vulnerability crudely exposed by riots and bombings. They saw their political saviour, Prime Minister Hendrik Frensch Verwoerd, swinging behind a microphone with blood streaming down his face. They saw his body being carried out of Parliament— stabbed in the heart like a pig by a non-white.

They were tightening apartheid legislation into an iron grip: banning the ANC and the PAC under the Unlawful Organizations Act No. 34; incarcerating activists under the 90-day detention law, to be followed by the 180-day deten- tion and re-detention thereafter law; detaining indefinitely without trial suspected 'terrorists' under the Suppression of Communism Act No. 24 and the Terror-ism Act No. 83; and prohibiting non-racial political parties under the Prohibition of Political Interference Act No. 51.

They declared two states of emergency, which gave the president rule by decree and heightened the powers of both the defence force and the police. Reportage of any political unrest was restricted.

They set up commissions of inquiry into the Sharpe-ville massacre and the riots at Evaton, Vanderbijlpark and Langa, which saw thousands of people detained, as well as three other commissions into secret organizations, improper political interference and the circumstances of Verwoerd's death.

They knew all too well how they were being perceived by the South African English. One of our country's Nobel Prize–winning writers formulated the disgust in Afrikaners by one of his characters:

> I have only to see the heavy, blank faces so familiar since childhood to feel gloom and nausea. The bullies in the last row of school-desks, rawboned, lumpish boys, grown up now and promoted to rule the land. They with their fathers and mothers, their aunts and uncles, their brothers and sisters: a locust horde, a plague of black locusts infesting the country, munching without cease, devouring lives. Why, in a spirit of horror and loathing, do I watch them? [. . .] Heavy eyelids, piggish eyes, shrewd with the shrewdness of generations of peasants. Plotting against each other too: slow peasant plots that take decades to mature [. . .]. Cetshwayo, Dingane in white skins [. . .]. Huge bull-testicles pressing down on their wives, their children, pressing the spark out of them [. . .]. Their feat [. . .] to have raised stupidity to a virtue. To stupefy [. . .] The Boar War (Coetzee 1990: 25–6).

But between the rising middle class and the peasantry was another group—people who understood enough to feel unsafe but knew too little to have a choice.

They're neither inside nor at peace with being outside. They are intimidated and abused by the rising middle class while they themselves despise the peasants. They lack the perceptiveness and skills of the powerful group as well as solidarity with the land of the other group. They have neither land nor power. They are being pressured to rally behind the powerful in order to set foot in the hallowed domain of the bourgeoisie.

The price they have to pay is to do the dirty work. They group together into bands and keep the neighbourhoods and beaches white. They rule their households and, at night, they 'remove terrorists'. After such a night, when they drive into the white suburbs in the mornings, they think: 'See how peaceful people drive in the traffic, listen how inspiringly our leaders have spoken last night, see how the white children blissfully walk to school. Look at the beautiful gardens, the neat open streets. Because of us. We kept all this safe through the night.'

*

As a boy, he hovers on leguan arms. Electricity tears from his skin. Ecstatically, he pierces the water. His eyes target like a predator.

Now he wears a jacket. His hair is cropped. He's *baas*.

He has stepped out of a Jungian textbook:

One does not really know who one is: one feels inferior somewhere and yet does not wish to know where the inferiority lies, with the result that a new inferiority is added to the original one. This sense of insecurity is the source of the hysteric's prestige psychology, of his need to make an impression, to flaunt his merits and insist on them, of his insatiable thirst for recognition, admiration, adulation, and longing to be loved (Jung 1964: 208).

These were the men who testified as perpetrators in their amnesty applications before the TRC.

Jeffrey Benzien, senior member of the South African Police anti-terrorist unit, became a national legend. He could get any information from anyone within 30 minutes of wet-bag torture. (A wet bag is placed over a victim's head, which results in suffocation and the sensation of drowning.) During his hearing, one of his former victims, Gary Kruser, director in the new police force and in command of the VIP protection unit, asked permission to interrogate Benzien.

KRUSER. What happened after you arrested me?

BENZIEN. I didn't arrest you, sir, perhaps you confuse me.

KRUSER. I KNOW YOU. It was you!

BENZIEN. I do not remember ever arresting you.

(South African Press Association 1997a)

After Benzien repeatedly denied having arrested Kruser, the latter broke down. It was clearly too much for flesh and feelings that this experience, which had nearly destroyed his life, did not make the slightest imprint on Benzien's memory. Or was he lying to torture an old victim one last time? One of the requirements for a successful amnesty application was to tell the full truth.

Benzien's psychologist told me afterwards that Benzien was suffering from a severe debilitating form of self-loathing. She was contacted one evening after he had a flashback while he was sitting outside on his veranda smoking a cigarette. The flashback was so intense and real that he burst into tears. Benzien's wife then called her. He just said repeatedly: 'I cannot tell you—I'm too ashamed.'

Sitting at Benzien's amnesty hearing, I was taking notes as a journalist. I knew that the next victim to question Benzien would be a long-time activist and current member of Parliament, Tony Yengeni. As a journalist who also reported from Parliament, I got to know Yengeni's voice as being fluent with confidence and somewhat tinged with arrogance. When he started to speak, I had to look up to ascertain whether this strange choking and stumbling voice was indeed that of Yengeni. He wanted to know exactly how Benzien knew when to release the wet bag so that a victim could breathe. It was well known in activist circles that Yengeni himself was tortured until he informed on a very important comrade. Now he wanted to understand how Benzien fathomed that exact point of being on the brink of dying. Was it something in the body, the breathing, the sounds?

This caused Benzien to demonstrate, with a mixture of anguish and keen concentration, to a flabbergasted Amnesty Committee and Yengeni the wet-bag method —sitting on a volunteer's back, pulling the bag over his face.

Soon after this very hearing, Yengeni appeared on enormous billboard-size posters, dressed in one of the silk suits sold by the most expensive shop at the V&A Waterfront in Cape Town. The face that once was suffocating within a wet bag was smiling confidently in those spaces where the rich shopped, looking radiant, chic and completely at ease in the luxurious outfit. A few years later, he was found guilty of receiving an expensive four-wheel drive vehicle as a bribe to facilitate the bidding of a particular European company to provide South Africa with arms. On the day he had to present himself at the jail, he was carried sky-high by singing comrades who hailed him as a hero.

What are the invisible links between being tortured into breaking your own moral codes and later corruption; between giving up everything in the fight for freedom and eventual greed? German poet Hans Magnus Enzensberger asks, where do monsters come from? He answers: from humiliated nations, from masses of permanent losers being humiliated for too long, intellectual failures, people too deep in poverty and powerlessness to influence their own lives (cited in Buruma 1994: 33).

At her hearing as a victim of torture, another activist, Deborah Matshoba, recognized all her former comrades laughing and hugging one another. When it was her turn to testify, she remarked: 'When I look round this room, I marvel at how we battle to be normal . . . and no one knows how shattered we are inside' (Krog 1998: 185).

Later, when I made a documentary on Deborah's life, I found her holding down a highly successful job at the head office of an insurance company but living alone in a big house in a white suburb with a stagnant swimming pool and no food in the kitchen cupboards or fridge. Her children preferred to live with her family. Her brother explained how, since her incarceration, she would be always alone: 'You can see her crying, and she will be far, far, far away, and when you touch her, she would just become violent. She would be crying from the chest, you know, not from the mouth or the eyes.'

According to the TRC's report, torture leaves no part of a victim's life untouched. Depression, anxiety, sleep disorders, sexual dysfunction, irritability and physical illness are common. Victims of torture have their faith in humanity eroded, their capacity to cope overwhelmed and their sense of self destroyed. After release, they feel alienated from others and have enduring difficulties in forming relationships.

Memory seems also able to protect one by letting shards through that are true but somehow less traumatizing— substituting those that cannot be brought to mind with those that can be borne. Captain Jacques Hechter was applying for amnesty for killing many people. Three of them—Jackson Maake, Harold Sefolo and Andrew Makupe—were singing 'Nkosi Sikelel iAfrika' (now South Africa's national anthem) when he killed them. This he could not remember:

> JUDGE BERNARD NGOEPE. Are you able to remember that on a certain day in 1987 on a farm near Pienaarsrivier, you electrocuted three people?
>
> HECHTER. I can . . . the electrocution . . . I can remember after it was told to me. But it was completely out of my thoughts . . . I consciously banned these things from my thoughts . . . I haven't thought about it for ten years . . .
>
> NGOEPE. But you remember trivialities.

HECHTER. Yes, I remember terribly . . . I can
    remember the path . . . it was a white chalky
    road . . . and there were guinea-fowl. I can
    remember things like that, but really . . . the
    worse deeds . . . those I do not remember.

(South African Broadcasting Corporation 2000)

Hechter worked alone. During the day, he was a cop in an office. By night, he became a hangman, killing activists. He could remember the guineafowl but not the people he killed. He openly said: 'I am saying yes to all you suggest, Your Honour, because I was told by my lawyer and fellow policemen that I have killed these people' (ibid.).

In a famous photograph of the Vlakplaas Five killers taken by Jillian Edelstein (2002), Hechter appears to be attractive but bristling with hostility. I interviewed many perpetrators but found him totally inaccessible. When asked for an interview, he irritably swung round on his crutches and marched off. Somehow I never wondered why he was on crutches. According to his psychiatric report, he has developed a personality disassociation. Before the commission, he delivered his testimony about scores of murders without any emotion. Right through his testimony, his eyes were glued on the table in front of him. Those eyes (he told the psychiatrist) were always open. He could not close them, neither to sleep, nor to pray.

★

Often the healing of memory seemed to need words. At a workshop for victims, a white man testified how he was sitting next to his wife and saw her slumping across his lap after being shot in what he described as a terrorist attack. On her back, he saw a red butterfly spreading across her yellow blouse.

Butterfly! I had problems with the image. Was that not a bit too frivolous or carefree to describe the blood from a fatal wound?

It took the man three years to arrive at that image, his psychologist told me. And the moment he arrived at it, she knew that he could begin the process of healing. This image, this word 'butterfly', meant that he at long last had a handle on the experience. Now he could perhaps stop an invading memory and say: No, wait, I do not want to have you rush through me at this very moment in which I am trying to lead a normal life.

Add to this that every violent death causes extensive trauma to parents who feel they have failed to protect their child or are now bereft because a breadwinner is dead. It causes siblings to be traumatized by survivor guilt. It affects the communities in which these deaths took place. If it is true that more than 21,000 South Africans died as a result of apartheid violence, then it means that quite a number of our population is directly and indirectly affected by trauma. What, then, are the accumulative effects of 300 years of colonialism, the many frontier wars, the Anglo-Boer War, the millions displaced after being forcibly removed from the places they lived, racism and capitalist exploitation?

The South African past is eating away at us. It is the fire stoking the crime and corruption which are consuming our soul.

*

'Why don't you forget, like this whole country is forgetting, and start afresh?' His black face is immobile as he loosens panels from my computer hard drive.

'And find myself also surprised over the high crime rate, the violence in families, the moral chaos in South Africa,' I respond. 'If you don't know where things come from, you won't be able to deal with them.'

'So you are a believer that God visits the iniquity of the fathers upon the children unto the third and fourth generation! Well, I believe that God banished the Israelites to 40 years in the desert, because he did not want those who *knew* slavery to build the promised land. But you misunderstood me. The only valid reason to keep remembering is to get a kind of moral immunity for yourself. It goes like this: because this is the suffering recorded in my memory, I may do as I please. Because I suffered, I may now make others suffer and you dare not do anything to me.'

I am surprised at the direction the discussion is taking.

'My father was arrested during the apartheid years,' he continues. 'To this day, I hate to see him. He still has that look, of surrender and humiliation, and I cannot stand that. I refuse to live my life within this state of victimhood. I have bought him a separate house. Out of my way. I don't want to see his shrunken selfhood. Actually, what I hate most is that when I lash out against whites, he would say, All whites are not like that, and would want to tell me about a kind warder or other who gave him a newspaper. A newspaper, for God's sake!'

'But maybe he knew whites in a more intimate way than you,' I say. 'He could distinguish between good and bad whites. I see only black people here round where you work. How many whites do you know?'

'That is not the point. He is too soft on the likes of you. We, the children of that generation, we are more realistic. We are not interested in maybe there is a wonderful white person out there somewhere. We don't care. We want a country without whites.'

What a toxic mix we have become, I say to myself as I leave the repair shop.

CHAPTER FIVE

Redefinition and the Battlefield of Guilt and Shame

In 2006, 12 years into the South African democracy, three young and unknown Afrikaner men, Bok van Blerk, Johan Vorster and Sean Else, produced a song about one of the lesser-known generals of the Anglo-Boer War: General Koos de la Rey. Through simple lyrics, a somewhat mediocre tune, a cabaret-like rhythm and a homemade digital video, we see de la Rey, addressed by his praise name 'The Lion of the West Transvaal', portrayed in romantic, heroic terms. On horseback, he rushes towards the Boers in their trenches (the trenches themselves were an invention of General de la Rey) and the women and children in the concentration camps.

Two phenomena characterized the release of 'De la Rey'.[1] It became the first Afrikaans song ever to sell 122,000 copies in less than six months, more than 100 copies per day, which indicated that it was probably popular to more people than right-wingers representing about 0.83 per cent of the population. Second, while Afrikaners were still arguing among themselves about whether the song was conservative or not, 'De la Rey' became the object of what

---

1 The song is included on a CD with the same title (Bok van Blerk, Johan Vorster and Sean Else 2005).

can only be described as obsessive media attention, locally as well as internationally. It made front-page headlines in the US and UK and an extraordinary number of radio and television hosts, intellectuals, commentators, editors, journalists, politicians and ordinary letter writers felt obliged to give their interpretation of the song. And they were not in doubt: they read the song, almost unanimously, as an ethnic call for an Afrikaner uprising.

I was one of those who bought a copy. While watching the music video, I was surprised to find that my hair suddenly stood on end. What was going on here? What nodes of sentiment, what hidden manufactured layers were being pushed so that a person oversensitive and resistant to Afrikaner manip-ulation felt moved by it?

The music video opens in silence.[2] On a black backdrop appears the numbers 82,742 Boers against 346,693 Khakis. Then the music begins and one sees a man lying in a war trench in the dark. Behind him are the iconic sandstone mountains of the Eastern Free State and the ruins of a burnt-down house. He sings in a somewhat forced low voice:

> On a mountain in the night
> We lie in the darkness and wait.
> In the mud and blood I lie cold,
> Grain bag and rain cling to me.
>
> My house and my farm burned to ashes
> So that they could catch us,

---

2 The music video is available at: http:// www.youtube.com/-watch?v=vtKKJSfYraU (last accessed on 23 June 2013).

But those flames and that fire
Now burn deep, deep within me.
(translation from Groenewald 2007)

Then the song jumps to the appealing chorus as one sees
a much older but impressive and intense-looking man gal-
loping over a wide savannah. But somehow the chorus
feels set in the present. The Afrikaners did have leaders
during the Anglo-Boer War but they do not have any
prominent, and especially no brave, leader in the new
South Africa.

De la Rey, De la Rey
Will you come and lead the Boers?
De la Rey, De la Rey
General, General as one man
We'll fall in around you General De la Rey.

The lyrics move from the man in the trench to the British:

And the Khakis that laugh
A handful of us against their great might
With the cliffs to our backs
They think it's all over.

But the heart of the Boer lies
Deeper and wider
That they'll discover.
At a gallop he comes,
The Lion of the West Transvaal.

Visually, the video moves to the face of a small boy peer-
ing through the wire of a concentration camp.

Because my wife and my child
Are perishing in a concentration camp

And the Khakis' reprisal is poured
Over a nation that will rise up again.

Behind the boy appears a young mother and, as the chorus swells again, she walks resolutely to the camp gates and, without a moment's wavering, simply pushes them open and walks out. The camera moves to the man lying in a trench in the opening scene of the song. He now jumps, or rather flies, out of the trench and joins those walking out of the camp.

It was the moment of pushing open the gates of the concentration camp that gave me gooseflesh. Initially, I thought my reaction tied up with the deep-seated desire to reverse history, to simply walk out of a camp—the anxiety of the oppressed that they were themselves responsible for what was happening to them. Why didn't we simply push open the gates?

I want to contextualize this song with the content of the CD as a whole and the reaction to it in order to explore three issues about the ways in which Afrikaners are approaching their past and future in the aftermath of apartheid: the role of memory in popular cultural practice and the ways in which the figure of the ancestor is being mobilized in popular art to integrate a violent past with a preferable present; the use of silences in signalling the burden of double guilt; and the role of particular interpretations in either opening or blocking negotiation for a new future and the entry of Afrikaners into the ethical debate about and of South Africa.

It is important to bear in mind that General de la Rey was known for several things: for being the last Boer general to enter the war because he believed a peaceful solution could be found; for being against the exclusionist policy of Paul Kruger, then president of the South African Republic (Transvaal); and known for the good treatment he gave to the wounded British officer Lord Methuen and other prisoners of war. Wounded and with a broken leg, Field Marshal Methuen was the only British general to be captured during the war. De la Rey released him due to the severity of his injuries, providing his personal cart to take Methuen to hospital in Klerksdorp. The two allegedly became lifelong friends as a result. After the war, de la Rey went into politics not as an Afrikaner nationalist, it was said, but with a vision of a broader South African nation.

After the song was released, the songwriters repeatedly distanced themselves from right-wing efforts to claim it as a kind of anthem. This should not be taken at face value; so, one has to take a closer look at the elements that were used in the song.

The songwriters mixed a variety of small shards chipped from well-known Afrikaner myths. The first of these was condensed in the line 'A handful of us against their great might'. The unequal numbers appearing in total silence on a black screen before the song begins forms the prelude to the essence of the song: an 'I' against 'them'. The 'I' lies alone in the night, his back against a cliff, one of a handful against a mighty army that is taunting, laughing and looting. The song speaks about 'they' who want to catch 'us'; 'they' think it is all over, but they don't know 'us'. 'We' will show 'them'.

This myth, presented through phrases or mythemes, is one of the strongest and oldest in Afrikaner culture, forged during the Groot Trek (as Afrikaans emigrants during the 1830s–40s left the British-ruled Cape Colony for the interior, where they came up against 'savage hordes'), proved during the Anglo-Boer War and internationalized during apartheid (with the belief in a worldwide total onslaught in which black South Africans would overwhelm and massacre whites).

The second mytheme embedded in the song is captured by the phrase 'My house and my farm burned to ashes'. This sentiment is older than the war. As frontier Afrikaners trekked away from the Cape, they often lost everything they owned in the many battles against indigenous groups. Soon, the Anglo-Boer War, the subsequent depression and the flu epidemic crushed most of them into a 'Poor White problem'. Every Afrikaner family has stories about the loss of family, the loss of land, the loss of diamond or gold concessions, the loss of livestock, porcelain and furniture.

On all the farms in my extended family, one can be (and often is) taken to a spot where 'the Tommies broke Grandma's porcelain', to pick up the most wonderful shards. A recurring image in documentaries and fictionalized accounts of the Anglo-Boer War is of a group of British soldiers bashing and destroying a piano with their rifle butts. This image conveys two things: that Afrikaners were/are civilized and that civilization is brittle and can easily be destroyed by barbarians. This double message is at the heart of much Afrikaner literature, though it is perhaps most perfectly distilled in P. G. du Plessis' recent and most popular novel *Fees van die Ongenooides* (Feast of the Uninvited, 2008).

In the terms of this mythical structure, these losses are the result of external forces and undeserved aggression. Except for the drought and pests that contributed to the Great Depression, all the incidents that supposedly stripped Afrikaners of what they had 'paid' for with 'innocent blood' were caused by deliberate and planned structures of attack and violence against them. For contemporary Afrikaners, who have only just recently moved out of the peasantry or working class into the middle class, this mythical shard of being-on-the-brink-of-losing-everything forms a powerful reality.

The third shard of myth is expressed in the lines 'And the Khakis' reprisal is poured / Over a nation that will rise up again'—a phoenix image. The notion of rising from the ashes was forged after the Anglo-Boer War. The Afrikaner nation grew from a deeply wounded and small group to a people who literally ran most of southern Africa. They rose from the ashes of the Anglo-Boer War and its 'scorched earth policy' to become the feared and terrible masters of the country.

The final mytheme is a plea for both leadership and liberation: 'De la Rey, De la Rey / Will you come and lead the Boers?' During the Groot Trek, a delegation was sent to ask Piet Retief, a prominent farmer, to come and 'lead' the Voortrekkers into the Promised Land of KwaZulu-Natal. Afrikaners, intones the song, always had a leader or believed that they should have one.

Koos de la Rey, as the Anglo-Boer War general, has a fixed location in history. But myth-making round his person, and therefore the dehistoricization of his life (what Claude Levi-Strauss would describe as his movement into reversible time [1968: 214]), had started at the time of his death in 1914, when he was shot by police at a roadblock set up to catch the infamous Foster gangsters. The shooting took place shortly after he concurred with the commandant-general of the South African defence forces, General C. F. Beyers, to resign rather than fight on the side of the British during the upcoming First World War. Beyers and de la Rey were on their way to convince General Kemp to join them and, despite evidence to the contrary, many Afrikaners believed that de la Rey had been deliberately shot to prevent a rebellion. In a call-in session to the main Afrikaans radio station during a programme discussing the song, many callers referred with some paranoia to de la Rey's last words: 'Christiaan [Boer General De Wet's first name], they *got* me!' (according to *Wikipedia* his last words were: 'Dit was raak!'—It hit!).

The second song on Van Blerk's album deals with the Afrikaans language. More than land, the language is regarded as the most definitive characteristic of Afrikaners. Nothing in South Africa's new dispensation embittered Afrikaners more than the marginalization of 'their' language. A panel discussion on television about accepting change elicited several calls of support when one member said: 'After the election I gave up my power, I gave up my land, I gave up my safety, I gave up the right of my children to have a job. But I am not prepared to give up my language.' (That he could still vote, that he could live where he wanted, that the police were no longer protecting only the whites, that unemployment was still less among white youth and that the majority of Afrikaans speakers were not white was clearly not part of this equation.)

The young songwriters confronted the language issue squarely in the song 'Jy praat nog steeds my taal' (You Still Speak My Language). They pose a question: 'How do you feel now, as we are building our language anew, / can I go with *pride* to where Afrikaners are?' (my translation; emphasis added). It is a strangely sensitive and tentative question, displaying nothing of the defiance usually surrounding Afrikaners when they deal with Afrikaans. It is noteworthy that the song refers specifically to a 'new' Afrikaans. In recent years, the majority of Afrikaans speakers are no longer white and they have become more audible in the language, both in terms of profile and destabilizing the so-called standard Afrikaans.

The word 'pride' is used again in the song 'So waai die wind' (So the Wind Blows), about a grandfather: 'He [my grandfather] doesn't need to say it, / Because it is in his eyes: / A *pride* that makes me ashamed, / A *pride* from above' (my translation; emphasis added). The lyrics are torn between love for the grandfather and dealing with the fact that he played a role in upholding and condoning apartheid. The grandfather is described as a good man and attempts are made to accommodate things that the lyricist and singer, as the grandson, finds problematic, such as the Broederbond (a secret society of Afrikaners that enhanced the interest of Afrikaners on all terrains). This time pride is directly linked to shame. So, after the honourable war led by de la Rey, why is the grandson *not* proud? Why the word 'ashamed'? Neither the song nor anything else on the album explains it.

The other songs range from ordinary student-friendly themes to a song about a liberated girlfriend, the black rugby player Brian Habana and reggae singer Bob Marley.

Let me now try to do a kind of Levi-Straussian reading, bringing together both the synchronic and the diachronic dimensions of the song-text as they appear in the song itself, in the song as part of the whole album, and the song read in the context of the historical position of Afrikaners today (Levi-Strauss 1968: 214).

Diachronically, the album opens with a historical forefather, de la Rey, followed by the genealogical grandfather, then jumps over the generation of the father straight into the new South Africa, with references to friends, a black rugby player and a reggae singer. In a synchronic reading, the album's time frame is the Anglo-Boer War; it then jumps over apartheid into the democratic South Africa. The lyrics are silent about the father and the apartheid past. Why?

What is at issue here is the strong sense of cultural identity which would normally lead to feelings of identification between the generations but, in the case of Afrikaners, generates a crisis in the form of a shame that is not desired.

In her conclusion to a book on transgenerational trauma, Yael Danieli uses her famous phrase 'a conspiracy of silence' (1998: 677) for the way in which individuals, parents, societies, nations and other groups 'expel troubling matter':

> According to most contributors, the conspiracy of silence is the most prevalent and effective mechanism for the transmission of trauma on all

dimensions [. . .] silence is profoundly destructive, for it attests to the person's, family's, society's, community's and nation's inability to
integrate trauma. They can find no words to narrate the trauma story and create a meaningful
dialogue around it (ibid.: 678).

Of course, what is at stake here is not so much
trauma as disavowal—although since 1994 and through
the TRC, Afrikaners have been confronted by parts of
their history which are 'non-ordinary' and many families
have been deeply traumatized through their fathers,
brothers and sons who served in the army, police and
security forces. One disavows what one cannot accommodate, given one's own ideal image of one's self. It may
be that the disavowal is born of trauma but in the case of
Afrikaner identity (as we have seen in the text of the
album) it has more to do with shame.

One could also say that the trauma suffered during
the Anglo-Boer War has been transmitted perfectly onto
the next generations but what has been denied/dis-
avowed is the parents' perpetration of violence through
and during apartheid. Afrikaners have failed to find a
structure which could navigate their movement from the
honourable Anglo-Boer War past through the shameful
apartheid past into a new identity within the new South
Africa.

As the song about love for the grandfather and shame
about his apartheid links shows, these contradictory feelings cause havoc in the formation of young Afrikaner
identity. In postwar contexts, '[c]hildren [. . .] developed,
in place of their parents, feelings of guilt and shame,'

says Gertrud Hardtmann in her study of the children of Nazis. 'The mutual defenses—denial, splitting and projection—tied the members of the family together like a sect' (1998: 89).

Studies directed at groups of Dutch collaborators who after the Second World War found themselves on the 'wrong' side of the war indicated that although they wanted to uphold and celebrate the 'right' side after the war, they felt excluded. They were happy that the values of civil order had been restored but felt 'depressed to live in a country [. . .] in which they were afraid to speak about their background, a country in which they have to stay out of conversations about the war [. . .]. To be silent about one of the most important and most emotional topics in Dutch memory means not to belong' (Lindt 1998: 169).

In efforts to 'obtain liberation', children often try to forget and ignore unacceptable parts of their history. In this way they become 'face- and history-less' and find themselves in a permanent state of restlessness and fear. They find it hard to live a different history, to show a different face and to develop a different identity. In order to develop the identity they long for, they have to question their parental models and thus the yearning and loving feelings attached to them. 'They are orphans inside,' says Hans Speier, 'reliant on surrogate mothers and fathers' (cited in Hardtmann 1998: 92). I want to suggest that in this song, de la Rey has become a surrogate father, not to inspire uprising but to assist young Afrikaners to deal with their guilt and shame in such a way that they can begin to try to successfully integrate into the new society.

188 | *Conditional Tense*

The songwriters have indeed sensed the dilemma: I cannot criticize my apartheid-supporting father because I see how insecure he has become in a country that he no longer understands or feels welcome in. I cannot criticize the new government because I have come to understand the devastation that racial discrimination did to the psyche. If the new government is greedy, paranoid, defensive, racist, angry, prone to stupid remarks and so forth, I know where much of it comes from. In other words: I suffer from double guilt. When I utter the words 'corruption' and 'discrimination', I feel how they die in my Afrikaner mouth. So how do I participate in the making of my country? What are the words that will legitimize my contribution as useful, worthy and equal? How will all the goodwill I have towards the land ever be heard and accepted?

A careful reading of the song, however, reveals that a new element has been added to the old myths, one that also hangs together with the notion of double guilt. The songwriters interlace the layer of the phoenix image with something that has not been used before in terms of the Anglo-Boer War: 'But the heart of the Boer lies / Deeper and wider / That they'll discover.'

These are interesting lines—because they pull the song from historical time into the present. In their fight against the British, Afrikaners were saying: We are as good as you are, we are also a people. They were clamouring for equality. In their oppression of black people, Afrikaners said: We are superior to you. They were clamouring for total *baasskap* (domination). The de la Rey song says something new: We are better than *you think we are.*

They are clamouring for the right to rectify a misconception. This, for me, is a significant change—a change that could only have been brought about by shame.

In conclusion, de la Rey, as a heroic figure, is used as a mediator between an honourable and a dishonourable past. The Anglo-Boer hero mediates not in highbrow drama or literature but via music. For the album's listeners, he sustains a coherence from trenches of shame to being proud of Afrikaans and a new South Africa. He negotiates his way past the grandfather, and the apartheid politicians, to a liveable and honourable present—he mediates between a problematic past and a complicated present.

It is, I believe, this mediating role that makes the song so popular. Afrikaners of all ages have grabbed or rejected or criticized or praised it to form and negotiate their own personal myth to deal with their past, understand their present and find guidance for the future.

It is therefore ironic that the interpretation of the dominant media hammered home the idea that the song calls for a vengeful uprising. At the time of its release, one got the distinct idea that journalists and some academics were actually *missing* the good old bad days of apartheid, when the Afrikaners made it easy for every one to determine who was evil and who were 'the Saviours'! White English-speaking South Africans, more and more under fire from a black government, are in desperate need of bad-racist-Afrikaners-on-the-rise. It completely confuses the white English media when Afrikaners try to work through their guilt or try to become part of the country.

The plea for forgiveness by former police minister Adriaan Vlok and, more recently, vice chancellor and rector of the University of the Free State Jonathan Jansen's forgiveness of four Afrikaner students who deeply humiliated four black workers are cases in point. Vlok, under whose jurisdiction hundreds of activists were killed, went to the office of one of the clergymen who was poisoned on his instruction. Vlok arrived with a bowl and towel and proceeded to wash the reverend's feet in an act of contrition. He subsequently washed the feet of a group of black women whose sons were killed. Both Vlok and Jansen have been mercilessly slated, scorned and satirized in the media. The reaction is so severe that for me it testifies to a desire that Afrikaners should not be allowed to escape the bondage of shame.

Such resistance to the idea that Afrikaners may change simply forces them back onto their old trajectories. What are the consequences of this negation?

Ronald S. Kraybill has identified several steps in what he regards as the cycle of reconciliation (1988). In order to live together to the advantage of everyone, people need to reconcile. Reconciliation is a process and has to happen again and again. The steps towards this, after groups have been harmed, is identified by Kraybill: a turning away from one another; a redefining of oneself within a safe space; then undertaking what he calls 'a small act of trust'; and then again a moment of redefinition in the light of the successes and failures of the act of trust.

Black people have been redefining themselves in important ways through the African Renaissance with its heroes, ancient civilizations, literature, affirmative action,

Black Economic Empowerment, Nelson Mandela, Desmond Tutu and so on. Initially, Afrikaners had to adapt to their loss of power, the shrinkage of their language, the emigration of their children and so on. It is only recently that Afrikaners have tried to redefine themselves in positive terms. In this the Afrikaans rock scene does not play a small role.

Due to democracy, gender equality and affirmative action, young white Afrikaner males feel themselves contested in all spheres of society as well as hampered by parents traumatized in their destabilized privileges. These young men employ two strategies: avoidance and the creation of uncontested space. They avoid the baggage of their surnames (but not of Afrikaans) by taking on pseudo-names such as Coke Kartel, Toast Coetzer, Snotkop, Angola Badprop. By creating, through Afrikaans and rock (not hip-hop as it is already occupied by young coloured rappers), an exclusive space, they can avoid the claims of politics and gender and feel safe enough to begin redefining—as is the case with 'De la Rey'.

Efforts like these have often been deliberately and heavily thwarted, as we have already seen. Research has found that in countries where people are *not* allowed to redefine themselves, groups solidify into intransigent ones which begin to function as though they have nothing to lose—with all the attendant insinuations of violence.

It is essential for Afrikaners to invest everything in redefining themselves in an honourable way. It is even more essential that their attempts are respected and accepted so that small acts of trust can begin to be undertaken in order for us to address the immense socioeconomic challenges facing South Africa. To try to address poverty while ignoring Afrikaners in which this country (albeit involuntarily) had invested three centuries of privilege seems not foolhardy but potentially disastrous. Van Blerk's 'De la Rey' touches me because it so powerfully tries to reach back to an honourable moment and an honourable man as if to insert the same kind of righteousness as the 'new' contribution of Afrikaners into the moral discourse of South Africa.

CHAPTER SIX

'This Thing Called Reconciliation': *Forgiveness as Part of an Interconnectedness-towards-Wholeness*

Introduction

In his Nobel Prize–acceptance speech in 1986, Wole Soyinka expresses astonishment at how some Africans seem able to forgive and reconcile enmity after much suffering and injustice. He links it to their world view:

> [T]here is a deep lesson for the world in the black races' capacity to forgive, one which, I often think, has much to do with the ethical precepts which spring from their world view and authentic religions, none which is ever totally eradicated by the accretions of foreign faiths and their implicit ethnocentrism (quoted in Bell 2002: 87)

Elsewhere, Soyinka warns that '[w]e should differentiate first of all between the deliberate use of Christian or Islamic symbolism, metaphors or historic archetypes' and the application of 'African indigenous values' (Soyinka 1976: 76).

According to David Bloomfield et al. (2003), the South African TRC differed in several important and useful ways from the previous (at least 15) commissions elsewhere in the world that investigated human rights abuses.

I want to focus on only two of those they mention and then another that they don't mention. The South African TRC was the first truth commission to individualize amnesty and to allow victims to testify in public. What, to my knowledge, is not mentioned anywhere is that it was also the first truth commission to allow people from both sides of the conflict to testify at the same forum as victims. In this chapter, I argue that these differences, also described by Boraine (2000: 362, 425–6) and others, were made possible at least partly by a particular cultural commonality. This is not to say that political and other factors did not play an important role in the transition to democracy in South Africa but the peaceful acceptance of the specific work of the TRC by the black community (whether as victims or perpetrators—more black perpetrators asked for amnesty than white perpetrators), as well as the way in which concepts such as amnesty, reconciliation and forgiveness were innovatively used and understood, is indicative of something broader and deeper than some of the critics of TRC would allow. Although they mention the word 'ubuntu', it hardly plays a role in the formulation of their critique. I will return to the criticism later but two examples are in order here.

First, probably the most oft-quoted analyst of the TRC, Richard A. Wilson, regards ubuntu as mere 'wrapping' for an ANC agenda to use the TRC to legitimize a new government:

> Ubuntu should be recognized for what it is: an ideological concept with multiple meanings which conjoins human rights, restorative justice, reconciliation and nation-building within the

populist language of pan-Africanism. In post-apartheid South Africa, it became the Africanist wrapping used to sell a reconciliatory version of human rights talk to black South Africans (2001: 13).

Second, in her published thesis on forgiveness at the TRC, Annelies Verdoolaege dedicates only three pages in her 238-page book to ubuntu and describes it as a mere 'political agenda' in the ANC's nation-building project (2008: 166).

In short, most critics see the world view of ubuntu as superficial and confusing, as agenda and ideology used by the powerful to present political, legal and/or personal religious schemes in palatable form to unsuspecting people. I want to argue that it was the other way round: the world view was the essence and foundation of the TRC process but it only became visible to some through the 'wrapping' of Christianity and restorative justice. In my argument, I adhere to the call of Kwame Gyekye that 'issues and problems unleashed by cultural and historical situations' should be responded to on a conceptual level (1987: 34).

Clarifications

There is tension between those who claim the word 'philosophy' for 'higher' arguments and those who feel that philosophy, world view, ethos and cosmology overlap. I prefer to use the term 'world view' (and not 'belief structures' or 'social imaginings') in the sense of 'a particular system of values, beliefs and attitudes held by a specific group' (Rapport and Overing 2000: 395). Of course, the term has its own baggage, but to define and develop the appropriate terminology for this kind of analysis in the space of a chapter is impossible, especially when one is mindful of further contestations round terms such as 'African', 'pan-African', 'sub-Saharan African' and so on. Similarly, the overuse and exploitation of the term ubuntu makes it nearly unusable as well.

Aware, therefore, of the risks of 'ethnophilosophy' (Hountondji 1983: 39) in taking the route of theoretically understanding something that is so abundantly and pervasively present yet so grapplingly and tentatively theorized, I prefer in this chapter to use the term 'inter-connectedness-towards-wholeness' and place it firmly within the well-defined and formulated broader African 'communitarianism' as well as the more southern African localized term ubuntu.

Interconnectedness-towards-wholeness is more than just a theoretical knowledge that all things in the world are linked. It means both a mental and physical awareness that one can only 'become' who one is, or could be, through the fullness of that which is round one—both physical and metaphysical. Wholeness is thus not a passive state of nirvana but a process of becoming in which everyone and everything moves towards its fullest self, building itself. One can, however, only reach that fullest self through and with others, which include ancestors and the universe.

Finally, I use the terms 'forgiveness' and 'reconcilia-tion' within the concept of interconnectedness-towards-wholeness. Much has been written about the difference between forgiveness (letting go, personally, of resentment and the past) and reconciliation (mutual commitment to an improved ethical future). In their research on these concepts in Rwanda, Ervin Staub et al. define forgiveness as presenting a change in the harmed party while reconciliation as presenting a change in *both* parties:

> Forgiving involves letting go of anger and the desire for revenge. It can help in diminishing the pain that results from victimization and in moving away from an identity as a victim [. . .] Since the definition of forgiving usually includes the development of a more positive attitude toward the other [. . .] reconciliation and forgiveness are clearly connected. We define reconciliation as mutual acceptance by members of formerly hostile groups of each other. Such acceptance includes positive attitudes, but also positive actions that express them, as circumstances allow and require (2005: 301).

Within the concept of interconnectedness-towards-wholeness, the notions of forgiveness and reconciliation can never be separated. They are not only closely linked but are also mutually dependent: the one begins, or opens up, a process of becoming, while the other is the crucial next step into this becoming. As the TRC testimonies and texts discussed in this chapter show, within the world view of interconnectedness-towards-wholeness, in order to grow into one's fullest self, one's fullest potential personhood, the deed of asking for forgiveness, and forgiveness itself, needs to lead to recovery, reconciliation and, eventually, a fuller personhood.

It is important to remember that the isiXhosa word for reconciliation, in the context of truth and reconciliation, is *uxolelwano* (forgiveness). In isiXhosa, the TRC literally means the Truth and Forgiveness Commission. Looked at from a human rights perspective, one could say that forgiveness was forced on isiXhosa speakers through the mere choice of the word *uxolelwano*. But looked at from an interconnected perspective, *uxolelwano* indicates the first step towards reconciliation, towards changing into a more humane self—for both victim and perpetrator.

I will use testimonies from the second week of the TRC hearings as well as some other TRC texts to illustrate the unobtrusive traces of interconnectedness in them and how awareness of these traces contributes to a powerfully coherent, yet often unnoticed, logic. My focus includes the participants in the process, not just those who set up and ran the commission.

Formulations of Forgiveness and Reconciliation during the TRC

For me, the most coherent and deeply understood sense of interconnectedness related to forgiveness had been articulated during the second week of TRC human rights violations hearings by one of the Gugulethu Seven mothers, Cynthia Ngewu, whose son, Christopher Piet, member of Umkhonto we Sizwe or MK, had been killed by *askaris*. (See Chapter 1 for more on this case.) One of the black perpetrators, the *askari* Thapelo Mbele, requested a private meeting with the Gugulethu mothers in order to ask for forgiveness. Pumla Gobodo-Madikizela, a member of the TRC's Human Rights Violations Committee, oversaw the meeting between the killer and the mothers of those who died. Mrs Ngewu, who spoke after the meeting, was heard on SABC radio:

> This thing called reconciliation . . . if I am understanding it correctly . . . if it means this perpetrator, this man who has killed Christopher Piet, if it means he becomes human again, this man, so that I, so that all of us, get our humanity back . . . then I agree, then I support it all (Krog 1998: 109).

In simple terms, Mrs Ngewu spells out the full, complex implications of being interconnected-towards-wholeness and the role of reconciliation in it. Her words mean that she understood, first, that the killer of her child could, and did, kill because he had lost his humanity—he was no longer human; second, that to forgive him would open up the possibility for him to regain his humanity, to change profoundly; third, that the loss of her son also affected her own humanity; fourth, and most important, that if indeed the perpetrator felt himself driven by her forgiveness to regain his humanity, then it would open up for her the possibility to become fully human again.

This is a remarkable formulation! It affirms how someone who would be regarded by many as not effectively literate, let alone schooled in African philosophy, intimately understood her interconnectedness and could formulate it succinctly. I argue that it is precisely this understanding and knowledge of interconnectedness-towards-wholeness that underpinned most of the testimonies delivered before the TRC and accounted for the way anger was articulated—without vengefulness. (To put it more bluntly, the daily living of interconnected-ness, and not simply Christianity, was the determining factor both in 'making the TRC work' and the tone of the hearings.)

So what is the main difference between forgiveness inspired by Christ and forgiveness inspired by intercon-nectedness-towards-wholeness? At the risk of gross over-simplification, I want to suggest that the basic difference is that Christian forgiveness says: I forgive you, because Jesus has forgiven me ('Forgive us our trespasses as we forgive those who trespass against us'). Although it has consequences for one's daily life, the real reward of this forgiveness will be in Heaven. Interconnected forgiveness says: I forgive you so that you can change/heal here on earth, and then I can start on my interconnected path towards healing. The effort is towards achieving full per-sonhood *on earth*.

In his biography *Rabble-Rouser for Peace* (2007), Tutu describes reconciliation as involving three separate actions: the perpetrator has to say I'm sorry, the victim is under the gospel imperative to forgive and the perpetra-tor then has to make restitution (Allen 2007: 342). This is Christianity.

On the very next page, however, Tutu quotes Malusi Mphumlwana, who said that while he was being tortured by police he looked up at them and thought: 'By the way, these are God's children too, and . . . they need you to help them to recover the humanity they are losing' (ibid.: 343). This is ubuntu.

This means that forgiveness can never be without the next step—reconciliation—and reconciliation cannot take place unless it fundamentally changes the life of the one that forgave as well as the forgiven one. Although it allows for the perpetrator to ask for forgiveness (and, in fact, prefers the perpetrator's quest for forgiveness to be the beginning of the process), it also lets the first step to be the victim's forgiveness—in other words, the victim may forgive without even being asked and thus the power to move towards wholeness stays firmly in the hands of the victim. After the act of forgiveness, however, the perpetrator must change.

Of course, one recognizes strong Christian elements in this explanation, but I want to make space for the possibility of forgiving sourced from or based in an indigenous humaneness. I believe that even the Christian forgiveness in southern Africa would have this interconnectedness-towards-wholeness as a main source and not the individual relationship between a Christian and Christ as a decisive source.

Another example of how interconnectedness informed forgiveness came from Reverend Frank Chikane, cleric, activist and general secretary of the South African Council of Churches during apartheid. The trial of Wouter Basson, South African cardiologist and former head of the country's secret chemical and biological warfare project, revealed that he had provided the poison used to line the clothes of the reverend in efforts to kill him. Speaking outside the Pretoria High Court after the trial, Chikane said that he had forgiven his tormentors but 'until the perpetrator says "I'm sorry" and wants to change and lead a different life, he becomes a prisoner for ever, even if I have forgiven him. So my forgiveness does not liberate the perpetrator' (Brand 2002: 90). So the circle of forgiveness can only be completed when the perpetrator tries to restore his own wholeness (wants to change) and, through that, restores the wholeness of society (actively contributes to producing a better society).

When, on 3 August 2006, former minister of police Adriaan Vlok, in an act of asking forgiveness that was derided by many as being too little too late, washed the feet of Reverend Chikane, the latter responded: 'I shared it with the congregation and people just broke down and cried. And there is no way that you can have that experience and keep it quiet' (MNET Television 2006).

TRC Testimonial Responses to Forgiveness

As part of its first round of hearings throughout the country, the TRC held a four-day hearing in Cape Town between 22 and 25 April 1996. A total of 44 testimonies focusing on 25 cases were heard over those days, focusing on some important and well-known names such as MK commander Anton Fransch and Namibian advocate and South West Africa People's Organization (SWAPO) member Anton Lubowski, well-known massacres including the Gugulethu Seven incident and the attack on St James Church in Kenilworth, Cape Town, which left 11 dead and 58 wounded, as well as acts of violence committed during the infamous years between 1976 and 86.

Although it was only the second week of hearings, the cumulative effect of listening to the human rights violations was already beginning to exact its toll on the commissioners and staff. Both Archbishop Tutu (in East London) and Mary Burton (in Cape Town) had broken down in public and attempts were made to counsel commissioners and staff.

Earlier chapters have shown how slippages in meaning can result during simultaneous interpretation and how difficult it is for philosophical concepts to survive across languages that do not share the same cultural references. With this in mind, one can observe from the English transcripts of testimonies delivered during the second week of hearings in Cape Town that not once in any of the isiXhosa and Tswana testimonies was Christ mentioned in terms of forgiveness. This could indicate that the 'reason' to forgive was not located in Christ but elsewhere. (In contrast to this, the coloured victims as well as their white minister explicitly said that they had forgiven the perpetrators because Jesus had forgiven them.) On the other hand, at least nine direct references were made to interconnectedness—four by Chairperson Tutu, two by Commissioner Dumisa Ntsebeza and three by victims. The references made by the commissioners spoke of the sharing of pain and loss:

> [. . .] we need to keep reminding ourselves we do belong in one family. And to help those who lost their humanity to recover their old [*sic*] (*Tutu to Kwisomba family of which two men were shot*) (TRC 1996e).

> This is not just your pain only, it is shared by all of us (*Tutu to Elsie Gishi whose husband was killed*) (TRC 1996f).

> Your wound is ours too (*Ntsebeza to Juqu family of which a young man was killed*) (TRC 1996g).

> Nomatise, now I am going to speak Xhosa with
> you, I am going to ask you to please bear with
> me, your pain is our pain as well (*Ntsebeza to
> Nomatise Tsobileyo who was severely wounded*)
> (TRC 1996b).

The idea here is not to classify these expressions as
uniquely ubuntu-esque in content but to warn that they
should also not be read as mere expressions of people
misled, pressurized or confused into a kind of Christian
forgiveness—because within a particular 'social imagining' they could well be signifiers of a hitherto unnoticed
world view. Note further that although these may sound
like common sentences, Commissioner Boraine, in his
kind, welcoming words to testifiers, never made this kind
of claim on interconnectedness—not even to white victims. (I would certainly have found it difficult to believe
if he had said that Mrs Ngewu's pain was also *his* pain.
But I realize that I would have had the same difficulty if
he had said that the pain of the mother of Namibian
advocate Anton Lubowski was his pain too. Yet when
Tutu and Ntsebeza shared the pain of black and white victims alike, I believed it.)

Tutu made two references to the healing that forgiveness, through sharing, would bring:

> [. . .] thank you very much my sister, please have
> forgiveness in you. We hope that you will be
> healed spiritually and physically, thank you (*Tutu
> to Mrs Tsobileyo*) (ibid.).

> Thank you for your spirit of forgiveness which
> joins the spirit of forgiveness of so many others

(*Tutu to Bishop Retief who was testifying as head of St James Church where a massacre took place*) (TRC 1996i).

While the commissioners emphasized the interconnectedness of pain, the victims underscored the *breakdown* in interconnectedness but often, at the same time, suggested how it could be healed. Mrs Ngewu and Mr Maliti especially articulated the need of victims to grant forgiveness in order to rehumanize themselves:

[. . .] we still have this big lump in our throats. If—if they can be put here in front of us maybe that lump can go away (*Mrs Ngewu in the Gugulethu Seven case*) (TRC 1996i).

Nobody even bothered to ask for forgiveness. When we saw each other, they just looked down (*Mr Maliti, whose aunt was burnt to death*) (TRC 1996d).

[If] the Truth Commission [can] assist in the education of that boy, as well as accommodation of that boy. Because in the old end, he is got to contribute maybe to peace—towards peace in this country, he will have felt the pain, and he will have felt maybe how to forgive, thank you (*Mr Kama, in the case of the brutal killing of his friend Mzimkulu Johnson*) (TRC 1996c).

It is important to keep in mind that the above quotations are all taken from English transcriptions. At the hearings, the remarks on interconnectedness were made in the testifiers' mother tongues, by educated and uneducated people alike.

Restoring Wholeness in Psychology

The need to restore wholeness is also articulated in the work of psychologist Pumla Gobodo-Madikizela. The post-Holocaust notion that it is impossible to forgive the unforgivable is 'unhelpful', she writes in her book *A Human Being Died That Night* (2003). She wants forgiveness to be a normalizing factor: '[T]o say that some evil deeds are simply unforgivable does not capture the complexity and richness of all the social contexts within which gross evil is committed' (2003: 124). She insists that '[p]hilosophical questions can and should give way and be subsumed to human questions, for in the end we are a society of people and not of ideas, *a fragile web of interdependent humans, not of stances*' (ibid.: 125; emphasis added). She also gives several reasons a victim would want to interact in a non-vengeful way with those who violated his or her rights:

> We are induced to empathy because there is something in the other that is felt to be part of the self, and something in the self that is felt to belong to the other [. . .]. The victim in a sense *needs* forgiveness as part of the process of becoming rehumanized. The victim needs it in order to complete himself and wrest away from the perpetrator the fiat power to destroy or to spare [. . .]. Far from being an unnerving proposition and a burdensome moral sacrifice, then, compassion for many is deeply therapeutic and restorative (ibid.: 127–9).

She points out that in this way the victim becomes the gatekeeper to what the outcast desires—readmission

into the human community: '[F]orgiveness does not overlook the deed: it rises above it. "This is what it means to
be human," it says. "I cannot and will not return the evil
you inflicted on me." And that is the victim's triumph'
(ibid.: 117).

Interconnectedness-towards-Wholeness as Part of a Commu-
nitarian African World View

The importance of interconnectedness has been stressed
many times by African philosophers (Kwame Gyekye,
Pauline J. Hountondji, Kwasi Wiredu), theologians
(Gabriel M. Setiloane, Desmond Tutu, Placide Tempels)
and sociologists (Pumla Gobodo-Madikizela, Kopano
Ratele), but often seems to fall on deaf Western ears as
far as using it in scholarly analysis and assessment is concerned. (I suspect, though, that many may be concerned
about being accused of essentialism.)

Thus, ubuntu or interconnectedness is not an isolated, exceptional phenomenon but part of a much
broader, more general context found in a variety of forms
under a variety of names, manifesting in a variety of cultures across the large African continent. In his famous
Essay on African Philosophical Thought (1987), Gyekye says
that communitarianism is held by most of the scholarship
on African cultures as the most outstanding trademark as
well as the most defining characteristic. He approvingly
quotes Kwesi Dickson's (somewhat essentialist) remark
that this sense of community is a 'characteristic of African
life to which attention had been drawn again and again
by both African and non-African writers on Africa.
Indeed, to many this characteristic defines Africanness'
(Gyekye 1987: 36). Ifeanyi Menkiti also maintains that 'as

far as Africans are concerned, the reality of the communal
world takes precedence over the reality of the individual
life histories,' and he therefore comes to three conclusions: the community defines the individual; personhood
is not bestowed on someone simply through birth but is
acquired; and personhood is something at which an individual could fail (cited in ibid.: 37). Gyekye states that
communitarian logic 'assumes a great concern for communal values, for the good of the wider society as such
[. . . It] deeply cherishes the social values of peace, harmony, stability, solidarity and mutual reciprocities and
sympathy' (ibid.: 65). He says that the basis of a caring
society need not be religious: 'It is also possible to derive
a conception of human dignity [. . .] not from theism but
from reflections on human nature, particularly on the
qualities that will dispose the human being to function at
his best in human society and realize his potentials to the
full' (ibid.: 63). Moreover, he makes a stern distinction
between being driven by 'caring or compassion or generosity' rather than by justice (ibid.: 70).

If one were to look for a pervasive and fundamental
concept in African socio-ethical thought in general—a
concept that animates other intellectual activities and
forms of behaviour, including religious behaviour, and
provides continuity, resilience, nourishment and meaning
to life—that concept would most probably be closer to
humanism: a philosophy that sees human needs, interests
and dignity as of fundamental importance and concern.

Taking this interconnectedness, from which a person
'builds' himself into a caring being, as a basis, theologian
Setiloane, in his seminal work on the image of God

among the Sotho-Tswana, suggests that Christianity became embedded within this communitarian spirituality: '[W]hile passing all the orthodox criteria to make it "Christian" [it] is nevertheless understood within the assumptions of the *mekgwa ya bo-rra rona*' (customs, beliefs and ways of life)' (1976: 161). In other words, Christianity (or human rights or restorative justice or, for that matter, the theology of Tutu or the politics of Mandela) is not simply linked to, or forms an add-on to, a pagan or animistic interconnectedness, but is, in fact, embedded therein—that is, interconnectedness forms the interpretive foundation of Christianity. It is this foundation that enabled people to reinterpret Western concepts such as forgiveness, reconciliation, amnesty and justice and in a new and practical way. These concepts moved across cultural borders and were infused and energized by a sense of interconnectedness-towards-wholeness. Setiloane stresses that the Sotho-Tswana have 'taken over Christian concepts and understandings and moulded them anew giving them an interpretation more reminiscent of their traditional practice' (ibid.: 185).

In *Understanding African Philosophy* (2002), Richard H. Bell deals extensively with moderate communalism and describes ubuntu as a notion rooted in 'whatever form of communalism that may have survived in South Africa'. He quotes Boraine, who described ubuntu as an ancient philosophy that gave rise to a need 'for a more community-orientated jurisprudence that acknowledges the reality that individuals are part of a much larger social context' (2002: 89). After the Rwandan genocide, Tutu noted that it was clearly not a mechanical and inevitable process to know that one has to build oneself into a good person by caring for others. Not to know that, however, could be regarded 'as a moral deficiency' (ibid.).

This pervasive world view throws a different light on some of the remarks about the failures of the TRC. When Mahmood Mamdani asks, 'If truth has replaced justice in South Africa—has reconciliation then turned into an embrace of evil?' (cited in Krog 1998: 112; see also Mamdani 1997), he ignores a world view which suggests that embracing the evil could be the beginning of a humanizing process in which compassion and change bring the ultimate form of justice. The fact that just a few perpetrators became scapegoats and that land reparations were not properly addressed during the TRC process becomes deeply problematic only within a human rights and Western post–Second World War milieu. Within a communitarian world view, however, one could have assumed that everyone would feel themselves interconnected with the scapegoats and that amnesty would therefore be the beginning of a process of change leading to reparation that involved everyone. That this did not happen is perhaps more an indication of a dominating non-interconnecting culture clashing with an indigenous one than of a moral failure or confusion on the part of those involved in the TRC process from a grassroots level. (Even the TRC legislation itself could imagine no reciprocal connection between amnesty seeker and victim.)

Perhaps even Derrida would not have regarded it as a 'confusion' on Tutu's part 'to oscillate between a non-penal and non-reparative logic of "forgiveness" (he calls it "restorative") and a judicial logic of amnesty' (Derrida

2001: 32). Tutu was not simply linking human rights and amnesty to religion but using the foundation of interconnectedness to allow people back into humanity through processes such as forgiveness and amnesty.

Amnesty, as a process of admitting a wrong and wanting it to be set aside, fits in neatly with the victims' desire to rebuild a humane and caring community. The fact that many, mostly white and Western people, did not read amnesty in that way and preferred to see it as being 'let off the hook' is rather to be laid at the feet of a Christianity-emphasizing individualism and a particular understanding of human rights, instead of suggesting that the majority of South Africans were coerced by Archbishop Tutu into forgiving.

Within a communitarian framework, the term 'religious-redemptive ethos' (Wilson 2001: 109) is also out of place, as well as the suggestion that the TRC was used to politically legitimize the new ANC government (ibid.; see also Verdoolaege 2008). Ordinary people, attending and participating in the TRC process in their thousands, knew that one could only fully 'build' oneself within a caring reconciled community which drove the process rather than any political agenda or pact among the new elites (Van Binsbergen 2001). The commission did not necessarily have a 'dual consciousness' with practical justice and forgiveness on the one hand and a confused understanding of human rights on the other (Wilson 2001: 153). It functioned from a sense of interconnectedness which lit up such concepts in a particular, new and, I would suggest, very coherent way.

When Verdoolaege notes that the ruling ANC is using the TRC and reconciliation as a nation-building exercise, she is ignoring the possibility that many of the 40 million non- white South Africans could be interested in restoring a traumatized community through affirming its interconnectedness-towards-wholeness, which would entail equal sharing of resources. The striking features of the South African TRC—public hearings, individualized amnesty and allowing victims fighting for and against apartheid to testify on the same forum—can all be traced back to the desire to restore the interconnectedness of a community: because people share each other's pain, the audience has as much right to be in the presence of the testimony as the testifier; because people who are prepared to apply for amnesty are willing to admit that they have done wrong, they could begin to change and eventually be readmitted into society; because mothers who lost their loved ones fighting for the 'right' or the 'wrong' side suffer alike, they are interconnected.

The Interconnected Moral Self

As a white South African, I am disturbed by the fact that I always notice this interconnectedness as a kind of second thought. Something does not make sense and then I realize that it is because I think as an unattached individual. In order to learn interconnectedness and live appropriately within it, I need to philosophically understand two things: What is the community to which I am interconnected? And how is the interconnected moral self formed?

THE COMMUNITY. Prominent Xhosa intellectual Tiyo Soga lamented in the loss of wholeness after the entry of Christianity into southern Africa. In his essay 'The Believers and the Pagans' (1864), he pointed to the widening gulf between the pagan and converted—the latter not allowing pagans into their houses (Sanders 2002: 124).

A hundred years later, A. C. Jordan, the author of *The Wrath of the Ancestors* (1968), took this idea one step further by redefining interconnectedness in terms of African hospitality. He said ubuntu was no longer merely what was expected of the people of a community towards members of that community but also encompassed what took place between the community and strangers. For Jordan, as formulated by Mark Sanders, hospitality and reconciliation were synonyms; it was a way of becoming, in a limited sense, the one who was not one's own, the one through whom one owned oneself and became who one was. One was a person through others and became a person through the stranger (Sanders 2002: 125).

Jordan warned that the figure of the stranger ought to be continually reinvented because there would always be an outsider who ought to be remembered, or not forgotten, who called into question the existence of the collectivity. Jordan seemed to conclude that in terms of the African world view, it was the task of the intellectual to be an advocate for the figure of the stranger—to insist on responsibility for the stranger as constitutive of collectivity itself (ibid.: 129). The stranger, who threatens the stability of society, who puts society at risk, also provides the possibility of restoring and saving it (ibid.: 129; see also Gyekye 1987: 74).

MORAL SELF (SELF-IN-ONE). After the Holocaust, Hannah
Arendt took up Socrates' proposition: It is better to suffer
wrong than to do wrong. But who decides what is wrong?
The self. For Arendt, the self stands in the centre of the
moral consideration of human conduct (2003: xx). Even
religious commands such as 'Love thy neighbour as thy-
self' or 'Don't do unto others what you don't want done
to yourself' cannot get away from the self (ibid.: 68).
Arendt points out that Socrates said that it would be better for him that most men disagree with him than for him
to contradict himself. In other words, Socrates was arguing with himself. He was two-within-one. Arendt
rephrased this: 'Though I am one, I am two-in-one and
there can be harmony or disharmony with the self [. . .]
(but) I cannot walk away from myself [. . . I]f I do wrong,
I am condemned to live together with a wrongdoer in
unbearable intimacy' (ibid.: 90). The conversation with
the self was the beginning of thinking and knowing
which would make a moral entity possible (ibid.: 91, 95,
101, 112, 162).

Perhaps it is at this point that an African awareness
could say: I constitute the self in another way. Of course
there is an 'I'. Of course there should be the mind-chang-
ing conversation. But the conversation that eventually creates the moral entity is not with the self but with the
people around one, the stranger-accommodating community. One's self-awareness is not formed by splitting
oneself into two but by becoming one-in-many—dispersed, as it were, among those around one.

The fundamental point of departure between an
African and a Western world view could be in the place

and the way the moral compass is formed. For Arendt, it is formed in the *self* through conversations with the *self*. For African awareness, it is formed in the *self* but through conversations with *those around one*. The departure point for Arendt lies inside the individual moving towards the self. The departure point for African awareness also lies inside the individual but the individual moving towards the community.

Arendt suggests that an individual who would like to be 'good' should become completely selfless and then embark 'upon the most lonely career there can be for man', with only God as company (ibid.: 117). According to my hypothesis of African awareness, however, it is precisely this moment of doing good towards others which makes one belong in the world as a full human being—it is this working for others that gives one a soul. The selfer one gets, the more self-focused, the less aware of one's community and the more spiritually dead one becomes (Comaroff and Comaroff 1991: 143; Brown 1926: 137–8).

Conclusion

Why is it important to disentangle interconnectedness-towards-wholeness from the other credited driving forces of the TRC such as Christianity, human rights, legitimizing liberation politics and so on?

First, it would assist a more complex interpretation of the TRC process and testimonies instead of assuming that they were mainly or exclusively informed by Christianity and therefore vulnerable to a whole range of judgements.

Second, it could make those adopting the South African version of the TRC in their own countries aware of the presence of a decisive element in the process that, although deeply spiritual, does not (yet) fall into one of the main religious or legal categories of the world.

Third, (some)one (like me) could begin to learn how to 'read' interconnectedness as the core value and bedrock of many of the actions of South Africans in different fields and at last begin to effectively critique and value the groundbreaking ways developed here. It is this almost a priori sense of interconnectedness that enabled the South African oppressed to redefine concepts such as reconciliation and forgiveness, and even amnesty, which have become trapped in unusable religious and aggressive social or legal contexts in many parts of the world. It means turning round Samuel Imbo's warning against emphasizing differences, for 'in the dominant frameworks of Western philosophy, "different" means "inferior"' (1998: 139). In the case of the TRC, difference brought a creative tension that produced effective results.

Fourth, being aware of this particular world view also makes it possible to understand the current groundswell of anger and frustration of victims—the very same people who seemed to have been so forgiving during the TRC process—expressed in letters to the media and group actions demanding compensation. Although their anger is used as proof that the TRC pressurized them into forgiving, interconnectedness means that they could well have been expecting the perpetrators to show signs of regaining humanity after forgiveness was extended to them. This seldom happened. Many perpetrators expressed surprise at a sentiment of 'I want to forgive but I do not know whom'—in other words, that there was such a readiness to forgive. To many perpetrators, it seemed to indicate that they could continue their lives as unperturbed as before. Initially, interconnectedness made victims forgive. But since no reciprocal sign of change and *widergutmachen* (literally, 'to make good again, to restore') came from the interconnected perpetrators, victims have now become angry. So, only by identifying interconnectedness-towards-wholeness as the foundation of the TRC process would one be able to understand that TRC resentment has more to do with thwarted beliefs now than with the abuse of Christianity to suppress anger at that time.

The usurpation of the TRC process into Christianity and a human rights culture obscures the fact that a radically new way, embedded in an indigenous view, had been suggested of dealing with gross injustice and cycles of violence. This throws a sharp light on a different way of becoming and being. Sustained scholarship into the formation, sustainability, integrity and moral compass of interconnectedness-towards-wholeness could lead to a more informed discourse round events happening on the African continent.

CHAPTER SEVEN

The Letters in the Body: Manifestations of
Interconnectedness and an Indigenous Humanism

On 13 April 1872, a short, yellow-skinned man with high
cheekbones and a wrinkled face began telling a story of
the death of a fellow hunter while the group was hunting
springbok. Opposite him sat a man and a woman who
were writing down what he was saying in a large exercise
book. It would take them five months to tell, record and
translate the story.

The teller of the narrative was //kabbo. He was a
member of the /xam, a subgroup of the Bushmen.[1] He
lived in the Kenhardt district, in the arid Northern Cape,
as part of the last generation living a hunter-gatherer existence. Like the Bushmen all over southern Africa,
//kabbo found the land where his people had roamed
freely for thousands of years invaded by settlers. The specific area where //kabbo came from was called Bushman-
land, where place names like Gifberg (poison mountain),
Keelafsnyleegte (cut-the-throat valley), Rugseer (sore

---

1 The word 'Bushmen' is controversial. Some academics view it as
insulting and prefer the word 'San'. Recently, however, it was pointed
out that San means 'vagabond', which could be even more pejora-
tive. That is why some San groups prefer to be called Bushmen.

back), Loerkop (peep head), Putsonderwater (waterless well), Verneukpan (cheat pan) and Kulsberg (cheat mountain) told the story of the dire life of its inhabitants. Drinking from the old waterholes or hunting game turned the Bushmen into trespassers and thieves, many finding themselves inmates at the Breakwater Prison in Cape Town. It was from this jail that / /kabbo was taken to the house where he told many of his stories.

The house belonged to Dr Wilhelm H. I. Bleek, a linguist from Berlin who was interested in the relationship among languages from Africa. With his sister-in-law Lucy C. Lloyd, he asked permission to bring / /kabbo, and others, to his home, where they wrote down—first lists of words and phrases devising an alphabet, then stories and narratives—accounts of the lives, history, folklore and remembered beliefs and customs of the / xam. Their documentation filled 138 notebooks—more than 12,000 pages—and is deemed the most impressive and complete ethnographical record of the life of hunter-gatherers in the world. By the early twentieth century, both the / xam culture and the language became extinct. If it weren't for Bleek and Lloyd's thorough and in-depth documents, Bushmen rock art would almost be the only evidence today of the sophisticated aesthetic and philosophy of the / xam and other Bushmen groups.

The narrative about an accident on the hunting ground was recorded and translated by Bleek and Lloyd between 13 April and 19 September 1872. It describes the fatal wounding of a fellow hunter and includes a moving testament of the dying man to his young wife as well as her beautiful, tender soliloquy (1911: 52–75). The

narrative concludes with the wife and the children moving back to her father and brothers, as her husband's
clan no longer has enough hunters to look after an extra
family. The death is described:

> (*13 April*) Another man shoots a man while they
> are shooting springbok. The man is wounded.
> All the other men leave the springbok and run to
> him as he sits in pain, weeping they stand over
> him. 'What is this thing here which shot our
> brother?' they ask. The other man answers: 'I did
> not mean to shoot him, I was busy shooting
> springbok. Our brother was wounded when he
> was behind the springbok's back. (*15 April*) I did
> not mean to shoot our brother. I was shooting
> at the springbok. The arrow went into the
> springboks' dust. Our brother was near and did
> not see. He could not avoid it, because he was
> looking at the springbok. He did not see the
> arrow. I weep for our brother, because he is our
> friend. He is not a stranger who is different, he
> is our friend. So I worry about our brother, my
> heart cries for our brother, my heart is not happy
> about our brother.'
>
> One of them says to him: 'It seems to me,
> you did not think of our brother's children, you
> shot him among the springbok when he could
> not see because of the dust. You did not wait to
> shoot the springbok as it passed by this side—so
> that you could shoot the springbok in this place.
> I saw how you came near to our brother. I saw
> our brother and I saw you both stooping as you

approached each other while the springbok moved between you (*16 April*) you did not seem to see our brother.' The other man says: 'I did not see our brother, the dust had shut in, for the springbok were many.'

The wounded man says: 'Our brother is angry with you, but I am the one who did not see well because of the dust. The dust was dense, for the springbok were many. I am wounded because I was watching the springbok. I did not look carefully on that side, for, if I had, I should have avoided the arrow. You scold our brother as if the arrow did not come in through the dust but that is how it was: I did not see the arrow. I could have avoided it and prevented our brother's pain. Lift me up and carry me away to my house. I do not feel as if I can walk. I am in great pain. I must go to lie by myself in pain at the house. Leave the springbok. You will shoot another day. My blood is out. I was wounded early, that is why I cannot see well, although it is early. The shade is great, the shade of the tree. The springboks' dust shut my eyes. We did not see each other.'

'We know we are right' says one of the other. (*17 April*) 'Our brother did not see you. We said: that man sitting far over there looks as if he is wounded. Over there another man is running to him as he sits. The other man helps him to sit yonder, he looks at the other man. He turns him over so that he can look at the wound. They are both sitting, let us go and see, (*18 April*) because the man over there beckons, he knows there is much blood. We must be correct when we talk to the people at home, when the women question us. The women will not speak nicely. They will ask things. The wound seems to be large for the arrow point is still on the shaft—so the wound is deep.'

The other man says: 'The wound is like that. We must run very fast to see so that we can speak nicely to the women. As we speak making their hearts stand still.' (*19 April*) They run strongly; they run fast.

[. . .] The wounded man tells them to speak gently, not angrily to the man who shot him. 'Remember that it was the arrow's fault. The arrow hit me of its own accord. Our brother here speaks the truth. He did not shoot me. We say truly, we did not see each other. (*20 April*) If I had looked I might have seen him coming, then stooping I should have gone round and sat down, for we approached each other in a direct line. The springbok ran through between us. The dust was dense. The springbok were in the dust, the dust of the springboks' feet was dense. I sat drawing the bow. I was completely still while I waited, because I did not shoot.'

The people carry him to the house. His wife cries, the other women cry. They ask: 'You others, your friend seems to have been fighting: you have shot your friend.'

The men say to the women: 'We did not do it on purpose. It was a false shooting; a false shot's arrow it was. You did not tell the children to play away from the house, that is why the man accidentally shot the other man.' 'My wife is stupid' says one. (*22 April*) 'She does not listen when I speak to her. She does not behave in the way her father and mother taught her.'

The other man says: 'My wife is doing foolish things, but I want her to see that it was a false shot's wound. This is how it happened. It is ugly. The wound makes people afraid. I might also have been wounded, because she did not say to my boys: "go out of the house". Dust covered my bed when I returned. My house was as if she has gone away' (Bleek and Lloyd 1911: 55).

What is of interest here is how the incident of the wounding is deliberately retold in a specific way every time so that the blame for the killing *shifts* smoothly from one to the next. The responsibility passes from:

the killer → the wounded → dust and arrow →
women → children

Blame moves from the most powerful to the most vulnerable. Why? Could one say that, for their survival, the group *needed* to remove the blame from the grown-ups? The grown men needed every man for hunting in order to feed the group. Perhaps it was best to send the blame lower down, where division could not cause severe survival problems. In other words, one forfeits moral responsibility in order to fulfil survival responsibility—a mere pragmatic execution of responsibility in the interdependent context of hunter-gatherers.

But this shifting of blame raises many questions for South Africans today who are coping with high crime rates and violence that is unusually brutal and excessive. What are the ethical implications of always blaming the women and children? How could moral codes of right and wrong be established in a context where the indigenous people have for centuries astutely avoided responsibility for a death? How *do* they see right and wrong?

The Bushmen are the First People of southern Africa. Several historical accounts are given of how the south-moving black groups peacefully mingled with the Bushmen (the Batlokwa tribe had Bushman healers; the Basotho king Moshoeshoe married one; Mandela's facial features have been traced to First People blood). One can assume that much more than the click sounds (which are unique to southern African indigenous languages) became part of a larger indigenous ontology.

Southern Africa was also noted in particular by missionaries for its pervasive spirituality, which forced them to change their evangelizing tactics. They found that black people here did not conform to their idea of heathens. Scottish missionary Robert Moffat complained that among the Tswana he could find 'no idols to shatter, no altars to seize, no fetishes to smash' (Comaroff and Comaroff 1992: 271). They were deeply spiritual but did not pray to physical icons. I want to argue that this difference came about under the influence of the First People.

But what is it that the /xam believed? Many studies have explored the specific belief systems of different indigenous groups, but for my purposes, I am interested in text which relates to an interconnectedness-towards-wholeness.

One of the Bushman informants recorded by Bleek and Lloyd, Díä!kwãin, suggests a profound interconnectedness with the universe:

> The star does it in this manner, at the time when our heart falls down, that is the time when the star falls down; while the star feels that our heart ( ) falls over [. . .]. For the stars know the time at which we die. The star tells the other people who do not ( ) know that we have died.
>
> The hammerkop acts in this manner, when a star has fallen, it comes; when it flies over us, it cries: γák γáäk, γák γáäk. The people say: Did you not hear the hammerkop when the star fell? ( ) It came to tell us that our person is dead (Bleek and Lloyd 1911: 389–91; parentheses in the original).

Díä!kwãin goes further:

> If we (Mother and I) are sitting in the shade when the place is not particularly warm, and we feel that the summer seems as if it would be hot [. . .] I will sit a little while in the shade: (then) we make clouds, our liver goes out from the place where we are sitting in the shade, if the place is not hot. Therefore, we make clouds on account of it. For, when it is really summer, then we (may) sit in the shade (ibid.: 399).

Another informant, /Han≠kassó, describes:

The Wind (i.e. the wind's son) was formerly a man. He became a bird. And he was flying, while he no longer walked, as he used to do . . . (ibid.: 107).

The /xam felt themselves intricately but thoroughly interconnected not only to stars, the wind, mist and moon but also to animals. Díä!kwãin says:

Baboons speak Bushman [. . .]. When we hear them talking there, we are apt to think that other people are to be found there, though we did not know of them [. . .] My father was the one who told me that baboons speak Bushman (quoted in Hollman 2004: 10).

A remark like this suggests a kind of communication that is more than a mere imitation of animal sounds: one does not speak like a baboon, but one speaks baboon! Jeremy C. Hollmann proposes that for the Bushmen, animals became an extension of people's senses: '[B]y observing the behaviour of animals, the /Xam transcended the limitations of their own sense perceptions and tapped into those of other species' (2004: 66). The eland, hartebeest, gemsbok and springbok

have such acute senses that people not familiar with scientific thinking may believe that these animals have extra-sensory perception. Antelope often seem to be in a continual state of nervous tension because their senses are so acute that they respond noticeably to stimuli too faint for most humans to detect. Their sensory abilities allow non-human mammals to communicate, navigate, find food and avoid enemies by signals that humans cannot even detect (ibid.).

In an effort to explain the complexity of this interconnectedness to his interpreters, / / kabbo says:

> The Bushmen's letters are in their bodies. They (the letters) speak, they move, they make their (the Bushmen's) bodies move. They (the Bushmen) order the others to be silent; a man is altogether still, when he feels that ( ) his body is tapping (inside) [. . .]. The Bushmen perceive people coming by means of it [. . .]. He feels a tapping (at) his ribs (Bleek and Lloyd 1911: 334).

With their hunter-gatherer lifestyle destroyed by the incoming white settlers and dispossessed of their waterholes and access to game, Díä!kwãin describes how this unravelled the rituals and belief systems of their lives by destroying their complex interwovenness with everything. The string, used to make music and call the rain or used in a bow to hunt, was no longer making a sound (ringing through the air), and this changed their whole relationship to the cosmos and made them feel displaced. This disturbed interconnectedness is reminiscent of Father Tempels' explanation that the African universe of forces is 'held like a spider's web of which no single thread can be caused to vibrate without shaking the whole network' (quoted in Gibson 2001: 36). Central to the lament of the broken string is the fact that it was people—not animals—who caused this destruction.

> People were those who
> Broke for me the string.

Therefore,
The place ( ) became like this for me
On account of it.
Because the string was that which broke for me.
Therefore,
The place does not feel to me,
As the place used to feel to me,
On account of it.
For,
The place feels as if it stood open before me,
( ) Because the string has broken for me.
Therefore,
The place does not feel pleasant to me,
On account of it.
(Bleek and Lloyd 1911: 237)

Is it possible that such a spiritual link with the cosmos was what made indigenous people of southern Africa capable of living an interconnectedness without the need for altars, idols or fetishes?

With this possibility of complete and complex inter-connectedness, let us rethink the Bushman narrative—this time as if it is embedded in the world view of interconnectedness or ubuntu. Let us see how a philosophy that says all things are interrelated in a dynamic process of transmitting life, changes the perception of the ethics in this narrative, which, at first reading, appears to be about moral evasion.

Could one say that the story is retold not to *remove* or *shift* the blame, but the opposite: To *distribute* it? In terms of interconnectedness-towards-wholeness, the death of the hunter became everyone's business. Everyone, even the youngest woman and child, was responsible when someone died. Every death affects us all. We have to care about everyone who dies, to feel affected by every bit of spilt blood on earth, because we are all interconnected towards wholeness.

This very notion was succinctly described by Coetzee in *Age of Iron*:

> Because blood is precious, more precious than gold or diamonds. Because blood is one: a pool of life dispersed among us in separate existences, but belonging by nature together: lent, not given: held in common, in trust, to be preserved: seeming to live in us, but only seeming, for in truth we live in it (1990: 58).

My point is: a narrative can easily be interpreted as discriminatory and ethically problematic when read through a particular framework. But the moment there is an attempt to interpret the narrative through its embeddedness in an indigenous world view, it becomes ethical and fair. One also realizes the impossibility of having any meaningful reciprocal interaction when the philosophy underpinning a narrative is not known or understood by one of the parties.

*

In *African Ethics: An Anthology of Comparative and Applied Ethics* (2009), several philosophers formulate their thoughts on the basis of an indigenous world view. Neville Richardson says: 'African thought does not regard ethics as a separate discipline, because morality is indistinguishable from the rest of African social life' (2009: 31).

He quotes Augustine Shutte: 'The goal of morality according to this ethical vision is fullness of humanity; the moral life is seen as a process of personal growth. And just as participation in community with others is the essential means to personal growth, so participation in community with others is the motive and fulfilment of the process. Everything that promotes personal growth and participation in community is good, everything that prevents it is bad' (quoted in ibid.: 30). Shutte further describes the way in which a moral life builds personhood: 'I am a potential person. [. . .] So I must see my life as a process of becoming a person. It is not just that I change and grow. I am being built up, constructed. My life is a progressive increase in vital force. That depends on the moral quality of my life (2009: 92).

This 'building up' is intimately connected with what kind of work one does and how one does it, suggests John and Jean Comaroff:

> The concept of self-construction—of *tiro*, 'work' and *iti re la*, 'to make [for] oneself'—then, projected a world in which the 'building up' of persons in relation to each other, the accumulation of wealth and rank, and the sustenance of a strong, centralized polity (*morafe*) were indivisible aspects of everyday practice. The object of that practice, minimally, was to avoid social death, to continue producing oneself by producing people and things. Maximally, it was to do 'great works' (2001: 268).

Moral behaviour of people living on the African continent had been recorded as far back as 1497 when Vasco da Gama came ashore on the coast of south-east Africa to repair a vessel. Somewhere between the current border of South Africa and Mozambique, the Portuguese sailors met indigenous black people. The kindness, assistance and generosity of the local people led the foreigners to call the area *Terra da boa gente*, 'The land of the Good People' (Axelson 1973: 24). 'This striking but little-known episode of great moral goodness of Africans towards outsiders should be seen as a powerful indication of the importance of Africa's ancient moral wisdom and practice in today's globalizing and all too uncaring world,' says Martin Prozesky (2009: 3). Luis Vaz de Camões' famous poem *Lusiads* (1572), based on the voyage of Vasco da Gama, describes an earlier meeting:

> The people who owned the country here
> Though they were likewise Ethiopians,[2]
> Were cordial and humane, [. . .]
> They came towards us on the sandy beach
> With dancing and an air of festival
> [. . .]
> These, as their smiling faces promised,
> Dealt with us as fellow humans,
> With the Universe (2001: 5.62–4).

Interconnectedness-towards-wholeness includes the living dead and the not yet born. Augustine Shutte suggests that the 'ancestors are also part of the extended family. [. . .] When one dies one does not leave the earth but moves deeper towards the centre. So the earth is one's

---

2 Near Mosselbay. All Africans south of the Sahara were called Ethiopians though in this case they must have been Khoi.

eternal home. Because of this it is also the common property of all people. No one can own part of it simply for themselves' (Shutte 2009: 96). The poet Birago Diop:

> Those who are dead have never gone away.
> They are at the breast of the wife.
> They are the child's cry of dismay
> And the firebrand bursting into life.
> The dead are not under the ground.
> They are in the fire that burns low
> They are in the grass with tears to shed,
> In the rock where whining winds blow
> They are in the forest, they are in the homestead.
> The dead are never dead (1964: 25).

During a TRC hearing, one of the Gugulethu Seven mothers Cynthia Ngewu spelt out the moral implications of reconciliation embedded in interconnectedness-towards-wholeness:

> MS NGEWU. What we are hoping for when we embrace the notion of reconciliation is that we restore the humanity to those who were perpetrators. We do not want to return evil by another evil. We simply want to ensure that the perpetrators are returned to humanity.
>
> MS PUMLA GOBODO-MADIKIZELA. Many people in this country would like to see perpetrators going to prison and serving long sentences. What is your view on this?
>
> MS NGEWU. In my opinion, I do not agree with this view. We do not want to see people suffer

in the same way that we did suffer, and we did not want our families to have suffered. We do not want to return the suffering that was imposed upon us. So, I do not agree with that view at all. We would like to see peace in this country [. . .]. I think that all South Africans should be committed to the idea of re-accepting these people back into the community. We do not want to return the evil that perpetrators committed to the nation. We want to demonstrate humane-ness towards them, so that they in turn may restore their own humanity (TRC 1998: 5.366).

★

Looking at how Westerners are described in indigenous literatures gives an even better understanding of the pro-file of interconnectedness. The essence of these descrip-tions is how they are unable to act as if they are part of anything—in other words, unable to interconnect with a shared-ness.

The most famous of all indigenous poets, *imbongi* (praise singer) S. E. K. Mqhayi—recorded live by H. Tracey around 1943 characterized white people:[3]

Noko nibantu bangakwaziy' ukwabelana
Nisuke nenz' imfazwe yamaBhulu neyamaJamani.

---

3 The following excerpts have been translated by Koos Oosthuysen, Ncebakazi Saliwa and Antjie Krog.

You whites-with-an-inability-to-share-anything
Learn to share it with the Boers and the Germans.

The Tshivenda poet R. L. Ndlovu says whites are late-comers who soiled the water as they were grabbing everything for themselves: 'Nga mulandu wa nyeni dzo dzhavhulaho vhune ha danga / Dzi si fune tshisima tshi tshi vha tsha madilutshele' (1991: 145).

In his Sepedi poem, H. M. L. Lentsoeane describes white policemen in terms of the Afrikaans language itself:

A phatlalala le metsemeso,
A ipala ka magorogoro.
Polelo a boletše ya go tsebja ke beng,
Polelo ya go bolelwa ke mašela,
Polelo ya go bolelwa ke dipampiri,
Polelo ya go bolelwa o rokile molomo.

The red-beards were spreading in the township,
Posting themselves at the meeting-places of men.
They spoke a language only spoken by its masters,
A language spoken as if others were dirty linen,
A language spoken as if others were bundles
	of paper,
A language spoken as if the lips were sewn together
	(1981: 177).

What is at stake here is more than a description of attitudes of colonialism or racism—a sense of two ontologies is foregrounded: one is driven by a strong sense of individualism, a personal responsibility to master and control the surroundings through science and various forms of power; the other speaks of an interwovenness which determines personhood through different levels of simultaneous relationships, one that always felt, and still feels, itself affronted by the inhuman beingness brought to the continent by those described as 'latecomers'.

However, despite the invasion by slave traders, colonizers and racists, Prozesky concludes:

> In the light of its historical context, African ethics must thus be seen as a moral cluster that is immensely old, deeply embedded in the cultures of the continent, still strong, and the survivor of massively powerful, disruptive, outside influences. That indicates a resilience and inner strength which non-Africans need to know about (2009: 8).

Having said that, it is crucial to make the point that acknowledgement of the existence of interconnectedness does not mean a rosy uncomplicated togetherness. In fact, it is precisely the problematic notion of sin within interconnectedness which causes some of the perversions. Setiloane asserts that '(t)he greatest of all evils according to African Traditional Religion is to live in "careless disregard of others"' (cited in Brand 2002: 98).

Keith Fernado maintains that

> sin in many African cultures is defined not so much in terms of the nature of the act itself, but rather of its consequences [. . .]. Thus to say that 'sin' disrupts harmony and causes suffering is tautologous [. . .]. An act that disrupts the harmony of the cosmos in a way harmful to the interests of man, is ipso facto evil; if no harmful consequences are entailed it is therefore probably

inaccurate to speak in terms of 'offence' or 'sin' (cited in Brand 2002: 83).

Can one gather from this that to kill a useless drunk beggar has no harmful consequences for society and is therefore not to be condemned?

One is keenly aware how easily a multilayered inter-connectedness which had not yet been properly investigated and theorized had grown many permutations and even ugly distortions. When interconnectedness imagines and moves towards a humane wholeness, in other words, when humaneness is its compass, it elicits actions like building, caring, helping and so on. But if the community and/or its ecological setting has been disrupted and disconnected through slavery, colonialism, urbanization, displacements, apartheid and AIDS, to name a few, inter-connectedness becomes severely disturbed and even mon-strously immoral.

If a community is distraught or brutalized, the self has little to connect to in order to build a personhood. A common replacement for interconnectedness is to con-flate interconnectedness with race/religion/gender and build solidarity through skin colour, religious belief or sexism. It does not matter what you do, if you have the same colour/religion/ gender as me, you are not to be blamed, criticized or held accountable.

It may therefore also mean that for South Africans to truly accommodate those who work for the benefit of this society would be to ultimately accommodate, despite a different colour, religion or gender, the 'stranger'—espe-cially the black stranger.

CHAPTER EIGHT

A Vocabulary of Grace

The master translator of a young country's visions of a democratic and caring society into an accessible vocabulary of metaphor was Archbishop Desmond Tutu. The combination of his inspired speeches, along with the well-crafted ones of Nelson Mandela, animated a future into which South Africans could project themselves as citizens of a country capable of overcoming and imaginatively transcending terrible adversity and injustice. Over the years, consistently and with immense integrity, Tutu provided a language that moved us from defiant outspokenness against injustice to righteousness, freedom, caring and forgiveness. He created new words for a society that had been fed for centuries on the poisonous mix of race, exclusion, humiliation and greed.

Almost 20 years and two presidents later, many things have fallen by the wayside. For me, one of the first casualties was our new vocabulary. In speech after speech, Mandela's successor, Thabo Mbeki, in accomplished English, brought back the old, dreaded and suffocating cadences of race and humiliation. By the time he was replaced by a president with only a few years of schooling —Jacob Zuma—we found ourselves not only without a vocabulary but dumped into bad English as well. Despite the excellent English of many of our non-English mother-tongue speakers, most of us muddle through in our third or fourth language. Over time, we have become a nation without any language at all. So we began to sing—in our mother tongues.

Instead of delivering a speech, President Zuma struggled to get a minimum of coherency from his written English text, then put it aside and burst into the Zulu song he made famous: 'Umshini wami' (Bring me my machine gun). This everyone understood. The crowd were on their feet, energetically imitating firing machine guns from the hip. He was imitated by Julius Malema, then president of the ANC Youth League, who, while singing the anti-apartheid song 'Ayasab' amagwala' (The cowards are scared) regularly diverted to a line from a Zulu song for which he had been taken to court to have it declared hate speech: 'Dubul' ibhunu' (Kill the Boer). Afrikaner youth began to sing the song 'De la Rey' at school and national sports events; it was played loudly in cars packed with young Afrikaner men, driving slowly, windows open, along streets frequented by black people.

The absence of an adequate English vocabulary with which speakers from different backgrounds and of varying proficiency could reach one another manifested disastrously one evening in 2010. A television debate was on, the subject was the murders of farmers—up to 3,000 of them since the end of apartheid, as cited by the broadcaster. The secretary of the right-wing Afrikaner resistance movement, the Afrikaner Weerstandsbeweging (AWB), was accused by a black female political commentator of being narrow-minded. The white man jumped up, plucked the wired microphone from his jacket, flung it on the ground and shouted, 'You will not speak to me like that!' As he was storming out, everything deftly captured on camera, the black host of the programme tried to stop him. The Afrikaner pushed him back, and the host responded, 'Sir, don't touch me on my studio!' The Afrikaner shouted back, '*You* touched *me* [on my studio].' Security appeared on the scene, and the last we saw was the Afrikaner turning back to the black woman, pointing his finger menacingly and declaring, 'I am not finished with *you*.'

Within minutes the phrase 'Don't touch me on my studio,' and the body language of the Afrikaner, became part of various hip-hop songs and jokes: 'Will somebody ple-e-e-ase touch my studio?'[1]

Although the black woman commentator was fluent in English, one wondered whether she would have sounded so disparaging if her comment had been translated from her mother tongue. The frustration of the white man trying unsuccessfully to translate his Afrikaans into English while being constantly interrupted was clear to see. The television host, a dynamic black man able to wield some power in intellectual debates, was left exposed as someone who could not 'hold his grammar' as it were—the originator of 'Don't touch me on my studio.'

★

1 Video available at: http://www.youtube.com/watch?v=Tcexnp-mei9E and http://www.youtube.com/watch?v=ZOFkSktQDFQ (last accessed on 23 July 2013).

It was Easter weekend, 10 April 1993. I was standing in a small supermarket in the rural town where I lived, buying a few items to bake a rhubarb tart. As usual, a radio was piping in muzak from somewhere. Suddenly, it was broken off for a special news bulletin: Chris Hani, the charismatic head of the South African Communist Party, had been assassinated in his driveway that morning. A car with two white men had been seen speeding away from the scene. Details would be provided as events unfolded.

It was as if a bomb had been detonated in the supermarket. The black women behind the till, two others standing next to me, an old black man at the entrance and I turned to stone. All was dead quiet. Although it was still a year before the first democratic elections, Hani was already regarded as the one who would take over after Mandela had finished his term as president. As I slowly put my basket down, I could feel how shock, anguish and suspicion mounted in the shop. Then, chaos! People ran, others shouted, some burst into tears. Doors slammed. Whites fled to their cars.

Driving home, I felt physically ill. After the tentative reaching out to one another since Mandela's release, it was as if one could feel how white and black South Africans, in fear, betrayal and horror, were tearing away from one another.

Over the long weekend, everyone mostly stayed indoors. Whenever I drove past the township, it was ominously quiet and empty. It was as if all South Africans felt that we were on the brink of the unspeakable.

The killers were soon arrested because Hani's white neighbour wrote down the car's registration number and phoned the police. The two men, who were ultimately found guilty and sentenced to life in prison, were Clive Derby-Lewis, a South African politician from the Conservative Party and former member of Parliament, and Janusz Waluś, a Polish citizen who had fled to South Africa some years before to get away from communism in his homeland.

As tensions and fears grew, and President de Klerk, the official political head of the country, could not see a legitimate way open to plead for calm, Mandela stepped in and, with a face set in steel, asked on television and radio for people to honour the memory of a comrade who decided to put his gun down in order to negotiate for a country's peaceful life.

Hani's funeral took place soon afterwards. A massive crowd gathered at the FNB Stadium in Soweto and, on our television screens, it soon became clear that people were beyond anger and were visibly volatile. Some of the speakers were reticent with emotion, others fierce with deep-seated anger. I sat on the edge of my sofa. Many white South Africans, like me, watched with sinking hearts. The crowd was ready to explode. Then it was Tutu's turn to speak. He raised his hands in the air. We recognized the one hand slightly distorted by polio that he had as a youth. He stretched his hands full length and in front of this swirling aggressive crowd, he cried powerfully into the microphone, 'We are all God's people.' Swaying his arms, he repeated it until the crowd became a massive sea of hands, chanting, later yelling, 'We are all God's people.'

Then I heard Tutu say, 'We are all God's people—black *and white.*' The word 'white' fell like a stone into the ether. I felt my blood turn ice cold. Everything became slow motion—one could literally see a wavering in the hands of the crowd—and I thought to myself, this is the end, the real end of us all.

But, after what felt like a century's hesitation, the crowd repeated en masse, 'black *and white.*' It was a terrifying, awe-inspiring moment, looking down into the abyss and then being pulled back by the priest in the purple robe.

I interviewed the archbishop about this event many years later. How was it that he was prepared to risk his entire reputation—even his life—at that moment in front of millions of people? If the crowd rejected him, booed him, broke into a furious rampage, it would have been the end of him—and of many other things as well. Tutu gave two explanations. First, that people prayed for him. Second, that he believed that when you were with and among the people through their lives, they would remember you, so that even when you took them where they didn't necessarily think they wanted to go, they would trust you.

In an interview with Tutu titled 'Moral Anchor', Njabulo Ndebele confirms this in an assessment of the moral authority of the archbishop, which was

> successfully tested in the long and bitter struggle against apartheid. It is authority derived from having actively intervened in many difficult moments during the struggle: the activist man-of-God who would fearlessly hold both the

oppressor and the oppressed to account. In this context, whatever political or philosophical limitations can be pointed out [. . .] they come up against an almost unassailable moral authority [. . .]. You are overwhelmed by the feeling that this man has earned the right to his words (Ndebele 2007b: 82–3).

In his book *Made for Goodness* (2010), co-authored with his daughter, Tutu clarifies such a moment of speaking as 'God-pressure', a feeling of being compelled to act, even against the voice of reason. There was outrage at the funeral. Whites were responsible for Hani's assassination, yet everyone refrained from broaching the subject of outrage. The archbishop spoke directly into that absence.

What is important is not only that he did it but *how* he did it: he did not single out whites for criticism or put them forward in order to reprimand them or distance himself and the crowd from them. Although whites killed Mandela's successor (and who knows what kind of country South Africa would be today if Hani had been our second president), through gesture and words, Tutu linked whites irretrievably to blacks: black and white, all God's children.

The opposite of wrong, says the archbishop in this book, is not 'right', but 'solidarity with goodness'; 'we are tuned to the key of goodness' (2010: 5). Goodness suggests a moral universe, a possibility of wholeness, which is also 'an invitation to the beauty of the world' (ibid.: 48). Whatever we do based on goodness may be a drop in the bucket but it contributes to an evolvement of human agency that could reshape the course of history. Being on the side of goodness means to tap in and to be interconnected to a powerful, already existing force.

One forgives not necessarily because one is performing a miracle but because one has surrendered to goodness. Even more unexpectedly, Tutu says, one sees the good God standing over there in solidarity with the sinner —which reveals the possibility of goodness in the sinner.

Does this mean impunity, allowing people to 'get away' with what is wrong and unjust? No, says Tutu, because of goodness, we forgive. We had to learn that God was standing on the side of whites that day of the funeral, appealing to the goodness in them.

★

'*Why* am I so shocked about Terre'Blanche's death?' I asked my husband as we watched on television the news of the murder of the Afrikaner Weerstandsbeweging (AWB) extremist and charismatic leader Eugène Terre' Blanche on 3 April 2010.

'Perhaps you regard him as the Number One Boer,' he suggested. 'If *he* gets killed, then where are you as number 100,000?'

I have always argued against the term 'Boer': it has been, and still is, a construct which is manipulated and abused by those who want to claim exclusive rights to privileges. But it became an interesting exercise over the following weeks. Confronted with images of Terre'Blanche's dilapidated house and meagre possessions, one had to face up to the fact that the Number One Boer was poor, he underpaid his workers, he bought alcohol and cigarettes for his killers. When stories did the rounds that he had a sexual relationship with one of them, it became truly interesting: the Number One Boer was bisexual. When his black fellow inmates testified how kind and generous he was in jail and that he kept in contact with them afterwards, I felt elated. Could it be? Could the Number One Boer perhaps have been a liberated person, living a fuller, much more integrated 'new South African' life than most of us number umpteenth?

But the images on television were frightening: Boers with desperate anger and fear on their faces, women crying or shouting, fleshy arms toting guns and hitting at cameras, at police, at black bystanders in front of the local courtroom where the accused briefly appeared.

Who will step in this time to ask for calm? I wondered. Do we still have the language 16 years into democracy to pull ourselves back from the brink?

That evening, seated in a God-awful chair, dressed in a crumpled shirt exposing his ageing neck, our president busked his way through a meaningless five minutes. I wanted to cry. Did no one in government *care* enough— if not about the Afrikaners, or about the possible violence that might erupt, then at least about the impression given by the president? 'Write the man a paragraph! Or let him sing!' I wanted to shout, as Zuma's vacuous statements puffed away in the air.

The news bulletin following the speech carried the first language of compassion to be heard during that week. The black men who shared a cell with Terre' Blanche after he was jailed for viciously assaulting a worker on his farm said that they got to know him as a kind man and that they sympathized with his wife and daughter.

The last interview that was ever done with Terre' Blanche was rebroadcast and there he was—red-nosed and bedraggled but a racist in full rhetorical force, calling black people *die goed* (these things). What was happening here? Was the Number One Boer a total hypocrite? A shrewd survivor? Did he lead a double life? How was he integrating his racist rhetoric with his comradeship with black prison inmates?

After the funeral, all suggestions of his sexual engagement with his killers were rejected outright by the AWB and, to my surprise, also by the same defence lawyer who initially could not wait to tell journalists about how Terre'Blanche was found with his pants pulled down and semen all over his clothes.

Again I had to think about language. Terre'Blanche spoke the same mother tongue as I. Did a vocabulary exist in Afrikaans in which the Number One Boer could reconcile his complex and variegated life? The context which gave someone like Terre'Blanche the norms according to which he lived projected him as moral and concerned about the plight of the poor Afrikaner. When the context became democratized and expressive of universal moral norms, he suddenly found himself seen as immoral. How was he then to vocabularize his life? Did he know the words in which to reconcile the 'good' parts of his past, such as his caring for others, his non-racial friendships and his bisexuality? My suspicion was that, during his last days, he had to fall back on the past with its seducing rhetoric of race, because he (and the Afrikaans language) was failing more and more at forging an adequate vocabulary of grace for living with the complexities of freedom.

★

During the TRC hearings, we saw how Tutu, instead of condemning Winnie Mandela like so many others did, recalled her bravery and then led her, step by step, into uttering words of accepting responsibility and acknowledging guilt and the need for subsequent contrition.[2]

After one of Winnie Mandela's many denials that she knew anything about the atrocities that she was being accused of, Tutu stood up and said: 'We need to demonstrate qualitatively that this new dispensation is different morally. We need to stand up to be counted for goodness, for truth, for compassion . . . I acknowledge Madikizela-Mandela's role in the history of our struggle. And yet one used to say that something went wrong . . . horribly, badly wrong.' He then turned to her: 'I speak to someone who loves you very deeply . . . I want you to stand up and say: "There are things that went wrong . . ."' At the end of his plea his voice fell to a whisper: 'I beg you' (South African Press Association 1997b).

After what felt like ages, she said: 'I am saying it is true: things went horribly wrong and we are aware that there were factors that led to that. For that I am deeply sorry.'

Even if Winnie 'play-acted' her apology, as she has been so often accused of, she bent her knee in public to

---

2 For a full discussion of Winnie Mandela's appearance before the TRC, see Krog (1998: Chapter 20)

what Tutu called 'our new morality'. It was irrelevant whether she truly meant it. When the chips were down, she had to agree to Tutu's moral outline.

Someone who found himself without this moral outline was Tony Yengeni on the day that he entered jail to serve his sentence for receiving bribes as part of the arms deal (a US$4.8 billion purchase of weaponry by the South African government, finalized in 1999, which has been subject to allegations of gross corruption). He stood in front of the prison, microphone in hand, clearly fumbling for the right words to talk about his activist past and his corrupt present to the all-important camera and the energetic, supportive crowd. Unlike Winnie, he had no one to assist him in uttering the difficult words of acknowledgement and regret, pride and shame. Yengeni was under pressure and unable to formulate a coherent navigation from the illegitimate context of apartheid to the legitimate one of democracy. He chose to conflate his plight into that of his once-innocent anti-apartheid self being destroyed by a legitimate democracy.

But it is not only those who are stumbling round in the morasses of power and corruption who find themselves without a vocabulary of resistance, integrity and goodness. Those reporting on attempts of finding a moral equilibrium also seem at a loss of words. We have seen, or rather heard of, Adriaan Vlok washing the feet of Reverend Frank Chikane and a group of black women. As described in Chapter 6, he was widely criticized for this act.

I found surprising the vehemence, especially from white liberal quarters, with which this gesture was rejected. Why? Since the dawn of the South African democracy, there was a need for a white man to respond adequately to the convincing reconciliatory gestures of people like Tutu and Mandela. Every South African had in his or her head a picture of Mandela wearing the Springbok rugby jersey, a much-contested symbol recalling apartheid, or holding up the hand of De Klerk together with that of Mbeki as his two deputy presidents during his inauguration. A powerful black man reached out to whites on behalf of blacks.

Who was going to make whites' rejection of and regret about apartheid visible? What picture was living in the back of millions of South Africans' heads when we said the word 'reconciliation'? Those who were so quick to torture and kill in our name were nowhere to be found to say sorry in our name. Ordinary people had asked for, been given or refused forgiveness in many visible and invisible ways, but in a patriarchal vocabulary-less society such as ours, we needed a gesture and this gesture needed to be performed by a powerful white *man*—a 'white prince of reconciliation' as it were.

In 1970, the then West German chancellor Willy Brandt visited the Warsaw Ghetto Memorial. While laying a wreath, he suddenly knelt down. For many Jews, that was the most important moment of the postwar era—the moment that the repentance of the German nation was made visible.

I had hoped that, like Brandt, De Klerk, during the time when he had stature, power and support, would be big-hearted enough to take all the guilt on himself. I had hoped that he would be imaginative enough to do it in a way more powerful than words. He didn't. And as regular as clockwork, every year around National Reconciliation Day, someone would say that the whites had never asked for forgiveness. And before long, De Klerk's name would come up and he, or lately the head of his foundation, would reiterate his long, dry, threadbare legal explanations of exculpation.

So, for what its worth, Vlok, in his way, made the gesture for whites. Although most of us would have preferred a more innocent scapegoat, his gesture was surprising and effective for three reasons. One, he was the first once-powerful, guilty white male who showed contrition that could not be linked to a TRC submission or an upcoming amnesty application. Second, without inviting television cameras, he chose a gesture that everyone could instinctively picture and understand. Apart from the biblical connotation, the act of washing feet also recalled the time when South African slaves washed the feet of their masters. And third, he didn't say that he was doing it on behalf of whites but that he was reaching out to all those he had hurt, pointing to an acceptance of being interconnected with them. However inadequate and pathetic some may have deemed this act, it was, after 10 years, the best that whites had come up with.

Why was it so viciously spurned? Were we saying that we don't want the guilty to change? That even if they go to jail, like convicted cleric and activist Alan Boesak and Tony Yengeni, we would continue to reject them?

Were we saying that because *we* were not guilty, because *our* hands were clean, we did not want someone as guilty as Vlok to suddenly join our holy ranks—we, the righteous and the self-righteous? Were we—we who so easily said Vlok did not do enough—saying that we actually knew how much contrition would be enough? Were we, who said he should wash many other feet, saying that *we* had already washed the feet we should have washed? Were we, who said too little too late, saying that anyone who ever contemplated dealing with his or her guilt should rather shut up and do nothing, because any action would always remain a futile gesture?

How were we treating those who didn't do right? To have ridiculed Vlok and Yengeni was an abdication of the responsibility to forge a vocabulary, as Tutu so often did, for the disgraced. One wants them to change; one wants to put in their mouths the language of integrity and care. They will not learn this under a torrent of ridicule, condemnation and rejection.

The dehumanization of the stigmatized often corresponds to the dehumanization of language and discourse. In a country emerging from centuries of fractured morality and dehumanization, it seems that this destructive vocabulary accrued from countless generations forms the very plausibility structures we have to extract ourselves from. If we don't, if we continue to assume that we do not need a vocabulary of care—also and especially for the disgraced—we will destroy everything good that we have achieved over the past 20 years.

★

To care for the disgraced is not, of course, altogether unproblematic. Claudia Braude writes that having avoided a Nuremberg Trials route in dealing with the crimes of the past, South Africa has entrenched a pervasive culture of impunity that uses the 'template of forgiveness', which allows many South African criminals to claim the right to be forgiven. 'Since amnesty cannot be granted for crimes against humanity, descriptions of apartheid mutated from being an internationally recognized crime against humanity into a "gross human rights violation"' (2009: 36).

Braude agrees with several scholars who accuse Tutu of using a language of forgiveness to give a moral overlay to what essentially has been a political compromise—a pact between elites. No wonder, her article continues, that the democratically elected leaders of the new South Africa who were involved in a corrupt arms deal a few years ago now demand amnesty. Using the language of amnesty, political context and forgiveness, South Africans have been asked to refrain from prosecuting the president (accused of raping a young woman), his financial adviser (accused of corrupt activities in the arms deal) and xenophobic attackers (accused of attacking and looting the businesses and houses of people from other African countries).

The article gives examples of how TRC vocabulary is being used by politicians who advocate for amnesty for tax evasion, illegal possession of guns and driving unlicensed taxis. A political commentator blatantly says that just as South Africa had bargained with the devil during the TRC, we can now bargain with those who committed serious political crimes during the arms deal. 'If perpetrators of heinous deeds who demonstrated neither commitment to democracy nor human decency could get amnesty and special pardons, why not our president, for the lesser alleged crime of corruption?' (ibid.: 43).

So, according to this criticism, those who benefited from crimes against humanity have walked off scot-free and those who killed, maimed and tortured have been given amnesty. Since the structural injustice which black people suffered has not been addressed, South Africans have concluded that crime does in fact pay handsomely.

Does the 'template of forgiveness' provide impunity for the corrupt? Yes, if amnesty is regarded as an individual desire to simply wipe out a deed. No, if amnesty is regarded as an expression of interconnectedness which involves the public admittance of wrongdoing and the assertion to be willing to 'make up for it' in order to become part of the human community again. In the latter case, it means profound change. It would therefore be an oversimplification to regard all those who ask for amnesty as merely seeking impunity. I want to suggest that much of the support for 'criminals' in South Africa stems not from base corruption and immorality but from a willingness to listen to the appeal of the disgraced to become, through negotiated making up, part of the community of respectable citizens. To rephrase Ndebele: The choice of reconciliation should never be an alternative to justice, or vengeance, but a means to enrich human conduct (2007b: 82).

During the TRC process, the concept of interconnectedness became a springboard for terms to be re-launched into a more caring vision: justice became restorative justice, amnesty became admittance of wrongdoing, forgiveness and reconciliation became a quest to be re-admitted into the community of humanity, and human rights became responsibilities towards a more humane society. The TRC allowed justice to be interpreted from the perspective of interconnectedness. Justice entered the equation and became rejuvenated through a radical rethinking of its grammar and through human compassion that is understood to be as important as, and part of, the rule of law.

★

While taking a walk recently after a rainstorm on the farm where I grew up, I found myself suddenly confronted with a rainbow splendidly poised over the endless plain of tussled and wet-stalked golden grass. I could smell the earth and see the first flying termites letting their transparent wings flit like breaths of glass. The earth, the grass, the insects—all of it was real. But the rainbow?

Of course I knew that one of the few truly original metaphors to come out of South Africa was 'Rainbow Nation'. Coined by Tutu, the metaphor has been criticized, praised, used to death in popular songs and ridiculed for having neither white nor black as part of its colour constellation. More recently, it was condemned as indoctrinating South Africans to live in false and unjust peace and, in light of the country's high crime and murder statistics, dismissed as nothing but a sentimental utterance.

Looking at the rainbow, I had to retreat from automatically classifying it as similar to Father Christmas or the tooth fairy; I had to stop my inner ear hearing 'Somewhere over the rainbow . . .' or my mind imagining the Irish pot of gold. This rainbow, here in the veld, was real. As real as myself and the land I was walking on. As real as the South African nation, I thought, throwing myself head first into the metaphor. The rainbow appeared at that moment not because the storm had passed but because so much of it was still present—behind me the sun was setting, but the last thunderclouds were unstable and restless behind the rainbow. For the rainbow to exist, I realized, it had to be raining while the sun shone. There had to be water drops in the air, so that the sunlight could pour in from behind me at a low angle. The real rainbow was always linked to contradiction and instability.

I walked so far into the veld that I could no longer see the farmhouse, yet I could still see the rainbow. That evening, I learnt that my mother also saw the rainbow from the house. Was every observer then seeing his or her own rainbow, and yet seeing a different rainbow depending on his or her position? How wonderful that no one could or would ever see a rainbow from the side or in profile! No one can be forced to live with skewed angles of the rainbow.

But if someone does not *see* the rainbow, then there *is* no rainbow—no matter who says what.

With parts of it fading, I tried to identify the different colours and observe how these colours transformed the simple landscape with its undulating grass, its few dishevelled blue gums, the wind pump, the small cement dam and the vast sky into something beyond reality. The overwhelming intensity and variety of the colours, the position, the formation of a bow—none of it related to what

I saw round me. The flat landscape and the immense sweep of sky—for me, that belonged together. The grass-flowing landscape and the big, tumbling, late-afternoon clouds with their blue dewlaps—that belonged together. But the rainbow seemed to have come from another world. Real, but a startling image from somewhere else. The logic forged in me over years of living in this landscape left me unprepared to accept the rainbow as a simple, natural and integral part of my world.

Like a bad oil painting, nothing in the execution of the 'total picture' reflected or harmonized with the rainbow. The rainbow didn't contain only blue and yellow to link to the landscape. The red wasn't weaker because there was no red round me.

The rainbow haunted me. How could I begin to understand 'us' in terms of the rainbow if I was so uncomfortably unclear about what it entailed?

'Yes, the rainbow cannot be formed with, say, only orange and violet. *All* the identified colours are always present and in the same order,' says the professor at the science department of UWC, giving me a crash course in the rainbow. I interpret metaphorically: so the rainbow cannot be what it is if some colours are invisible, powerless or allowed to suffer or die; it can only exist inclusively.

'There are no separate or impenetrable "bands" of colour in the rainbow spectrum. All raindrops refract and reflect the sunlight in the same way, but only some of the colours in the raindrops reach the observer's eye at a particular moment,' the professor continues. I look at her in astonishment. 'Yes,' she says. 'Colours are continuously spilling over into one another. There's no dominant colour, and when sunlight enters the droplet, red is at the top and blue is at the bottom. During the inversion, blue comes out at the top and red at the bottom.

'But now for the real magic—the essence of why the rainbow confronts our comfort zones of colour.' Am I imagining it, or has she also slipped into metaphoric mode? If one has grown up with Noah's ark, perhaps it is impossible ever to regard the rainbow as a pure scientific fact.

'Imagine the following: all the droplets, tiny as they are, as they fall, reflect and refract the full rainbow spectrum, every one of them. As they fall, your eye picks up a million droplets of only one colour, then another, then another until *you* see the rainbow in its iconic shape. But *all* the droplets have to disperse all the colours all the time, in order for you to fully see the rainbow.'

I was in a daze. Exhilarated.

Walking back to my office, a white face among black and coloured students, I wondered: Do I reflect all the colours all the time? Do I walk here, teach here on campus as a white Afrikaner woman, or am I reflecting the full South African spectrum—so that when the students see my one colour, they know that the *only* reason why they can see that one colour is because I refracted *all* the colours? If I am to refract exclusively Afrikaner female whiteness, I'll disappear. But—and this is even more radical—if I prefer to absorb only my 'own colour', I'll disappear . . . but so will they.

★

I belong to this land. It made me. I have no other land than this one. My feeling for this land is overwhelming. It is gnarled and tough, but unambiguous.

I do not believe in miracles, I say with David Grossman (2006), but the existence of my country is a miracle: this I do not forget—not for one single moment. There is blood in my feeling for this land, baptized in the dreams of ancestors and the nightmare of ethnic survival.

I know that my country is a man-made miracle. I never forget that—not for one single moment. Even if the miracle seems to be falling apart, even if the land starts to resemble a parody on a miracle, even when it falls apart in chunks of crime, suffering, greed, corruption, cynicism, I will still remember the miracle.

How wasteful do we want to be? How many ill people, how many murdered ones do we want to bury at the feet of this miracle? In criminal ways, we waste each other's lives, year after year—not only sons, not only daughters, not only babies, not only old people, it is the miracle itself that we are starting to waste, the big and rare opportunity we received from history to create a structure that is a refuge for the poor, the talented, the dreamers, the ordinary ones, the maimed: a state in Africa that cares.

I belong to this land. It made me. I have no other land than this one.

Why are we in such a permanent state of feeling offended, weak, wasting opportunities? Have we even lost hope that solidarity with the poor is at all possible? Why do we keep looking as if hypnotized at how criminality, madness, violence and racism breed as commonplace attitudes in our workplaces and homes?

How does it happen that a country with so much creativity, such a capacity for rebirth and nurturing of the slightest creativities can find itself in such a brutal state?

My feeling for this land is overwhelming. It is gnarled and tough, but unambiguous.

We are becoming victims of ourselves. Our leaders are being caught up in the despair of short-sightedness. It is as if we do not have an idea of the inspirational component of humaneness that can serve as an antidote to our violent behaviour towards one another. Our public voices are becoming nothing but packets filled with intimidation and exclusion—anxious, suspicious, sweating, despising, dishonest.

We grieve for and bury our dead in this land, while we hear how the miracle is being squandered in the name of the poor or of 'our people' or of Afrikaner culture.

I belong to this land. It made me. I have no other land than this one. My feeling for this land is overwhelming. It is gnarled and tough, but unambiguous.

I do not believe in miracles, but the existence of my country is a miracle.

This I do not forget—not for one single moment.

CHAPTER NINE

Suske en Wiske: Sequential Comic Panels and the
Iconization of Nelson Mandela

With rumours surfacing at regular intervals about the
imminent death of Nelson Mandela, this chapter explores
how this icon is often honoured in ways that emaciate,
distort and even destroy the very things he stands for. I
intend to use a few sequential panels depicting Mandela
in a popular comics series titled Suske en Wiske in Dutch
(the American title is Willy and Wanda) to pinpoint some
of the consequences of this kind of iconization within a
global discourse round tolerance, forgiveness and reconciliation.

Aware of Charles Hatfield's warning that comics are
'a complex means of communication and are always characterized by a plurality of messages' (2009: 132), I need
to underscore my purpose: precisely because of this
thickly woven fabric of visual and verbal material, I do
not regard my exploration of some panels of Suske en
Wiske in any way exhaustive or conclusive as far as comics
are concerned. In fact, my purpose is precisely to make a
particular point about perceptions round Mandela and
not about comics. I use comic-strip panels merely as effective torches to throw some light on representations of
Mandela in general.

According to Pascal Lefèvre, readers encounter two broad types of 'spaces' when reading a comic: diegetic space (the fictive space in which the comic-strip characters live and act) and extra-diegetic space (the space outside the fictive world of the comic—not only the white spaces between the panels, but also the real space in which the reader is located) (2009: 157, 160). Working in this extra-diegetic space, I want to mention a few historical contexts in which this comic strip has to be read: the long, successful history of the series itself as the brainchild of the Belgian artist Willy Vandersteen in the 1940s; the specific characteristics of the characters—Suske, Wiske, Sidonia, Lambik, Jerom and Professor Barabas; the country in which the plot plays itself out; and European and colonial history combined with the growing intolerance against Islamic culture in the Netherlands and Belgium.

The Dutch have a particularly complicated, interwoven, centuries-old history with South Africa: through the Afrikaners as their descendants, who became colonial exploiters and later installers of official apartheid; through black people, whose struggle for liberation was supported by the Dutch government and a variety of NGOs; and through the presence of many emigrant Afrikaners in current, everyday Dutch life.

Thus, a Dutch comic using the 'new' South Africa as part of its plot inevitably carries traceable sediments of these pasts and presents in a variety of generic conventions. To analyse Vandersteen's *Suske en Wiske*: *Kaapse Kaalkoppen* (Cape Town Baldheads) is to enter an archive of perceptions and normative assumptions and stores of sense-making.

262 | *Conditional Tense*

I want to re-emphasize that although I focus on this specific comic, I could have chosen any number of other texts to demonstrate the same—that is, how to make it possible to admire Mandela while making it impossible to take seriously the example he sets. I chose a comic because the visuality and the presence of both diegetic and extra-diegetic space help unravel multiple, intersecting strands that illustrate the uneven ways in which transnational collaborations coin the radical challenge that someone like Mandela poses for current mass consumption, social justice and sharing with the poor.

The tools I use for unravelling some of these ambiguities are two of the most important building blocks of comics: formula and style.

In narrative theory, 'formula' has a specialized meaning, says Marion Saraceni (2003). It invites us to look at the rules of construction that underlie the form of the story and at how those rules influence the interaction among characters as the story develops. Hence, to look for formula is therefore 'to look for common elements within the stories which govern more than the pace at which stories unfold' (ibid.: 36). Saraceni further argues that the exceptions are as revealing of the predicaments and the motives of the text makers as the formula is.

So what is the broad formula of the Suske en Wiske comics? *Wikipedia* describes the series as a strip dealing with the adventures of two young people (Suske and Wiske) and their friends and family, mostly in foreign countries.

In *Het Aruba-Dossier* (The Aruba File), the team visits the Netherlands Antilles, where they expose the mining of cancer-inducing fertilizers. The story ends with police arresting the thugs and the team being thanked by scientists and the local government.

In *De Mompelende Mummie* (The Mumbling Mummy), the team exposes a mining company's exploitation of raw materials, local inhabitants and a pristine jungle in Indonesia. The story ends with the arrest of those responsible in front of an international media contingent.

In *De Laatste Vloek* (The Last Swear Word), the team prevents the earth from being destroyed after the seven hundred seventy-seven thousand billionth swear word is being uttered in Belgium. The character Jerom, the strongman of the group, literally holds the world together with immense chains.

In *De Krakende Carcas* (The Creaking Carcass), the team helps a town in the south of France to live out its proper history during the Crusades.

In *De Razende Race* (The Hysterical Race), illegal weapon smugglers are brought to book by the team during a race in Flanders.

In short, the team unselfishly sets out to assist and fight on the side of those who support the 'good cause'.

In his superb analysis of the practical elements of comic-strip texts, Scott McCloud distinguishes between comics artists who want 'to say something about life through art' and those who want 'to say something about art itself' (1993: 178). He classifies Hergé, the creator of the Adventures of Tintin, as the former kind; in other words, the power of Tintin lies in the power of its ideas about life: 'This is the path of great storytellers who have something to say through comics and devote all their energies to controlling their medium, refining its ability to convey messages effectively' (ibid.: 180).

Hergé shares a history with Vandersteen. After a few years of publishing his work in several newspapers, Vandersteen was approached by Hergé who wanted *Suske en Wiske* for his stable. It is therefore reasonably safe to suggest that the *Suske en Wiske* series in general represents the kind of comic that says something about life and, to do it, uses the formula of 'group setting out to fight the good fight'. In *Kaapse Kaalkoppen*, they do it in South Africa.

In the opening frames of *Kaapse Kaalkoppen*, we learn that Professor Barabas is working on a cure for arachnophobia. The choice of arachnophobia among all the phobias is an interesting one to which I will return. The only thing the professor still needs to complete the formula is a flower called the 'be-not-anxious violet'. A colleague in South Africa, Professor Hector Wildebeest, finds this rare flower but warns Barabas that the elixir from the violet produces a completely different effect: instead of alleviating the fear of spiders, it removes prejudice. He says, 'Your formula will mean a turning point in the history of humanity. An irreversible positive turn.'[1]

Professor Wildebeest is kidnapped and the team decides to go to South Africa to rescue him, save the rare flower and finalize the content and effect of the elixir. Once they arrive, Sidonia (Wiske's aunt), Jerom (the

---

1 All translations from *Suske en Wiske*: *Kaapse Kaalkoppen* are by Antjie Krog.

strongman) and Lambik (the father figure) stroll round Pretoria. They learn the complete Afrikaner-as-settler history through a dazzling summary in Jerom's typically cryptic sentences filled with information he picked up, as he readily confesses, from the KLM in-flight magazine.

The other three members of the group—Suske, Wiske and Barabas—go to Khayelitsha, the black township outside Cape Town, looking for clues that could lead them to the kidnapped Wildebeest. Margaret, a woman in the township, explains apartheid to Suske and Wiske, who are visibly stunned by the poverty round them. The black woman points out the improvements brought about by the ANC government —crèches, clinics, houses—but adds, 'Dat is een werk van lange adem . . .' (That is work which will take some time . . .).

Thus, as readers move to the final scenes in the comic, they have been given a reasonable version of how Afrikaners instigated apartheid, how systemic violence created poverty in the townships and how inequality is still being maintained.

In their search for Wildebeest, the team is relentlessly followed and harassed by men with blue, yellow, green and red masks. These men are operating for bosses who make money from arms deals or those who benefit from conflict.

In *Comics: Ideology, Power and the Critics*, Martin Barker stresses that it is important to ask questions about the logic in a comic: What kind of logic works in the strip and what is its significance? How are the bad guys transformed for the purposes of fitting this logic or formula?

(1989: 77). To portray bad guys in a country infamous for its high crime rate and a staggering number of young black men convicted of crime is a very tricky business. Marc Verhaegen, the artist for *Kaapse Kaalkoppen*, creatively provides multicoloured masks, probably signalling that the bad guys are not race specific but are of all colours. Yet one immediately notices that the hair and hands of the crooks are those of whites. To distinguish between good whites and bad whites in South Africa is a complicated business. The mask is a brilliant device to convey that these guys are bad white, as opposed to bad black, yet not South African bad white but international bad white. It is not without its problems, however: it not only makes immediate racial identification difficult but it also obstructs possibilities of accountability. As the comic's panels include no visual account anywhere of blacks and whites mingling in the street or in public spaces, the impression is created that the only good whites interacting with blacks in South Africa are the six unmasked Belgians. The only bad people in South Africa are the masked internationals, whose emotions or intentions the reader cannot clearly discern.

Consequently, the whites who benefited so richly from apartheid and who now benefit from reconciliation are absent from the comic. This allows the reader to stay as innocent as Suske and Wiske, who ask the woman in the township why the people are so poor. Judging from what is being said and portrayed, the answer is: people are poor because the ANC government is still busy fixing things.

This lets not only the whites and especially Afrikaners off the hook but also the Dutch and Flemish who have benefited handsomely from their colonial pasts in Africa and the East. The absence of South African whites misleads the (young?) reader into thinking that poverty is not attributable to concrete steps set in motion by particular identifiable individuals and groups, but is, in the words of Slavoj Žižek, purely 'objective', systemic and anonymous (2009: 11). Žižek urges us to identify the invisible objective violence (caused by capitalists) which sustains inequality, so that we do not become distracted 'from the true locus of trouble, by obliterating from view other forms of violence and thus actively participating in them' (ibid.: 9). How do we participate in this violence? By propagating tolerance and reconciliation, suggests Žižek, in a chapter titled 'Tolerance as an Ideological Category' (ibid.: 119–150). I will return to this idea later.

With the accountability of white South Africans out of the way, forgiveness and reconciliation become the determining motive of the plot, and of course the final scene *has* to take place on the internationally accepted semantic field of forgiveness—Robben Island, where Mandela and other political undesirables were imprisoned. The team catches up with Professor Wildebeest as he runs into the quarry, infamous for being the place where political prisoners, including Mandela, quarried limestone and where the professor has built a secret laboratory in the back of the cave.

Wildebeest describes his findings to only five of the team: 'Whoever drinks from this elixir loses any built-in anxieties about people who are different from oneself.' The elixir means the end of homophobia, xenophobia, Islamophobia—Verhaegen is setting foot on the road to imagining the consequences of an idea which has been the material of countless philosophers and artists.

But what is the team's response to such astonishing news? Lambik says, almost facetiously, 'No one needs to fear my exceptional intelligence any more.' 'What I mean,' Wildebeest tries again, 'is that people stand open to other people who have another skin colour, another culture and other ideas . . .' This inoffensive version of tolerance, that doesn't mention religion or sexual orientation, has Suske and Wiske in ecstasy: 'Oh, but that is wonderful news. Most conflicts round the world start with these differences.'

One cannot help but think this is a terribly unfortunate observation, especially in Dutch (the language linked to the French-speaking Belgian king Leopold II and spoken by the owners of the Dutch East India Company [VOC]), as it ignores the fact that conflicts are mainly about resources, using difference as a tool for inclusion or exclusion. One wants to ask with Žižek: 'Why are so many problems today perceived as problems of intolerance, rather than as problems of inequality, exploitation or justice? . . . Why is the proposed remedy tolerance, rather than emancipation, political struggle, even armed struggle?' (2009: 119). He says the immediate answer lies in the 'liberal multiculturalist's basic ideological operation', which naturalizes and therefore neutralizes differences initially conditioned by political inequality or economic exploitation. In other words, instead of trying to remedy inequality with radical, even revolutionary steps, differences in culture or skin are presented as the only differences—these differences cannot be surmounted, '[t]hey can only be tolerated' (ibid.). Again, this removes any responsibility for former plundering and current inequality.

Enter the masked bad guy: he shoots and shatters the glass vial containing the elixir. This scene makes imaginative use of one of the most important tools of comic-making, namely, the gutter, or the white space between the panels. McCloud regards the gutter as the ultimate device which makes comics unique among art forms: '[t]he [imagined] blood in the gutter' in the extra-diegetic space is what draws readers to comics (1993: 60). The world is experienced through the senses, yet the senses can only truly reveal a fragmented and incomplete world. The perception of reality as a coherent and whole entity is an act of faith, based on these fragments (ibid.: 63). Comics also work with fragments. They are called panels and they build the diegetic space in which the characters function. The space of the gutter plays 'host to much of the magic and mystery that are at the very heart of comics' (ibid.: 66; see also Saraceni 2003: 50–3 and Lefèvre 2009: 157–61). 'Here in the limbo of the gutter, human imagination takes two separate images and transforms them into a single idea' (McCloud 1993: 67).

In the showdown at the limestone quarry on Robben Island, we see the bullet shattering the vial holding the elixir, the last remnants of an already destroyed formula. We read Wildebeest's description of the elixir flowing among the stones; we do not actually see it. The gutter (enhanced by the jump to the next page) leaves it to us to imagine how this remarkable fluid, which could have changed the world, seeps into the stone floor and disappears for ever.

FIGURE 1. Wildebeest and the flowing elixir

Because we do not see the elixir flowing away but imagine it taking place in the space between the panels, the loss feels immensely real. It is as if one cannot continue to the next panel. One stares 'into the gutter' as it were, trying to think of ways to stop the fluid from disappearing. Was not a drop of elixir on a piece of shattered glass perhaps enough to recover the formula?

This is what you and I may wonder but not the Belgian writers.

The unarmed Wildebeest storms forward, his fists raised, but he is grabbed by Professor Barabas. Such a fight would be senseless, Barabas says. Suske runs towards the bad guy but Sidonia prevents him from getting there. Let us not make more victims, she says. Although they are five against one, they do nothing, even when the thug turns his back to pour acid over the only surviving specimen of the crucial violet. Risking their lives for one of the most important inventions in history is clearly not part of the plot. Thus, *not* exposing the wrong and *not* fighting for the good mitigates the Suske-and-Wiske formula of supporting the 'good cause'.

Barker stresses that it is important to know where and how so-called reality enters the strip and how it is treated. What is the particular role set for the reader by the strip? What happens when the characters fail against the functions set for them in the formula and what does this say about the formula itself? (1989: 77)

In several similar situations in other editions of Suske en Wiske, strongman Jerom would do the necessary in order to have a mission accomplished. At this moment in the cave, however, he is conveniently absent on another mission. This is the first manipulation of the formula.

Instead of safeguarding something that will enable human- kind to live in tolerance of difference, the team watches its destruction. The general formula is changed from 'we will save the good' into 'tolerance is not possible.' This is the second manipulation of the formula and can be read as the place where a double-layered reality sets in. The first layer makes it clear that tolerance by such superficial means as drinking an elixir is not possible. (Hurrah! one wants to say, as this neatly deals with the illusion that tolerance is simply a kind of trickery.) The second layer reveals the unspoken contract between the comics and the reader: we, the makers of the comics, are (like) you and will never critique or confront you with an unpleasant, unpopular reality, such as—if one really works hard and mobilizes round an inclusive interconnected vision to address injustice, tolerance might just be possible.

The rest of the bad guys arrive and so, finally, does Jerom, accompanied by a batch of neatly dressed, non-overweight, effective South African policemen. The bad guys are arrested. Suske and Wiske embrace each other, and Wiske says, 'We were close to something beautiful. Yes, it could have made a big difference to the world.' As they leave the limestone quarry, we see Wiske crying.

The story could have ended here: inculcating tolerance through an elixir is fantasy. But the writer now has a dilemma. On the one hand, he started off by posing reconciliation and tolerance as the main ingredients of his plot, so they cannot suddenly be rejected as worthless pursuits. He also knows his audience—how the Dutch people had poured out their adoration when Mandela visited Holland and the very warm relationship that exists between Mandela, Queen Beatrix and her family. On the other hand, he possibly knows the boundaries. Within the general atmosphere of growing conservatism and intolerance in Europe, he dare not, even in fantasy, affront his readers by forcing them to consider tolerance as a reality within justice.

To please his readers, he needs to bring in Mandela, but in a way that has no unpleasant implications for them. So, as the team sadly walks out of the cave with Wiske saying 'It was perhaps too beautiful to be true. Such miracles [of tolerance] do not happen any more . . .', lo and behold—they hear a voice behind them: 'It still does happen, dear child. That miracle happens here in South Africa every day . . . In the rainbow all the colours form one unity.'

The children are flabbergasted as they recognize the great icon of tolerance and forgiveness. Again it is Lambik who makes an untoward remark (see Figure 5), but he is

Ik heb alle Zuid-Afrikanen opgeroepen tot verzoening,... en ze hebben geluisterd. Wij leven nu als broeders en zusters, ongeacht onze verschillen. Dat bedoelde ik met het wonder dat zich hier alle dagen voltrekt...

FIGURE 2. Mandela from the back

immediately forgiven. Mandela declares that Lambik's 'heart is in the right place'.

In the panel above, Mandela gives his personal version of reconciliation in South Africa: 'I called on all South Africans to reconcile, and they listened. We now live as brothers and sisters, despite our differences. This is what I mean with the miracle that is happening here every day.'

But let us take a re-look at the panel in which Mandela makes his appearance and explore the second building block in comics culture: pictorial icons. For this, we need to focus on the specific drawing technique used in *Kaapse Kaalkoppen*. Suske en Wiske comics are executed in the popularized and much-loved 'clear-line' style of the European comic tradition (labelled *Klare Lijn* by Dutch cartoonist Joost Swarte). One of the features of this style has been described by Hatfield as blurring the distinction between organic and inorganic form:

> Though the settings are often much more complex than the characters, the setting tends to be without shadow, except in the most diagrammatic sense, and also relatively textureless. The resultant tendency toward flatness produces what McCloud calls a 'democracy of form', in which each shape has the same clarity and value, conferring the same authority on cartoon figures as it does on meticulous scenic detail (2009: 145).

The drawing style used for Suske and Wiske could produce a democracy of figures between Mandela and Suske and Wiske which could make it easier for them (and us) to resist Mandela's call for tolerance. Mandela is not nature. The clear-line technique makes it possible for Suske and Wiske to be thrilled by Mandela's presence, while the democracy of form makes it possible not to feel compelled by him.

Let us move a step further. The Japanese comic culture has extended the split between background material and character (which appears in Tintin as well as in Suske en Wiske) to a split among characters as well: some characters are used for self-identification but others are 'drawn more realistically in order to objectify them, emphasizing their "otherness" from the reader' (McCloud 1993: 44). Verhaegen uses this technique.

So when Mandela enters the comic frame half in profile and with his back somewhat towards us, Verhaegen wants us to know that Mandela is not completely aware of us—he is not talking to us, his message is not related to us; we are looking over his shoulder at the main characters of the comic: Suske and Wiske. But because we are they, Mandela speaks also to us, although indirectly. Again, this indirect means makes it easier for us *not* to feel bulldozed by his vision.

In the panels where Mandela appears, we also see an example of how comics make use of the universality of pictorial icons. In McCloud's comics terminology, the pictorial icon represents a concept, idea, person or place. By stripping down an image, moving further away from the realistic version, to the essential 'meaning' of the icon, an artist amplifies the meaning (ibid.: 30). The more stripped-down a face, the more it can be read universally. The sparser the detail of the face, the better the chances that you will come to see it as yourself. 'The cartoonlike face is a vacuum into which our identity and awareness is pulled; an empty shell that we inhabit which enables us to travel in another realm' (ibid.: 36).

Mandela enters as a much more detailed icon than Suske and Wiske next to him. His hair is markedly grey and frizzled with individual curls. He has three lines on his forehead instead of the single one of the older Professor Barabas. He has an ordinary and formed nose, an upper and a lower lip, and his shirt is beautifully patterned with more lines of detail than are found on any other character in the comic.

FIGURE 3. The universality of cartoon imagery

When Mandela extends his hand, the fingers are elegantly separated and the small visible detail of a cuff button can be seen.

One even sees his high Khoisan cheekbones, but best of all are his eyes. Everyone in the comic has either dots or round white circles with a black dot for eyes. Mandela's eyes have a realistic form with a visible sclera and iris. (Interestingly, Professor Wildebeest starts off with 'normal' eyes but they soon become dots as he becomes part and parcel of the plot.)

Through these details, Verhaegen splits Mandela off from the other comic characters into a more realistic kind of icon. Because he is presented with otherness, one cannot identify with him (perhaps this was the exact

FIGURE 4. The individuality of Mandela's features

intention—no one should ever consider themselves 'being' Mandela but, at the same time, one is free from following his example); and one is more aware of the messenger than of the message—one is hardly mindful of his definition of reconciliation, because one is caught up in the fascinating detail.

If one finally manages to veer from the visual to the speech bubble, one is surprised by the oversimplified and, frankly, half-true account of the new South Africa living in daily peaceful harmony. Many readers of this comic are no doubt aware of South Africa's high crime rate, the stories of corruption, political tensions and extraordinary

FIGURE 5. Mandela's extended hand

inequalities. It pains me, I have to admit, to think that
thousands of readers will read Mandela's (Verhaegen's)
superficial and naive explanation of what he stood for.

What is happening in these panels?

In the comic's diegetic space, Suske and Wiske are fantasy. Arachnophobia, racism and xenophobia function in
the extra-diegetic space and are *not* fantasy. In fact, trying
to cure, undo, defuse and live with the consequences of
intolerance is the daily occupation and preoccupation of

millions of people across the world. Mandela is *not* fantasy. The reconciliation he led and stood for was real. But Mandela *could* be fantasy. He could have been used as a stripped-down icon to open up possibilities of seismic change within the diegetic space of Suske en Wiske. But his realistic representation has a threefold effect: his otherness prevents one from imbibing what he stands for; he becomes an exception—*he* can forgive, but *we* (and you can fill in here 9/11 victims, Palestinians, Bosnians, Holocaust survivors, etc.) need not; and tolerance achieved through an elixir is fantasy but by moving Mandela outside the fantasy world within which change is sought, the stringent condition for tolerance—that is, justice—is successfully sidestepped.

These few frames capture for me in an exemplary way everything that is suspect in most of the well-meaning accolades and interpretations of what Mandela stood for, which circulate non-stop and uninterrogated in the arteries of international networks of our daily extra-diegetic spaces. We attribute to him a kind of reconciliation that is so simple that it is almost mindless.

Ndebele, one of South Africa's most prominent and honoured intellectuals and writers, says that the characteristic feature of Mandela's moral authority is his ability 'to read a situation whose most observable logic points to a most likely (and expected) outcome, but then to detect in that very likely outcome not a solution but a compounding of the problem'. In order to prevent this outcome that seems to bring about worse things than what came before, a counter-intuitive step is required (2007a: 237).

As an example, Ndebele discusses a confrontation between Mandela and two Afrikaner generals of the South African Defence Force (see Sparks 1994: 202–04). The two generals described the apartheid army's impressive and well-equipped capacity, indicating readiness to indefinitely fight a war against the liberation movement. Mandela conceded their strength, but after sketching out their victory as of little worth to both sides, he suggested negotiations that would make them and their army part of something larger (Ndebele 2007a: 238). This counter-intuitive alternative changed the course of South Africa's history.

Why was it Mandela and not the generals who produced the counter-intuitive suggestion? Ndebele suggests that the generals had been 'socialized to defend white privilege' and that prevented them from imagining a common interest with 'outsiders' (ibid.: 239). I want to suggest that it was Mandela's innate sense of the collective which enabled him to formulate a vision of the country which included Afrikaners in its articulation. It is therefore his sense of being interconnected with others which led him to come up with a strategy which seems counter-intuitive. His forgiveness and reconciliation are first and foremost inclusive because they are embedded in his sense of interconnectedness.

One can suggest that Mandela, in the language of Gobodo-Madikizela, needed to forgive as part of the process of becoming rehumanized after his immense suffering at the hands of the apartheid regime. He needed it in order to complete himself and wrest away from his perpetrators the power to destroy him. Forgiveness or salvation does not overlook the deed, she says, but rises above it (2003: 117).

But a gesture of forgiveness embedded in interconnectedness has very precise implications: the rehumanization of the perpetrator. Forgiveness was granted, reconciliation was offered, with the assumption that reciprocating acts would follow in South Africa: the forgiven would regain their humanity through restoring what they have destroyed. But because the dominant world reads forgiveness primarily within a particular Christian context, Mandela's forgiveness is regarded as something unique, like Jesus', and, like Jesus', is bestowed on an undeserving group while, in fact, for some South Africans, forgiveness may be regarded as a natural extension of a belief in interconnectedness. One can say that Mandela has forgiven the beneficiaries of apartheid because he assumed they would try to rehumanize themselves by assisting in building a better life for impoverished South Africans.

But Mandela's collectiveness also works on another, more disruptive level. To insist that one is embedded in one's community is to impress on the world that one is not an exception. In one of his speeches, Mandela said:

> To the extent to which I was able to achieve anything, I know this is because I am a product of the people of South Africa. I am a product of the rural masses who inspired in me the pride in our past and the spirit of resistance. I am the product of the workers of South Africa, who in mines, factories, fields and offices of our country have pursued the principle that the interests of each are founded in the common interest of all (quoted in Krog 2003: 220).

In other words: you cannot admire me *and* reject or discriminate against black people; you cannot admire my stance on forgiveness (as Barack Obama did in the foreword to Mandela's recent book, 2010: xiii) *and* celebrate proudly the killing of another (as Obama did when he announced the death of Osama bin Laden). European leaders who had rushed to be seen with Mandela kept on instigating and doing things that were devoid of inclusiveness. The essence of what they bring across is their own intolerance—and so the cycle of intolerance continues.

Why is the essence of Mandela so consistently distorted? Indeed, why bother with him at all? Along the line of Žižek's argument of liberal communism, I want to suggest a reason the powerful in the world need an over-representation of the Mandela-as-forgiver icon: he is used to keep the conditions of the privileged intact. Through him we can talk tolerance while doing the opposite: telling immigrants that they are 'guests who must accommodate themselves to the cultural values that define the host society' (Žižek 2009: 35).

What is ultimately wrong with Mandela's portrayed tolerance is the intolerance of his portrayers about everything that appeals to a fundamental redress of inequality.

Near the end of *Kaapse Kaalkoppen*, the Suske and Wiske group is safely back in their suburban sitting room in Belgium and they express their sadness that they couldn't at least save something to cure arachnophobia. The doorbell rings. Aunt Sidonia opens the door. There, in the awful spider costume, is friend and father figure Lambik! Fear of spiders is misplaced: within the spider is one's own brother! Or is the comic saying something else? Is it

FIGURE 6. Arachnophobia

perhaps saying that one's brother is actually whom one should fear?

The choice of arachnophobia (in contrast to all the other phobias) to find a cure for begs analysis. One of the first philosophers attempting to explain African philosophy to Westerners was the priest Father Tempels (see Chapter 7), in this case also a Belgian. He used the term 'spider's web' to describe the African's sense of being interconnected: 'Nothing moves in this [African] universe of forces without influencing other forces by its movement. The world of forces is held like a spider's web of which no single thread can be caused to vibrate without shaking the whole network' (quoted in Gibson 2001: 36).

One can imagine that a society which places a high premium on individuality could feel uncomfortable about a 'web' of deeply interconnecting fields and forces. Implicit in this text, then, is that the desire for tolerance (accepting the interconnected web) is undermined and under attack by arachnophobia (fear of the interconnected web). Intellectually, the writer accepts that humanity should live as interconnected, but psychologically the text has to safeguard itself against the consequences of acknowledging the connectedness. The cure is destroyed; arachnophobia remains. And, by othering Mandela, the story carries no contradiction.

Both plot and style are used—had to be used—in such a way that Mandela's web-forming capacities are frozen.

CHAPTER TEN

Reading with the Skin:
Liberalism, Race and Power in J. M. Coetzee's
Age of Iron *and* Disgrace

It is a privilege for any serious reader to share a country with the kind of exceptional creativity that is recognized by a Nobel Prize. Grappling with the ways in which South African realities are used by remarkable authors to talk about the world is a rich and often disturbingly challenging experience.

I focus in this chapter on two novels by J. M. Coetzee that bookend the most revolutionary decade in South African history: *Age of Iron* (1990) and *Disgrace* (1999). Both novels, particularly the latter, have occasioned widely divergent interpretations and considerable controversy. It seems worthwhile exploring why.

Liberalism and Age of Iron

Age of Iron was published in 1990, the same year that F. W. de Klerk gave his groundbreaking speech announcing the release of Nelson Mandela and the unbanning or decriminalization of the liberation movements. However, the book reflects nothing of the new hope for South Africa. It is set in the 1980s, when South Africans were living through the iron age of what we called the 'Total

Onslaught', being told that the country was besieged militarily, politically, culturally, ideologically, economically and socially by communism and radical black nationalists. Reading *Age of Iron* in 1990 was like discovering at last the words to articulate this terrible period of cruelty and brutal debasement.

The 80s were a crucial period in the history of South African liberalism. As the struggle against apartheid intensified, so did the challenge to liberals to find appropriate ways in which to oppose a violent system. The 'true-blue liberals' of Jill Wentzel's *The Liberal Slideaway* (1995) opposed all violence (but without propagating pacifism) and articulated their disgust with those other liberals who 'sanctimoniously understood' the violence of the liberation struggle and refused to condemn the young comrades. As if this dissent inside the liberal fold was not enough, liberals became fair game everywhere.

Most Afrikaners had always heavily resented liberalism, seeing it as morally arrogant and condescending. From quite another perspective, the academic and revolutionary Neville Alexander had written as far back as 1974 that '[l]iberalism is a greater danger in the long run to the struggle of the oppressed than fascism; for the very reason that it seems to speak with the tongue of the people' (quoted in Husemeyer 1997: 8). The grassroots antiapartheid Black Consciousness Movement (BCM) and its leader Steve Biko (famous for the slogan 'Black is beautiful') made no bones about the fact that he regarded 'white liberals' in particular as the main danger to black emancipation. In the same vein, Itumeleng Mosala of the political movement called the Azanian People's Organization

(AZAPO) later said: 'White liberals love black people more than blacks love themselves, but they choose their blacks.' According to him, '[l]iberalism is rooted in individualism and that is part of the problem in our society, it is rooted in possessiveness' (quoted in ibid.: 225).

Age of Iron depicts Elizabeth Curren, an old classics professor who is slowly dying of cancer during the last terrible years of apartheid. She has been against the regime all her life but finds herself face-to-face with the horrors of the system as life in Cape Town disintegrates into violence. As the story unfolds, profound questions are being asked about liberal values and, as Coetzee himself suggests, the novel plays itself out in the last days of 'liberal-humanist posturing'. As protagonist, Mrs Curren does not posture, however—she cares. Her caring is not out of charity ('the spirit of charity had perished in this country [. . . T]hose who accept charity despise it, while those who give give with a despairing heart' [Coetzee 1990: 19]) but because she lives the essence of liberalism as a concern for all people. While stopping blood from a wound she comments: 'blood is one: a pool of life dispersed among us in separate existences, but belonging to nature together: lent, not given: held in common, in trust, to be preserved' (ibid.: 58).

Unlike Wentzel's 'slideaway' liberals, Elizabeth condemns all violence. She says, 'This killing, this bloodletting in the name of comradeship, I detest it with all my heart and soul' (ibid.: 136). But she is also increasingly aware of the institutionalized violence in which she is unavoidably complicit and can see the detestable inhumanity as its consequence:

Let me tell you, when I walk upon this land, this
South Africa, I have a gathering feeling of walking upon black faces. [. . .] They lie there heavy
and obdurate, waiting for my feet to pass, waiting for me to go, waiting to be raised up again.
Millions of figures of pig-iron floating under the
skin of the earth. The age of iron waiting to
return (ibid.: 115).

She links up with Mr Vercueil, whom she found on
the street in front of her house. In the novel he is a man
without property or ambition, belonging to no community, the kind of individual who refuses to 'earn' any rights
or to act in a responsible way to claim these rights. Yet
when two black boys beat him because of his drinking
habits, Elizabeth protects him against these 'new puritans,
holding to the rule, holding up the rule' (ibid.: 114).

Elizabeth insists on the right of the individual to have
an individual vocabulary and viewpoint: 'They are not
Yes, they are not No. What is living inside me is something else, another word. And I am fighting for it, in my
manner, fighting for it not to be stifled. [. . .] I am arguing
for the unheard' (ibid.: 133–4).

Liberals have often been accused of 'bending over
blackwards' to atone for their guilt. Elizabeth prefers the
word 'shame': 'I have cancer from the accumulation of
shame I have endured in my life' (ibid.: 132). 'As long as I
was ashamed I knew I had not wandered into dishonour.
That was the use of shame: as a touchstone' (ibid.: 150).

She also accepts being judged by others. Florence is
the black woman who has been her house servant and
Elizabeth recognizes that 'Florence is the judge [. . .]. The

court belongs to Florence; it is I who pass under review. If the life I live is an examined life, it is because for ten years I have been under examination in the court of Florence' (ibid.: 129).

In many ways, Elizabeth represents what was highly admirable in South African liberalism, trying to open up spaces in which individuals could stay humane within an inhumane system. In one of the most moving moments of the book, she articulates the enormous challenge facing any humane world view:

> How shall I be saved? By doing what I do not want to do. That is the first step: that I know. I must love, first of all, the unlovable. I must love, for instance, this child. Not the bright little Bheki, but this one. He is here for a reason. He is my salvation. But I do not love him [. . .] Nor do I want to love him enough to love him despite myself [. . .] I cannot find it in my heart to love, to want to love, to want to want to love [. . .] Therefore let me utter my second, dubious word. Not wanting to love him, how true can I say my love is for you? For love is not like hunger [. . .] When one loves, one loves more. The more I love you, the more I ought to love him. The less I love him, the less, perhaps, I love you (ibid.: 124–5).

To read Coetzee is also hard in a personal way. Inevitably, there are the moments where one's 'own' people (Afrikaners, blacks, coloureds) enter the narrative, and no matter how one distances oneself, there is no escaping the feeling of annihilation. In my case, it is Afrikaners:

'Cetshwayo, Dingane in white skins [. . .] Huge bull-testicles pressing down on their wives, their children, pressing the spark out of them [. . .] Their feat [. . .] to have raised stupidity to a virtue. To stupefy [. . .]. The Boar War' (1999: 25–6).

The self-horror is upon one before one manages to wedge a distance between oneself and the 'Boars'. I believe that most South Africans read Coetzee's work with pangs of recognition, to a greater or lesser extent, as Mrs Curren spares no one: 'We who marry South Africa become South Africans: ugly, sullen, torpid, the only sign of life in us a quick flash of fangs when we are crossed [. . .] A bad-tempered old hound snoozing in the doorway, taking its time to die' (1990: 64).

Disgrace *and the End of Liberalism*

Disgrace appeared at the end of a decade that saw, to the bewilderment and dismay of many liberals, how both they and their political beliefs had come under unprecedented attack from black intellectuals. In newspapers, academic magazines and television debates, liberals were characterized repeatedly as the hypocritical, arrogant and patronizing whites who had refused to get into the trenches during the liberation struggle yet now wanted to dictate the shape of post-apartheid South Africa.

The very word 'liberal' had come to mean its opposite. It no longer meant progressive or tolerant (or as in America the opposite of 'conservative', or as in Europe the opposite of 'socialist') but, in fact, racist and conservative—'South Africa's last credible instrument of privilege' was the label given to it by Kader Asmal and Ronald

Roberts (cited in Husemeyer 1997: 90). After the debate
between the judge Dennis Davis and University of South
Africa (UNISA) rector Barney Pityana and the incident in
which 12 white academics questioned the credentials of
Professor William Makgoba at the University of the Wit-
watersrand, the word 'liberal' was often used to refer to
all English-speaking white people. To their surprise, even
white radicals and activists (like Davis) found themselves
classified as liberal and the word came to exude the sort
of moral outrage associated with terms like 'fascist' and
'apartheid'. This usage was not confined to black South
Africans. Writing in *De Kat,* Dries van Heerden, an
Afrikaner and former deputy editor of the *Sunday Times*,
simply described liberals as the 'New Right' (cited in ibid.:
208). Margaret Legum, an activist and social reformer spe-
cializing in economics, spoke of liberal fundamentalists
who had become the political conservatives of our time
(ibid.: 117). Although liberal ideals were entrenched in the
new Constitution with its Bill of Rights, more and more
South Africans came, rightly or wrongly, to regard white
English-speaking 'liberals' as the biggest obstacle to real
power and real change.

Within this context, *Disgrace*, with its protagonist
David Lurie, ageing professor of Romantic poetry,
stepped into the world of South African readers. He
seduced Melanie, one of his students, and his refusal to
show any contrition saw him dismissed from his job. He
went to stay with his lesbian daughter in the Eastern Cape
but was forced to come to terms with an attack on the
farm in which Lucy was raped and impregnated and he
was violently assaulted. One of the attackers turned out

to be related to Petrus, the black man who lived on Lucy's farm. Lucy refused to report the incident to the police, decided to keep the child and made a deal with Petrus: he got the land in exchange for protection.

I am not aware of any other book that has been so incessantly discussed at so many gatherings and dinner tables and in informal conversations by so many different categories of readers. Even elsewhere in Africa and abroad, one came to expect that at some point someone would sit opposite one and ask, 'Now, what did you think of *Disgrace*?'

More interesting than the absolute obsession with trying to assess what the book was saying about the new South Africa was the sharp contrast in the interpretations it evoked. Like the O. J. Simpson case in the US, the book generally divided its readers—cleanly, as if cut by a very sharp knife—into a white group and a black group in terms of interpretation. It didn't matter how sensitively you read it; you would inevitably find that your final reading would lie close to the colour of your skin.

Disgrace also became the banner for those (whites) who prided themselves on being politically incorrect. Not only on the electronic literary-critical chat group LitNet but also in several reviews to be found on the Internet, it was claimed that *Disgrace* was evidence against what they regarded as the tyranny of the politically correct. It was brave of Coetzee, the reactionary language activist Dan Roodt would say, to tackle crime and the fact that blacks condone it (2003). While everyone else was wallowing in the past (referring to the TRC and the texts flowing from it), Coetzee looked at 'now' and spoke out about the atrocities. It was amazing and amusing to discover how many white readers, most of them probably facing the wrong end of affirmative action and transformation, simply regarded Lurie as an honourable bearer of white liberal values. It was equally amazing and amusing to discover how many black readers, most of them probably facing men like Lurie at their workplaces, simply regarded Lurie as the all-pervasive white eye judging black as evil. Neither of these groups grasps that the eye and behaviour of Lurie are virtually the same as the eye and behaviour of Petrus. But I will return to that later. I believe that the key to these opposing readings of the book lies within two issues: whether you regard Petrus as the antagonist or the mirror image of Professor Lurie, and whether you regard what happened between Lurie and Melanie as rape.

In the book's opening pages, Lurie introduces his colleagues and himself as 'burdened with upbringings inappropriate to the tasks they are set to perform; clerks in a post-religious age' (Coetzee 1999: 4). Their time has clearly passed. The rest of the book bears this out. Lurie flounders trying to find guidelines within the burnt-out wreck of a certain kind of liberal upbringing. Unlike Mrs Curren, Lurie refuses to do anything out of the goodness of his heart (charity): 'It sounds suspiciously like community service, trying to make reparation for past misdeeds. I'll do it as long as I don't have to become a better person. I am not prepared to be reformed' (ibid.: 77).

Following in the footsteps of his favourite Romantic poet, Byron, Lurie believes that '[a] woman's beauty does not belong to her alone. It is part of the bounty she brings to the world. She has a duty to share it' (ibid.: 16). Twice he says: 'She does not own herself' (ibid.: 18). Petrus sees women in the same way, in fact. He moves from 'bounty' to 'booty' and regards Lucy as his benefactor, someone who has to share what she has with him and his family.

When Lurie seduces his student, he glibly describes it in the least offensive terms possible: 'Not rape, not quite that, but undesired nevertheless, undesired to the core. As though she had decided to go slack, die within herself for the duration, like a rabbit when the jaws of the fox close on its neck' (ibid.: 25). Petrus makes a similar remark after the rape of Lucy: 'It is very bad, a very bad thing. But you are all right now' (ibid.: 114). Lurie thinks of Byron: 'Among the legions of countesses and kitchen-maids Byron pushed himself onto there were no doubt those who called it rape' (ibid.: 160). But he does once bring himself to link his actions directly to those of Petrus: 'Rape, god of chaos and mixture, violator of seclusions. Raping a lesbian worse than raping a virgin: more of a blow' (ibid.: 105).

Lucy likewise links the two acts by throwing the question to her father: 'Hatred [. . .] When it comes to men and sex, David, nothing surprises me any more. Maybe, for men, hating the woman makes sex more exciting. When you have sex with someone strange [. . .] Isn't it a bit like killing? [. . . D]oesn't it feel like murder, like getting away with murder?' (ibid.: 158)

Defending himself in his mind, Lurie uses all the attributes of Romanticism as reasons for his behaviour: like a true Romantic, he gives primacy to emotion over reason, to sensuality over sensibility, to rebellion over conformity, to mystery over revelation. It was an impulse. He had 'become the servant of Eros' (ibid.: 52). Melanie had 'enriched his life' (ibid.: 192). He would plead guilty but not admit that he was wrong. In the post-TRC era, when South Africans were quite obsessed with confession and forgiveness, Lurie refuses to express any contrition, offer any confession or, initially, any apology. Repentance belongs to another world: 'Recantation, self-criticism, public apology. I'm old-fashioned, I would prefer simply to be put against a wall and shot' (ibid.: 66). Unlike Mrs Curren, he refuses to use shame as a touchstone but attempts to search out the unattainable. Coleridge once said that the secret of Byron is in revolt; that to him nature and humanity are antagonists and he cleaves to nature, that he even would take her by violence to mark his alienation and severance from man.

Proudly Lurie cuts himself off from his colleagues. Unlike Mrs Curren, he refuses to be judged by the court of Florence. His attitude in front of the 'community of the righteous' is that of someone who believes that he is defending a crucial principle. Yet he is unable to profess any overriding principle when asked by Professor Manas Mathabane to agree to a simple straightforward paragraph: 'I acknowledge without reservation serious abuses of the human rights of the complainant, as well as abuse of the authority delegated to me by the University. I sincerely apologize to both parties and accept whatever appropriate penalty may be imposed' (ibid.: 57)

Does he deny that he abused Melanie? Why is it so impossible to apologize? Does he think everything should be as before? When his daughter confronts him, he says he stood for 'the rights of desire' (ibid.: 89), but he clearly does not consider how those very rights may infringe on the rights of others. When his ex-wife confronts him and urges him to name the principle he stood up for before the committee, he says: 'Freedom of speech. Freedom to remain silent' (ibid.: 188). Whereupon she responds: 'You have always been a great deceiver and a great self-deceiver' (ibid.: 188).

In a letter to the editor of the *Mail and Guardian*, Peter du Preez described a version of a liberal apparently once articulated at Cambridge: they believe 'the surest way to get other people to look up to them is to look down on themselves. There's no way to attack these people. You tell them they are exploiters and they agree brightly. They chalk it up to their credit' (1996). Lurie is this kind of liberal. But his real objection, of course, lies in the way in which his private life as an individual has been turned into a public affair with requirements straight from the TRC testimonies: 'These are puritanical times. Private life is public business [. . .]. They wanted a spectacle: breast-beating, remorse, tears if possible' (Coetzee 1999: 66).

The rape of his own daughter exposes the extent of Lurie's moral bankruptcy. He wants Lucy to make it public, to go to the police, to lay a charge. Like Melanie's boyfriend had confronted him, he wants to confront Petrus and make him acknowledge those very things he himself refused to acknowledge: 'Violation: that is the word he would like to force out of Petrus. Yes, it was a violation, he would like to hear Petrus say; yes it was an outrage' (ibid.: 119). Lucy rejects her father's request. The very man who refused any 'appropriate steps' against himself now wants to call the police, because 'if you buckle at this point, if you fail, you will not be able to live with yourself' (ibid.: 134). No universal values in this argument.

Gradually, the mirror moments multiply: during a confrontation, Petrus calls one of the rapists 'my people' and Lurie thinks, 'So that is it. No more lies. *My people*. As naked an answer as he could wish' (ibid.: 201). One page further Lurie says: '"This is not how we do things." *We*: he is on the point of saying, *We Westerners*' (ibid.: 202; italics in the original).

To return to the two assumptions above, I think there are enough indications that Professor Lurie is not a knight in shining liberal armour. Whites may empathize with his loss of power but he is a tattered shadow of the fierce courage of Mrs Curren in her relentless efforts to be a good person.

In a review of *Disgrace* published in Dutch, Salman Rushdie points out that it is a writer's prerogative to create a black character that is inarticulate and menacing (2000). But it becomes problematic when the author seems to be in cahoots with that sentiment. Is that the case here? Is Coetzee supporting Lurie's view of women and blacks? In a lecture on Coetzee, David Attwell reminds his audience to

> look for the subject [in Coetzee's work], locate that subject within the discourses of the culture being represented, and from that tension, try to understand the subject's ironies, longings, failures, triumphs of insight, linguistic implosions

and recoveries. There is seldom what we could call a positive philosophy that emerges from this struggle, but there is always an expansion of language, a breaking of rules, a re-thinking of dominant categories, and a creativity which is constantly in search of a place not previously known or understood, a place, in other words, of transformation (2004: 116).

In *Disgrace,* Coetzee does not give Lurie an insight beyond his deficient cultural and historical frame of reference. In Lucy's words, Lurie is like 'one of those three monkeys: who does not see'. Lurie doesn't see himself as a white version of Petrus but Coetzee provides the reader with enough convincing parallels to make Petrus and Lurie echo one another in troubling ways. In other words, Coetzee is not in cahoots with the sentiments of Lurie; he is, in fact, exposing Lurie by showing his doppelgänger in the image of Petrus protecting the rapists. That many readers read them as opposites and not parallels says less about the novel and more about the separate lives of whites and blacks in South Africa and our need to find an honourable position in relation to our past. It is because of the parallels Coetzee establishes between Petrus and Lurie (and Byron's characters) that he cannot be accused of being in support of racist stereotyping. Rather, it appears that Coetzee finds himself, like Byron, 'conflated with his own poetic creations' (1999: 31).

The rape of Lucy gives the reader occasion to ask deeper questions about the power relationships in the novel. I would like to refer briefly to three texts that deal with rape in a way that resonates particularly with Lucy's story as well as with the account of the earlier rape which we tend to forget: Lurie's rape of a woman of colour.

The first is the story of Lucrece. It is used by Shakespeare (and before him Livy, Ovid and Chaucer) as one of the founding myths of patriarchy. The text of Shakespeare's poem *The Rape of Lucrece* (1594) is important for two reasons: first, the rape of Lucrece is used in various ways to authorize revenge, revenge to comprise revolution and revolution to establish legitimate government; and second, the text of *Lucrece* is a site of struggle between speech and suppression of speech, between female and male control of the narrative (Kahn 1976; see also Higgins and Silver 1991).

The second text is from the work of Ida B. Wells, a black woman who devoted most of her activist career to the late nineteenth-century anti-lynching campaign in the US. She counselled white women: 'Write [say] nothing, nothing at all. It will be used against all black men and therefore against all of us' (Walker 1981: 94; see also Dorr 2004). Lucy's refusal to report her rape to the police can therefore be read as a strategy to stop a cycle of violence legitimated by the economy of vengeance.

The last text is that of Eldridge Cleaver, radical black activist and founder member of the militant Black Panthers, the African American revolutionary leftist organization. Cleaver said:

> Rape was an insurrectionary act. It delighted me that I was defying and trampling upon the white man's law, upon his system of values, and that I was defiling his women—and this point, I

believe, was the most satisfying to me because I was very resentful over the historical fact of how the white man has used black woman. I felt I was getting revenge (1968: 28).

Rape is a crime of power, anger or control. Lurie used his position of power to have sex with Melanie. The three black men used their positions of anger and control to have sex with Lucy. The differences lie in the outcome of these rapes and, for our purposes, the racial way in which they have been interpreted.

Husbands, brothers and fathers of rape victims usually exercise their social power by pressing charges, demanding that the legal system respond to the harm inflicted on their families. This happens in the case of Melanie. Her boyfriend physically reclaims her body by chasing Lurie away the moment he shows his face, while her father takes the case to the university authorities.

Narratives of black-on-white assault verbally map the contours round appropriate and inappropriate relations while at the same time drawing the boundaries of blackness and whiteness. Lucy's rapists act violently, brutally and are 'filled with hatred', while Lurie's sexual interactions with women of colour have the civilized veneer of literature, wine, music and services paid either in currency or with higher grades. It is these luxurious wrappings that, I believe, caused many readers to accept Lurie's act as reasonably 'appropriate' and the black rapists' act as grossly inappropriate.

The men in these two women's lives also have different levels or modes of access to old and new social power systems, and cases of black-on-white assault often constitute a vehicle through which black males can claim a place among white males under a different guise of power.

During the years of white rule, black men raping could be read as signalling their desire to share in the patriarchy, to lay claim to manhood with the same privileges as white men over women both white and black. But power has changed hands in South Africa. White men like Lurie no longer have that kind of politically legitimate power, while Melanie, through her father and friend, can now access power and receive justice. Melanie's father says: ' "How the mighty has fallen!" Fallen? Yes, there has been a fall. But mighty? Does mighty describe him? He [Lurie] thinks of himself as obscure and growing obscurer. A figure from the margins of history' (Coetzee 1999: 167).

Yet there is a twist. Melanie's family gets justice but she has handed her narrative over to the men in her life and to the new authorities. She has given up her own power to control it. Lucy, on the other hand, does not allow this to happen. She forbids her father to take over her narrative and safeguards the description of events she alone experienced, telling him, 'You weren't there. You don't know what happened' (ibid.: 140). She acts with impatience when he confesses: 'I did nothing. I did not save you' (ibid.: 157). It is not important, she implies. She does not expect men to protect her. She also does not report the rape to the police but uses it to negotiate a future for herself as an equal partner from an unequal past.

Initially, in responding to Melanie's charges, Lurie refuses to negotiate. His refusal has a larger significance.

By spurning the new human rights–sensitive authority at the university, he refuses to operate from a diminished power base. But the assault on Lucy confronts him with himself. He has failed in his duty as a father to protect his daughter. Topping this humiliation is Lucy's refusal to let him shape her account of the rape or see official justice done.

Following Cleaver's logic that rape is political revenge, and combining it with Coetzee's positioning and presenting of these two acts of violation, one could conclude that symbolically Lucy bears the brunt of the actions of her father—the deeds of one generation visited upon the next. In a sense, one could say that Lucy is raped by her own father.

When Lucy is raped, Lurie starts to change—a point in his life which Attwell calls a 'place of transformation'. Words like 'confess', 'guilt', 'contrition' enter his vocabulary. He confesses to Lucy, he asks forgiveness for being such an inadequate guide in her life, he asks pardon of Melanie's father, he bows to the ground in a gesture of pleading in front of Melanie's mother and sister—all of this done clumsily, insecurely, sometimes cynically. However, he is taking the 'appropriate steps' he so vehemently rejected at the beginning to lead a life of penitence.

> I am being punished for what happened between myself and your daughter. I am sunk into a state of disgrace from which it will not be easy to lift myself. It is not a punishment I have refused. I do not murmur against it. On the contrary I am living it out from day to day, trying to accept disgrace as my state of being. Is it enough for God,

do you think, that I live in disgrace without term?
(Coetzee 1999: 172)

But Melanie's father asks the big question: 'When we are found out then we are very sorry. The question is, what lesson have we learned? The question is, what are we going to do now that we are sorry?' (ibid.).

Lurie answers by spending the rest of his life near Lucy, hoping to assist her, by giving up his dream of the haunting opera ('Mad indeed. How can he ever explain, to them, to their parents, to D Village, what Teresa [the central character in the opera Lurie is writing] and her lover have done to deserve being brought back to this world?' [ibid.: 212]) and by being kind to dogs—those who do not claim anything, who did not ask for anything, who have given up everything ('like a dog' [ibid.: 156]). Lurie admits to himself that he takes over the role of the dog-man from Petrus.

Conclusion

The 'discourses of the culture being represented' in *Age of Iron* and *Disgrace* at the beginning and end of the 1990s are those of a changing liberalism. But while Elizabeth Curren infuses the liberal posture with genuine engagement and concern for the rights of all people, David Lurie is interested only in his own rights and resists all the buzzwords of the era, such as guilt, confession and accountability—until the rape of his daughter.

Disgrace also follows the unique event of the TRC. After three centuries of a dominant white discourse, suddenly, on a daily basis for a period of two to three years, thousands of black narratives were put out into the public domain: victim, perpetrator, horror and unimaginable suffering. No creative artist could have been immune to them. But whereas most subsequent texts preferred to deal with past political experiences, confessions and guilt, Coetzee masterfully took the very topical, but what was regarded as very apolitical, theme of crime and turned it into a powerful metaphor of injustice done to a continent. The consequences of that have taken their toll to such an extent that despite belated attempts at contrition, Professor Lurie has no role to play in the new relationships between Petrus, his family and Lucy, Melanie, her boyfriend and her family. One respects his final focus of care on the most powerless in his society.

But this change in himself and in his own view of what he has done does not seem to alter the racial reading of his actions. Many white readers feel great empathy with the academic (regarding him as perhaps a bit reckless, but who is perfect?) for being forced to live a life caring for dogs; many black readers feel uncomfortable that they are once again stereotyped as unfair brutes cruelly depriving well-educated white men of their rightful lives. Both these readings, black and white, are possible only if the reader chooses *not* to regard Lurie's intercourse with Melanie as rape.

Disgrace is a book filled with mirroring events. The scope of this chapter prevents me from comparing Lurie's sleeping with Soraya and his sleeping with Bev; Lurie 'peeping' at Melanie on stage, causing rage in her boyfriend, and Pollux 'peeping' at Lucy, causing rage in Lurie, etc. These are not opposing but mirroring events, which emphasize similarity: ways across the gulfs of social divisions. Coetzee explicitly allows Lurie to put himself in the rapist's mind when he says near the end of the book: 'He [Lurie] can be there, be the men [rapists], inhabit them, fill them with the ghost of himself. The question is, does he have it in him to be the woman' (ibid.: 160). Can he (and henceforth Petrus) be the Other? Mrs Curren forces herself to be the Other. She empathizes with everyone she comes in contact with. Lurie, who previously functioned well only in the presence of immature girls, is slowly learning how to listen to grown-up, ordinary women.

If there are more parallels between Lurie and Petrus than there are differences, then Coetzee has been subjected to grossly racialized readings in South Africa. However, if one considers most of the reviews by international scholars, these perceptions are also prevalent elsewhere. This means that people everywhere tend to read more with their skin than with the analytical side of their brain.

One dilemma remains. The mirror images of Lurie and Petrus may remove the racial discomfort about *Disgrace,* but they do not explain what is seen by many as an ending of unqualified bleakness. How does the decade in which a long history of oppression and conflict in South Africa shifts decisively in the direction of peaceful coexistence bring a writer to the point of not being able to give any character a tenable position? The informing vision of the shift in South Africa is something which several conflict-ridden countries seem unable to sustain, with devastating consequences. However, Coetzee seems to offer the scantest signs of hope for sustained change for the better in South Africa. If the university committee is as pathetic as Lurie, if Melanie's father is as pathetic as Petrus, if Lucy is nothing but a *boervrou* (farmer's wife), then it becomes difficult to find the 'space of transformation' Attwell refers to.

The beginning of the 90s had Mrs Curren burning like a flame. The end of the 90s—a decade in which, despite numerous difficulties, there had been a signal advance in humanity in South Africa—produces a morally bankrupt Professor Lurie and his morally bankrupt mirror image, Petrus. Coetzee warns with prophetic insight that an entire society cast in the same mould is only a step away.

CHAPTER ELEVEN

Pieces in the Anatomy of Loss

Chest

> *Vladso, West Flanders.*
> *The edge of the rustling Praatbos.*
> *In front of the* Treurende Ouderpaar, *kneeling in grief.*[1]

I feel heavy. As if grief has the weight of stone. As if grief has the hands of the father: one clenching the upper arm in petrifying rage, the other holding the ribs so that they do not burst with grief. Grief has the stone face of the father. Grief wears the pitiful shoes of stone. Grief has the bowed head of the mother. Grief is wrapped in the stone cloak, which wears her down. Unable to lift a face to the world. Arms and hands holding the chest, where the blunt grater of grief shreds and shreds and shreds all the heart and soul. The upper lip and cheeks are set in the loneliest of stone.

Grief drenches my bones. I turn away. I walk back to my whole life.

And as I am walking back across the killing fields of Flanders, I am puzzled by the fact that there is no contact

---

1 The *Treurende Ouderpaar* (*Grieving Parents*) sculpture by Käthe Kollwitz is in the Vladslo German war cemetery, near the Praatbos forest in West Flanders.

FIGURE 8. Käthe Kollwitz, *Treurende Ouderpaar*, Vladslo, Germany

between the grieving husband and wife. They are kneeling on two separate pedestals. Nothing in their body language or in their design gives them any contact. As if to say: there is no succour to be found anywhere after the death of a child, not even (and perhaps especially not) with your spouse. I find it odd. Surely the death of a child is the one moment where a father and mother are equally involved and can comfort one another because they both made and loved this child. I find the two parents hauntingly moving, but I baulk at the separateness of their grief.

★

The Afrikaners also have a well-known and much-revered statuary of two women expressing the grief emanating from the concentration camps of the Anglo-Boer War. The emaciated corpse of a little girl lies in the lap of an older, seated woman, sunken into sorrow, while a younger woman stands next to her, her hand on the older woman's shoulder in a gesture of comfort, as she looks straight ahead, into the future.

This statuary at the Women's Memorial in Bloemfontein taught me at a very young age that we can comfort one another in grief, because of life.

So I couldn't understand why Käthe Kollwitz was saying with her two figures: in grief, a father and a mother are absolutely alone.

Nervous System

About seven years after this visit to Flanders, I reported as a radio journalist on the testimonies of apartheid victims before the TRC. Many parents testified.

The testimonies soon made clear that the death of a child creates a grief unlike any other (see Schlosser 1997). The severest loss is of that sense of invulnerability that allows one to lead a normal life—to go out into the world, to drive a car, to let one's children visit others—this is totally destroyed. The death of a child brings existential despair: parents feel frightened, alone and incapacitated. Events that once brought families together, such as birthdays and holidays, become reminders of loss.

The grieving parents at the TRC taught us about guilt:

Immediately I noticed a trickle of blood on her shoulder as she was lying face down. I pressed her to the ground and counted to ten waiting for this explosion. Nothing happened. I turned her over and she just slumped in my arms (Krog 1998: 228).

I lifted my daughter up, felt for her pulse, but my hand just sunk in her neck. I laid her down on her back, tried to close her eyes, but they would not close. This is when the realisation really hit me that she was dead [. . .]. I feel responsible and guilty. I have lived with that for the past ten years (ibid.).

As Lindy's father, responsible for her existence, I accepted the responsibility of raising and caring for her to the best of my ability . . . [W]hen our children become adults, and more than equal to their parents, that is when the battles all seem worth it and many of life's mysteries [about our offspring] seem to fall into place . . . but I and my wife, Jeanette, have been robbed. Robbed of our own flesh and blood. Robbed of the most natural form of happiness that humans can experience . . . No longer do we hear the voice on the telephone say, 'Howdy Pops, how are the brother and the mother?' . . . You see, sir, we were ordinary people, doing ordinary work, in our own ordinary and uncomplicated manner . . . so why did she have to die so young and by such violent means? (Ibid.: 229)

It seems that grieving families are often plagued by their own guilt. The sudden death of a child leaves all sorts of issues between the dead and the family unresolved. Siblings feel guilty that they have survived. Parents are torn by self-doubt. Aren't parents supposed to keep their children safe from harm at any cost? It seems that the death of a child becomes a kind of looming icon of the profound failure of the parents to protect their child.

We learnt about the effects of grief on the body.

> I just had major surgery which I trace as a direct result of the stress and trauma that resulted after the Heidelberg incident [an attack on a restaurant in Cape Town by the Azanian People's Liberation Army in which four people were killed]. It has been demonstrated that cancer of the colon results from tremendous stress. First my heart was ripped out and now half my gut. I am happy that you are well. The day you killed my child you ripped my heart out (ibid.).

It seems that the internalized grief felt by parents brings about a variety of serious illnesses. Some parents soon follow their children to the grave.

> So the truth that Käthe drank from was illuminated over and over in the testimonies before the commission: 'My wife has told you her grief. She preferred to talk directly to the killers. My grief is different. I talk to you, Mr Chairman, as the person who decides on their amnesty' (ibid.: 230).

It seems that men and women grieve differently: 'Suffice to say, my marriage has suffered irreparable harm. My wife suffers from extreme anxiety and nervous tension. We are both on constant medication' (ibid.).

The differences and discrepancies in grieving often create resentment and there is a high divorce rate among grieving parents.

Käthe Kollwitz knew. She looked into a mirror darkly.

Hand

When Käthe came down the steps of her house in Berlin, she saw a man standing in the foyer and her husband in spasms of bewilderment. The man had come to tell them that their youngest son, Peter, had been killed in action at Diksmuide in West Flanders on 23 October 1914, early in the First World War. Käthe wrote:

> Everything has changed, forever, and I have become poorer. My whole motherlife already lies behind me. Many times I have such an unbearable longing to have my two sons with me again, the one on my right side and the other on my left, to dance with them, as before, when it became spring and Peter runs towards me with flowers (Seys and Kollwitz 1964: 35; my translation).

Two years after Peter's death, Käthe was trying to come to terms with it through her art. She made a drawing of a mother holding her dead son in her arms. 'I can make hundreds of similar drawings, without being able to approach Peter. *I search for him and know that I could find him in my work.* But everything I produce is so weak and unsatisfying' (ibid.: 39; my translation, emphasis added).

She wanted to make a relief of Peter—his body stretched out full length, with the father at one end and the mother at the other. Then her idea changed to Peter suspended above the parents, with his arms outstretched.

But nothing seemed to really work for her. She started with the father, then abandoned him and started with the mother. For weeks she worked on the exhaustion of the shoulders, the back, the arms—slowly and with difficulty. Then she took up the father again but stopped immediately: 'I cannot do it' (ibid.: 40; my translation).

Next she transformed Peter into a figure of the German Youth Movement, to accompany the slogan 'Never again war'. This generalization also didn't help her find him.

Ten years after Peter's death, Käthe decided to make two full separate figures—first moulded in clay and then carved in granite. She persevered through several mishaps and setbacks but, finally, on the evening before the work was finished, she could write in her diary: 'In this evening in my work I have been fully with you, my son' (ibid.: 53; my translation).

The sculptures of the mother and the father, without Peter, were moved to the cemetery at Praatbos. Both Käthe and her husband went with the stone parents. The two figures were hoisted onto pedestals with particular care such that the mother is tilted slightly forward, in contrast to the father, who is looking up, not towards the horizon, but at the grave. Two petrified parents kneeling at the entry to the cemetery. And that was the closest Käthe could come to regaining Peter: to plant a hawthorn rose on his grave in the presence of eternally grieving parents.

But grief for Käthe was not over. She lost her husband in 1940. She and her work were rejected by the Nazis for 'misportraying' German mothers. The worst blow was that her grandson, named after his uncle Peter, was killed in action in Russia during the Second World War. Two wars cost her a son and a grandson. She had to flee Berlin, after which her house and everything in it was destroyed by aerial bombing.

Vertebra

The TRC commissioner spreads the photos on the table. He is reporting on the digging up of the grave of MK commander Phila Ndwandwe. She disappeared during the years of the liberation struggle and her family was told that she had eloped with a boyfriend to Tanzania. It was only when one of the armed forces members who killed her asked for amnesty that her death and gravesite became public.

The photographs display a slope of *tamboekie* grass, a wind-blue sky, some fresh soil. The commissioner tells us:

> He showed us the place . . . we dug . . . we found red topsoil mixed with black subsoil . . . then we knew . . . and soon the spade hit something . . .
>
> 'She was brave this one, hell she was brave,' said the perpetrator who showed us the hidden grave. He whistled softly through his teeth as if admiring her for the first time. 'She simply would not talk' (quoted in Krog 1997).

Next photo: the earth holding a bundle of bones. Delicately they are chiselled loose. Cigarette butts, an empty beer bottle.

'"It's hard work, digging," the grave indicator said, so that we could know that he knew,' says the TRC commissioner (ibid.).

A man in short sleeves puts the bones on a small piece of canvas next to the grave. Building blocks: a vertebra

. . . the thin, flattened collarbone . . . the skull has a bullet hole right at the top.

'She must have been kneeling,' says the commissioner. He spreads out the photos.

Ribs. Breastbone, behind which the heart was once in place.

Round the pelvis is a blue bag. A blue plastic shopping bag. The commissioner told us: 'When he saw this, the grave indicator remembered: "We kept her naked and after ten days she made herself these panties." He even sniggered admiration. "God, she was brave"' (ibid.).

On television that night we saw the grieving parents of Phila Ndwandwe. The mother, who for years never knew whether her daughter might not still be alive, broke down as she said: 'I cannot bear the fact that all these years she was in a grave a mere ten kilometres away from me and I didn't know that. I didn't *feel* that. My previous grief suddenly seems like such a luxury.'

★

It's a peaceful weekday morning. As I ring the bell to the art gallery, the Cape Town suburb of Claremont comes to me in friendly domestic sounds of radio chatter and the hum of appliances. I am alone. Someone had suggested that I go and see the exhibition of painter Judith Mason 'because she has some Truth Commission stuff'. I know her work well and have always been drawn to the combination of violent and tender lines in some of her paintings.

I suddenly find myself in a room—completely empty at first glance, except for an ordinary wire coat hanger

316 | *Conditional Tense*

FIGURE 9. Judith Mason's triptych *The Man Who Sang and the Woman Who Kept Silent* (1998).

suspended in the middle. From it hangs a dress made of blue plastic—blue shopping-bag plastic. The pretty shoulder straps hold up a blue embroidered bodice. From the soft-pleated empire line, the skirt flows out light and carefree as if swaying in the soft morning breeze. As if in it a woman is running—lithe and lovely. It is so exquisite—this soft, twirling blue, delicately rustling dress—that I have to bend over. Kneel. Sit. Choke.

It is for her!

MK commander Phila Ndwande. This dress is for her. The blue plastic panties of shame and humiliation had been transformed into this haunting blue salute of beauty.

Perhaps this is the only thing art can do: try to transform pain into evocative beauty so that one can, at times, live with loss.

Judith Mason made a painting of this dress for South Africa's first Constitutional Court. There Phila's blue dress will forever float light and lovely in the heat generated from the burning *konkas* of memory while the hyena of death scowls in the background.

Hamba kahle, Phila . . .
may your spirit dance free
in this blue blessed dress
for you . . .
and perhaps
also
for us.

Heart

The conference at the Nexus Institute at Tilburg University is in full swing. The institute's mission is to gather intellectuals, artists and politicians to debate burning issues. This conference is about loss.

On the podium are philosophers, psychologists, experts in life and loss. I take notes. The words are many.

'In art the human form has lost its feeling of awe.'

'Loss of religion is the loss of loss—there is nothing to lose if you have done away with death.'

'Loss of religion is the gain of loss.'

'Suicide is the most fundamental question because you have to decide whether life is worth living.' 'Can we ever let go of the anguish of the self?' 'It is time for a new religion—the religion of art.' 'We have to rediscover the sacred.' 'Religion had never found an answer to suffering—it simply provided references to the "other world".'

Amid the melancholy are tea and music.

'One can have an ongoing conversation with the dead. The process is not separation, but it brings it inside. You relocate yourself with the dead in you.' 'Humiliation is the biggest loss, not death, but the loss of respect for the self.'

I take notes.

'Nobody is ever only a victim.' 'I prefer the power of the imagination to the power of experience.' 'Grief taught me nothing.' 'Sorrow has its own vanity.' 'Art is not useless in the face of death, but aestheticism is.' 'Loss is the first stage in the steps towards redemption.'

After one of the panel discussions I take a walk outside. The enormous maple trees are wrapped in autumn.

Although it is cold it feels as if I am walking among fires. I see someone following me. I walk faster. He keeps up with me. I turn into a parking lot. He follows me and I prepare myself for meeting an avid reader of South African literature.

'Uw bent Vrouw Krog?' he says more than asks. I nod. He is young, with dark hair and serious eyes.

'I am the brother of Retha, your cousin Dawid's wife.'

I look into his eyes and he doesn't have to speak further. Everything reels. I just know.

'When?'

'Yesterday. My mother phoned and I promised to tell you here today.'

I start walking again, out onto the cold cement of Tilburg University. And I see him: little Johan in my house, the bald head, the shy smile. I am massaging his feet. I see him on my veranda looking at the stars through a telescope. I see him returning from the sea with a fist full of fish. I see him in hospital, wan and weak. And I think of the many years of chemotherapy, the bone-marrow transplants, the tests, the wild flights of hope, the desperate holding on of his father and mother, the terrified eyes of his younger sister, and now he is dead. His tortured little body at rest.

I go back into the hall and listen to the theories round grief and loss and I know that there is nothing, absolutely nothing, I can offer Dawid and Retha. There is nothing this conference can offer. Because we are all dumb in front of the wall of death. There is, even in the most brilliant mind, a collapse of the imagination before death. And because we cannot access death through our imagination, we fear death.

I stop taking notes. Nobody can tell me where Johan is now, or why he had to suffer so cruelly.

But the pain stays in me in a kind of dry fury. I cannot sleep. Back in Amsterdam, I walk along the streets. Scorched by a need I recognize only when I take up a pen and write to my family:

Dear Dawid, Retha and Marie—

At this moment I know you are standing there where the hill slopes towards the river. It would still be spring with the first smell of mimosa blossoms, majestic clouds building up in the vast sky, the first bite of summer heat . . . And so I know it is all heart-cuttingly sore there in the small family graveyard where everyone in a way had died too soon. But suddenly I see your mother, Dawid. She waits at the corner of the enclosing wall. She wears a sober hat and her neatest shoes and she's clearly impatient for the funeral procession to come down the hill. It is she who will take Johantjie from you as she tries to touch you and comfort you and to say: shush now, it is me who takes him, his grandmother is with him. She takes him in her arms as she did when he was still small and she laughs with her head thrown back and her hands are pinkish as she touches his cheek.

Inside the graveyard waits our great-grandmother with her soft upper arms and fragrant lap. See it is true! No one can laugh like her with her eyes. She is excited because she already loves

Johan as she loves all her great-grandchildren unconditionally. She sits on one of the graves and takes Johan on her lap. She rocks him and kisses his forehead. She rubs his toes which look like his father's, the eyebrows of his mother. She sees he is tired of the journey. He has come from afar. She knows he knows about pain and hanging in and pain and hanging on, and being ill and brave, and having pain but comforting others with your eyes.

They will be with Johan when he wakes on the other side and he will be with them without pain or fear. See, already his forehead has lost its too serious frown, his hair has started growing . . . And when you walk back from the graveyard he waves at you shyly—as he once waved at me from the back of the car when he left for his first chemotherapy.

Dear Dawid and Retha, so I think of you here in Amsterdam, trying to breathe for a moment above this sorrow and grief.

Nothing replaces life.

Nothing takes away this terrible longing to hold him.

And in this we are completely alone.

Works Cited

ALLEN, John. 2007. *Rabble-Rouser for Peace*. London: Rider Books.

ANGELELLI, Claudia V. 2004. *Medical Interpreting and Cross-Cultural Communication*. Cambridge: Cambridge University Press.

ARENDT, Hannah. 2003. *Responsibility and Judgment*. New York: Schocken Books.

ATTWELL, David. 2004. 'J. M. Coetzee: South Africa and the Politics of Writing'. *English Academy Review: South African Journal of English Studies* 21(1): 105–17.

AUERHAHN, Nanette C., and Dori Laub. 1998. 'Intergenerational Memory of the Holocaust' in Yael Danieli (ed.), *International Handbook of Multigenerational Legacies of Trauma*. New York: Kluwer, pp. 21–43.

AXELSON, Eric. 1973. *Portuguese in South-East Africa, 1488–1600*. Johannesburg: Struik.

BARKER, Martin. 1989. *Comics: Ideology, Power and the Critics*. Manchester and New York: Manchester University Press.

BELL, Richard H. 2002. *Understanding African Philosophy: A Cross-Cultural Approach to Classical and Contemporary Issues*. New York: Routledge.

BENNINGTON, Geoffrey. 1990. 'Postal Politics and the Institution of the Nation' in Homi K. Bhabha (ed.), *Nation and Narration*. London: Routledge, pp. 121–37.

BLEEK, Wilhelm H. I., and Lucy C. Lloyd. 1911. *Specimens of Bushman Folklore*. London: George Allan.

BLOOMFIELD, David, Terri Barnes and Lucien Huyse (eds). 2003. *Reconciliation after Violent Conflict: A Handbook*. Stockholm: International Institute for Democracy and Electoral Assistance.

BOCK, Zannie, Ngwanya Mazwi, Sifundo Metula and Nosisi Mpolweni-Zantsi. 2006. 'An Analysis of What Has Been "Lost" in the Interpretation and Transcription Process of Selected TRC Testimonies'. *SPIL* 33: 1–26.

BOOI, Beauty Ntombizanele. 2004. 'Three Perspectives on *Ukuthwasa*: The View from Traditional Beliefs, Western Psychiatry and Transpersonal Psychology'. MA thesis, Department of Psychology, Rhodes University. Available at: http://eprints.ru.ac.za/175/1/booi-ma.pdf (last accessed on 22 June 2013).

BORAINE, Alex. 2000. *A Country Unmasked: Inside South Africa's Truth and Reconciliation Commission.* Oxford: Oxford University Press.

BRAND, Gerrit. 2002. *Speaking of a Fabulous Ghost: In Search of Theological Criteria with Special Reference to the Debate on Salvation in African Christian Theology.* Frankfurt am Main: Peter Lang.

BRAUDE, Claudia. 2009. 'Pervasive Impunity: From Amnesty to the Apartheid Lawsuit and Beyond'. *Focus* 55: 35–49.

BROWN, John Tom. 1926. *Among the Bantu Nomads: A Record of Forty Years Spent among the Bechuana.* London: Seeley Service.

BURUMA, Ian. 1994. *Het Loon van de Schuld* (Wages of Guilt). Amsterdam and Antwerp: Uitgeverij Atlas.

CAMÕES, Luis Vaz de. 2001. *The Lusiads* (1572) (Landeg White ed. and trans.). Oxford: Oxford University Press.

CARUTH, Cathy (ed.). 1995. *Trauma: Explorations in Memory.* Baltimore, MD, and London: Johns Hopkins University Press.

CLEAVER, Eldridge. 1968. *Soul on Ice.* New York: McGraw-Hill.

COETZEE, J. M. 1990. *Age of Iron.* London: Secker and Warburg.

——. 1999. *Disgrace.* London: Secker and Warburg.

COMAROFF, John L., and Jean Comaroff. 1991. *Of Revelation and Revolution*, VOL. 1, *Christianity, Colonialism and Consciousness in South Africa.* Chicago and London: University of Chicago Press.

——. 1992. *Ethnography and the Historical Imagination.* Boulder, CO: Westview Press.

——. 2001. 'On Personhood: An Anthropological Perspective from Africa'. *Social Identities* 7(2): 267–83.

COPLAN, David B. 1994. *In the Time of Cannibals: The Word Music of South Africa's Basotho Migrants.* Johannesburg: Wits University Press.

DANIELI, Yael. 1998. 'Conclusions and Future Directions' in Yael Danieli (ed.), *International Handbook of Multigenerational Legacies of Trauma*. New York: Kluwer, pp. 669–90.

DE KOCK, W. J. (ed.). 1968. *Suid-Afrikaanse Biografiese Woordeboek* (South African Biographical Dictionary). Bloemfontein, Port Elizabeth and Johannesburg: Nasionale Boekhandel.

DEGENAAR, Johan. 1995. 'Myth and the Collision of Cultures'. *Myth and Symbol* 2: 39–61.

DERRIDA, Jacques. 1993. *Memoirs of the Blind: The Self-Portrait and Other Ruins* (Pascale-Anne Brault and Michael Naas trans). Chicago: University of Chicago Press.

——. 2001. *On Cosmopolitanism and Forgiveness*. London: Routledge.

DES PRES, Terrence. 1977. *The Survivor: An Anatomy of Life in the Death Camps*. New York: Pocket Books.

DIOP, Birago. 1964. 'Breath' in *French African Verse* (John Reed and Clive Wake trans). London: Heinemann, p. 25.

DORR, Lisa Lindquist. 2004. *White Women, Rape and the Power of Race in Virginia: 1900–1960*. Chapel Hill: University of North Carolina Press.

DOUGLAS, Mary. 2002. *Purity and Danger: Analysis of the Concepts of Pollution and Taboo*. London: Routledge.

DU PLESSIS, P. G. 2008. *Fees van die Ongenooides* (Feast of the Uninvited). Cape Town: Tafelberg.

DU PLESSIS, T., and Chriss Wiegand. 1998. 'Interpreting at the Hearings of the Truth and Reconciliation Commission: April 1996 to February 1997' in Alet Kruger, Kim Wallmach and Marion Boers (eds), *Language Facilitation and Development in Southern Africa*. Pretoria: South African Translators Institute, pp. 25–30.

EDELSTEIN, Jillian. 2002. *Truth and Lies*. New York: New Press.

FELMAN, Shoshana, and Dori Laub. 1992. *Testimony: Crises of Witnessing in Literature, Psychoanalysis, and History*. New York: Routledge.

FULLARD, Madeleine, and Nick Rousseau. 2008. 'Uncertain Borders: The TRC and the (Un)Making of Public Myths'. *Kronos*

34(1). Available at: http://www.scielo.org.za/scielo.php?-pid=S0259019020080001000009&script=sci_arttext#1a (last accessed on 20 June 2013).

GIBSON, Kean. 2001. *Comfa Religion and Creole Language in a Caribbean Community*. Albany: State University of New York Press.

GOBODO-MADIKIZELA, Pumla. 2003. *A Human Being Died That Night*: *A South African Story of Forgiveness*. Cape Town: David Philip.

——. 2006. 'Healing', in Charles Villa-Vicencio and Fanie du Toit (eds), *Truth and Reconciliation in South Africa*: *10 Years On*. Cape Town: David Philip, pp. 71–6.

GOLDBLATT, David. 2007. *Some Afrikaners Revisited*. Cape Town: Umuzi.

GRAYBILL, Lyn S. 2002. *Truth and Reconciliation in South Africa*: *Miracle or Model?* Boulder, CO: Lynne Reinner.

GROENEWALD, Yolandi. 2007. 'The De la Rey Uprising'. *Mail and Guardian* (16 February). Available at: http://mg.co.za/article/2007-02-16-the-de-la-rey-uprising (last accessed on 23 June 2013).

GROSSMAN, David. 2006. 'A State of Missed Opportunities'. *Guardian* (7 November). Available at: http://www.guardian.co.uk/world/-2006/nov/07/israel (last accessed on 23 July 2013).

GYEKYE, Kwame. 1987. *An Essay on African Philosophical Thought*: *The Akan Conceptual Scheme*. Cambridge: Cambridge University Press.

HAMILTON, Carolyn, Verne Harris, Graeme Reid. 2002. 'Introduction' in Carolyn Hamilton, Verne Harris, Michèle Pickover, Graeme Reid, Razia Saleh and Jane Taylor (eds), *Refiguring the Archive*. Cape Town: David Phillip, pp. 7–18.

HAMILTON, Carolyn, Verne Harris, Michèle Pickover, Graeme Reid, Razia Saleh and Jane Taylor (eds). 2002. *Refiguring the Archive*. Cape Town: David Phillip.

HARDTMANN, Gertrud. 1998. 'Children of Nazis: A Psychodynamic Perspective' in Yael Danieli (ed.), *International Handbook of Multigenerational Legacies of Trauma*. New York: Kluwer, pp. 85–96.

HARRIS, Brent. 2002. 'The Archive, Public History, and the Essential Truth: The TRC Reading the Past' in Carolyn Hamilton, Verne Harris, Michèle Pickover, Graeme Reid, Razia Saleh and Jane Taylor (eds), *Refiguring the Archive*. Cape Town: David Phillip, pp. 161–78.

HARRIS, Verne. 2002. 'The Archival Sliver: A Perspective on the Construction of Social Memory in Archives and the Transition from Apartheid to Democracy' in Carolyn Hamilton, Verne Harris, Michèle Pickover, Graeme Reid, Razia Saleh and Jane Taylor (eds), *Refiguring the Archive*. Cape Town: David Phillip, pp. 135–60.

HATFIELD, Charles. 2009. 'An Art of Tensions' in Jeet Heer and Kent Worcester (eds), *A Comics Studies Reader*. Jackson: University Press of Mississippi, pp. 132–48.

HATIM, Basil. 2001. *Teaching and Researching Translation*. London: Pearson.

HAYNER, Priscilla B. 2001. *Unspeakable Truths: Confronting State Terror and Atrocity*. London: Routledge.

HERGÉ. 2007[1976]. *Tintin and the Picaros*. London: Egmont UK.

HIGGINS, Lynn A., and Brenda R. Silver (eds). 1991. *Rape and Representation*. New York: Columbia University Press.

HOFMEYR, Isabel. 1993. *We Spend Our Years as a Tale That Is Told*. Johannesburg: Wits University Press.

HOLLMANN, Jeremy C. 2004. *Customs and Beliefs of the / Xam Bushmen*. Johannesburg: Wits University Press.

HOUNTONDJI, Pauline J. 1983. *African Philosophy: Myth and Reality*. London: Hutchinson University Library for Africa.

HUSEMEYER, Libby. 1997. *Watchdogs or Hypocrites? The Amazing Debate on South African Liberals and Liberalism*. Johannesburg: Friedrich-Naumann Stiftung.

IMBO, Samuel. 1998. *An Introduction to African Philosophy*. New York: Rowman and Littlefield.

JANSEN, Willy. 1987. *Women without Men: Gender and Marginality in an Algerian Town*. Leiden: E. J. Brill.

JUNG, Carl Gustave. 1964. *The Collected Works of C. G. Jung*, VOL. 10, *Civilization in Transition* (Gerhard Adler and R. F. C. Hull trans). London: Routledge and Kegan Paul.

KAHN, Coppelia. 1976. 'The Rape in Shakespeare's *Lucrece.*' *Shakespeare Studies* 9: 45–72.

KRAYBILL, Ronald S. 1988. 'From Head to Heart: The Cycle of Reconciliation'. *Conciliation Quarterly* 7(4) (Fall): 2–3, 8.

KROG, Antjie. 1997. 'Unto the Third or Fourth Generation'. *Mail and Guardian* (13 June). Available at: http://mg.co.za/article/1997-06-13-unto-the-third-or-fourth-generation (last accessed on 23 July 2013).

———. 1998. *Country of My Skull*. Johannesburg: Random House.

———. 2003. *A Change of Tongue*. Johannesburg and Cape Town: Random House.

———, Nosisi Mpolweni-Zantsi and Kopano Ratele (eds). 2009. *There Was This Goat: Investigating the Truth Commission Testimony of Notrose Nobomvu Konile*. Pietermaritzburg: University of KwaZulu-Natal Press.

LALU, Premesh. 2009. *The Death of Hintsa: Post-Apartheid South Africa and the Shape of Recurring Pasts*. Cape Town: Human Sciences Research Council Press.

LEFÈVRE, Pascal. 2009. 'The Construction of Space in Comics' in Jeet Heer and Kent Worcester (eds), *A Comics Studies Reader*. Jackson: University Press of Mississippi, pp. 157–62.

LENTSOEANE, H. M. L. 1981. *Ihlo la Moreti*. Pretoria: Van Schaik.

LEVI-STRAUSS, Claude. 1968. *Structural Anthropology* (Claire Jacobson and Brooke Grundfest Schoepf trans). London: Allen Lane.

LINDT, Martijn W. J. 1998. 'Children of Collaborators: From Isolation toward Integration' in Yael Danieli (ed.), *International Handbook of Multigenerational Legacies of Trauma*. New York: Kluwer, pp. 163–74.

MAMDANI, Mahmood. 1997. 'Reconciliation without Justice'. *Southern African Review of Books* 10(6): 3–5.

MANDELA, Nelson. 2010. *Conversations with Myself* (with a foreword by Barack Obama). London: Pan Macmillan.

MBEMBE, Achille. 2001. *On the Postcolony*. Berkeley, Los Angeles and London: University of California Press.

McCLOUD, Scott. 1993. *Understanding Comics: The Invisible Art*. New York: HarperCollins.

MIKRO. 1936. *Ruiter in die Nag* (Rider in the Night). Cape Town: Nasionale Pers.

MKHIZE, Nhlanhla. 2004a. 'Psychology: An African Perspective' in D. Hook, N. Mkhize, P. Kiguwa and A. Collins (eds), *Critical Psychology*. Landsdowne, South Africa: University of Cape Town Press, pp. 24–52.

———. 2004b. 'Sociocultural Approaches to Psychology: Dialogism and African Conceptions of the Self' in D. Hook, N. Mkhize, P. Kiguwa and A. Collins (eds), *Critical Psychology*. Landsdowne, South Africa: University of Cape Town Press, pp. 53–83.

MNET TELEVISION. 2006. 'Vlok on His Hands and Knees', *Carte Blanche* (10 September). Available at: http://beta.mnet.co.za/-carteblanche/Article.aspx?Id=3164 (last accessed on 23 July 2013).

MQHAYI, S. E. K. 1943. *Inzuzo*. Johannesburg: Wits University Press.

MUROVE, Munyaradzi Felix. 2009. 'Beyond the Savage Evidence Ethic: A Vindication of African Ethics' in Munyaradzi Felix Murove (ed.), *African Ethics: An Anthology of Comparative and Applied Ethics*. Pietermaritzburg: University of KwaZulu-Natal Press, pp. 14–32.

NDEBELE, Njabulo S. 2007a. *Fine Lines from the Box: Further Thoughts about Our Country*. Johannesburg: Umuzi / Random House.

———. 2007b. 'Moral Anchor: An Interview with the Arch (1998)' in *Fine Lines from the Box: Further Thoughts about Our Country*. Johannesburg: Umuzi / Random House, pp. 77–83.

NDLOVU, R. L. 1991. *Mulisa*. Johannesburg: Out of Africa.

OPLAND, Jeff. 1977. 'Two Unpublished Poems by S. E. K. Mqhayi'. *Research in African Literatures* 8: 27–53.

POSEL, Deborah, and Graeme Simpson. 2002. *Commissioning the Past: Understanding South Africa's Truth and Reconciliation Commission*. Johannesburg: Wits University Press.

PREEZ, Peter du. 1996. 'Liberals Aren't all Whack Whiteys'. *Mail and Guardian* (26 March). Available at: http://mg.co.za/article/1996-03-29-liberals-arent-all-whacky-whiteys (last accessible on 22 June 2013).

PROZESKY, Martin H. 2009. 'Cinderella, Survivor and Saviour: African Ethics and the Quest for a Global Ethic' in Munyaradzi Felix Murove (ed.), *African Ethics: An Anthology of Comparative and Applied Ethics*. Pietermaritzburg: University of KwaZulu-Natal Press, pp. 3–13.

RAATH, A. G. W. 1991. *Die Konsentrasiekamp te Springfontein Gedurende die Anglo-Boereoorlog, 1899–1902* (The Concentration Camp of Springfontein During the Anglo-Boer War, 1899–1902). Bloemfontein: Prisca Uitgewers.

———. 1992. *Die Konsentrasiekamp te Vredefortweg Gedurende die Anglo-Boereoorlog, 1899–1902* (The Concentration Camp of Vredefort During the Anglo-Boer War, 1899–1902). Bloemfontein: Prisca Uitgewers.

———. 1993. *Vroueleed: Die Lotgevalle van die Vroue en Kinders Buite die Konsentrasiekampe, 1899–1902* (Women's Grief: The Plight of the Women and Children Outside the Concentration Camps, 1899–1902). Bloemfontein: Prisca Uitgewers.

RAPPORT, Nigel, and Joanna Overing. 2000. *Social and Cultural Anthropology: The Key Concepts*. London and New York: Routledge.

RATAZZI, E. A. 2005. 'Narrating Rape at the Truth and Reconciliation Commission in South Africa'. MA thesis, Department of Political Studies, University of Cape Town.

RICHARDSON, Neville. 2009. 'Can Christian Ethics Find Its Way and Itself in Africa?' in Munyaradzi Felix Murove (ed.), *African Ethics: An Anthology of Comparative and Applied Ethics*. Pietermaritzburg: University of KwaZulu-Natal Press, pp. 129–54.

ROODT, Dan. 2003. 'It's Young Black Men Who Rob, Rape and Murder'. Praag.org (17 August). Available at: http://www.praag.org/ It's%20young%20black%20men%20who%20rob,-%20rape%20and%20murder.htm (last accessed on 22 June 2013).

Ross, Fiona. 2003. *Bearing Witness: Women and the Truth and Reconciliation Commission in South Africa*. London: Pluto Press.

——. 2004. 'Testimony' in Charles Villa-Vicencio and Erik Doxater (eds), *Pieces of the Puzzle: Keywords on Reconciliation and Transitional Justice*. Cape Town: Institute for Justice and Reconciliation, pp. 58–64.

Rushdie, Salman. 2000. 'Het falen van Coetzees fictie' (The Failure of Coetzee's Fiction). *Vrij Nederland* (1 July).

Sanders, Mark. 2002. *Complicities: The Intellectual and Apartheid*. Durham, NC: Duke University Press.

Saraceni, Marion. 2003. *The Language of Comics*. London: Routledge.

Scarry, Elaine. 1985. *The Body in Pain: The Making and Unmaking of the World*. New York: Oxford University Press.

Schaffner, Christina, and Helen Kelly-Holmes. 1995. *Cultural Functions of Translation*. Philadelphia: Multilingual Matters.

Schlosser, Eric. 1997. 'A Grief Like No Other'. *Atlantic Monthly* (September). Available at: http://www.theatlantic.com/-past/docs/-issues/97sep/grief.htm (last accessed on 23 July 2013).

Scholtz, A. H. M. 2000. *A Place Called Vatmaar* (Chris van Wyk trans.). Cape Town: Kwela Books.

Serfontein, Dot. 1979. *Rang in der Staten Rij: Roman oor die Tweede Vryheidsoorlog* (Place in the Row of States: Novel about the Second Liberation War). Cape Town and Pretoria: Human and Rousseau.

——. 1990. *Keurskrif vir Kroonstad: 'n Kroniek van die Ontstaan, groei en Vooruitsigte van 'n Vrystaatse Plattelandse Dorp* (A Choice of the Best of Kroonstad: A Chronicle of the Beginning, Growth and Prospects of a Rural Town in the Free State). Kroonstad: Perskor.

Setiloane, Gabriel M. 1976. *The Image of God among the Sotho-Tswana*. Rotterdam: A. A. Balkema.

Seys, Raf, and Käthe Kollwitz. 1964. *Käthe Kollwitz in Vlaanderen*. Keokelare: De Rumberg.

SHUTTE, Augustine. 2009. 'Ubuntu as the African Ethical Vision' in Munyaradzi Felix Murove (ed.), *African Ethics: An Anthology of Comparative and Applied Ethics*. Pietermaritzburg: University of KwaZulu-Natal Press, pp. 85–99.

SOUTH AFRICAN BROADCASTING CORPORATION. 2000. 'Bits and Pieces' in *Worlds of Licence: Self-Confessed Violators of Human Rights From Across South Africa's Political Landscape*. Available at: http://www.-sabctruth.co.za/worlds.htm (last accessed on 23 June 2013).

SOUTH AFRICAN GOVERNMENT INFORMATION. 1993. 'Constitution of the Republic of South Africa Act 200 of 1993'. Available at: http://www.info.gov.za/documents/constitution/93cons.htm (last accessed on 19 June 2013).

SOUTH AFRICAN PRESS ASSOCIATION. 1997a. 'Traumatised Torture Cop Claims He Can't Remember Abuses' (15 July). Available at: http://www.justice.gov.za/trc/media/1997/9707/s9707-15g.htm (last accessed on 23 June 2013).

———. 1997b. 'Winnie Complies with Tutu's Appeal for Her to Say Sorry' (4 December). Available at: http://www.justice.gov.za-/-trc/media/1997/9712/s971204v.htm (last accessed on 23 July 2013).

SOYINKA, Wole. 1976. *Myth, Literature and the African World*. Cambridge: Cambridge University Press.

SPARKS, Allister. 1994. *Tomorrow is Another Country: The Inside Story of South Africa's Negotiated Revolution*. Sandton: Struik.

SPIVAK, Gayatri Chakravorty. 1988. 'Can the Subaltern Speak?' in Cary Nelson and Lawrence Grossberg (eds), *Marxism and the Interpretation of Culture*. Urbana and Chicago: University of Illinois Press, pp. 217–314.

———. 1993. *Outside in the Teaching Machine*. New York: Routledge.

STAUB, Ervin, Laurie Anne Pearlman, Alexandra Gubin and Athanase Hagengimana. 2005. 'Healing, Reconciliation, Forgiving and the Prevention of Violence after Genocide or Mass Killing: An Intervention and Its Experimental Evaluation in Rwanda'. *Journal of Social and Clinical Psychology* 24(3): 297–334. Available at: http://www.theworld.com/~gubin/-

Rwandafiles/Staub,%20Pearlman,%20Gubin%20and%20Hag
engimana.pdf (last accessed on 24 June 2013).

STOLER, Ann Laura. 2002. 'Colonial Archives and the Arts of Governance: On the Content in the Form' in Carolyn Hamilton, Verne Harris, Michèle Pickover, Graeme Reid, Razia Saleh and Jane Taylor (eds), *Refiguring the Archive*. Cape Town: David Phillip, pp. 83–102.

TRC (Truth and Reconciliation Commission of South Africa). 1996a. 'Human Rights Violation: Hearings and Submissions; Case No. CT/00100'. Available at: http://www.justice.gov.za/trc/hrvtrans/heide/ct00100.htm (last accessed on 21 June 2013).

——. 1996b. 'Human Rights Violation: Hearings and Submissions; Case No. CT/00205'. Available at: http://www.justice-.gov.za/-trc/hrvtrans/heide/ct00205.htm (last accessed on 21 June 2013).

——. 1996c. 'Human Rights Violation: Hearings and Submissions; Case No. CT/00505'. Available at: http://www.justice.gov.za/-trc/hrvtrans/heide/ct00505.htm (last accessed on 21 June 2013).

——. 1996d. 'Human Rights Violation: Hearings and Submissions; Case No. CT/00506'. Available at: http://www.justice.gov.za/trc/-hrvtrans/heide/ct00506.htm (last accessed on 21 June 2013).

——. 1996e. 'Human Rights Violation: Hearings and Submissions; Case No. CT/00603'. Available at: http://www.justice.gov.za/trc/-hrvtrans/heide/ct00603.htm (last accessed on 21 June 2013).

——. 1996f. 'Human Rights Violation: Hearings and Submissions; Case No. CT/00624'. Available at: http://www.justice.gov.za/trc/-hrvtrans/heide/ct00624.htm (last accessed on 21 June 2013).

——. 1996g. 'Human Rights Violation: Hearings and Submissions; Case No. CT/00712'. Available at: http://www.justice.gov.za/trc/-hrvtrans/heide/ct00712.htm (last accessed on 21 June 2013).

——. 1996h. 'Human Rights Violation: Hearings and Submissions; Case No. EC0028/96'. Available at: http://www.justice.gov.za/-trc/hrvtrans/hrvel1/calata.htm (last accessed on 4 September 2013).

——. 1996i. 'Human Rights Violation: Hearings and Submissions; Second Submission of the National Party to the Truth and Reconciliation Commission'. Available at: http://www.justice.gov.za/- trc/hrvtrans/heide/retief.htm (last accessed on 21 June 2013).

——. 1996j. 'Human Rights Violation: Hearings and Submissions; Statement from Bishop Retief'. Available at: http://www.justice.-gov.za/trc/hrvtrans/heide/retief.htm (last accessed on 21 June 2013).

——. 1997. 'Human Rights Violations: Women's Hearing; Case No. Jb04279/01 Gtsow'. Available at: http://www.justice.-gov.za/trc/-special/women/masote.htm (last accessed on 23 June 2013).

——. 1998. *Truth and Reconciliation Commission of South Africa Report*, 5 VOLS. Cape Town: Juta. Available at: http://abctrc.-saha.org.za/reports.htm (last accessed on 17 July 2013).

TUTU, Desmond, and Mpho Tutu. 2010. *Made for Goodness: And Why This Makes All the Difference*. Cape Town: Umuzi.

UYS, Hester Johanna Maria. 2007. 'A Boer Girl's Memories of the War'. Available at: http://www.erroluys.com/BoerWar-ChildsStory.htm (last accessed on 23 June 2013).

VAN BINSBERGEN, W. M. J. 2001. 'Ubuntu and the Globalization of Southern African Thought and Society'. *Quest* 15(1–2): 53–89.

VAN BLERK, Bok, Johan Vorster and Sean Else. 2005. *De la Rey*. Mozi Records, compact disc.

VANDERSTEEN, Willy, and Marc Verhaegen. 2003. *Suske en Wiske: De Laaste Vloek* No. 279. Antwerp: Standaard Uitgewerij.

——, and Marc Verhaegen. 2004. *Suske en Wiske: Kaapse Kaalkoppen* No. 284. Antwerp: Standaard Uitgewerij.

——, and Paul Geerts. 2000. *Suske en Wiske: De Krakende Carcas* No. 235. Antwerp: Standaard Uitgewerij.

——, and Paul Geerts. 2005. *Suske en Wiske: Het Aruba-Dossier* No. 241. Antwerp: Standaard Uitgewerij.

——, and Paul Geerts. 2008. *Suske en Wiske: De Razende Race* No. 249 (P. Geerts). Antwerp: Standaard Uitgewerij.

——, Peter van der Gucht and Luc Morjaeu. 2008. *Suske en Wiske: De Mompelende Mummie* No. 255. Antwerp: Standaard Uitgewerij.

VERDOOLAEGE, Annelies. 2008. *Reconciliation Discourse: The Case of the Truth and Reconciliation Commission*. Amsterdam: John Benjamins.

WALKER, Alice. 1981. 'Advancing Luna—and Ida B. Wells' in *You Can't Keep a Good Woman Down*. New York: Harcourt Brace Jovanovich, pp. 85–104.

WENTZEL, Jill. 1995. *The Liberal Slideaway*. Johannesburg: South African Institute of Race Relations.

WILLIAMS, Patrick, and Laura Chrisman (eds). 1993. *Colonial Discourse and Post-colonial Theory: A Reader*. New York: Harvester Wheatsheaf.

WILSON, Richard A. 2001. *The Politics of Truth and Reconciliation in South Africa: Legitimizing the Post-Apartheid State*. Cambridge: Cambridge University Press.

YELD, John, and Joseph Aranes. 1996. 'Mother's "Necklace" Killing Described'. *Argus* (25 April).

ŽIŽEK, Slavoj. 2009. *Violence*. London: Profile Books.